BUILDING
A
COMPANY

BUILDING
A
COMPANY

ROY O. DISNEY
AND THE CREATION OF AN
ENTERTAINMENT EMPIRE

BOB THOMAS

HYPERION

New York

Library of Congress Cataloging-in-Publication Data
Thomas, Bob, 1922-
    Building a company : Roy O. Disney and the creation of an
entertainment empire / Bob Thomas.—1st ed.
        p.   cm.
    Includes index.
    ISBN 0-7868-6200-9
    1. Walt Disney Productions.   2. Disney, Roy O. (Roy Oliver),
1893–1971.   3. Cheif executive officers—United States—Biography.
I. Title.
PN1999.W27T56   1998
384'.8'092—dc21
[B]   98-4405
                                                              CIP

Book design by Jennifer Daddio

FIRST EDITION

10 9 8 7 6 5 4 3 2 1

In 1967, Roy Disney reminisced about a time when he and Walt and their little sister Ruth stopped at their aunt's house in Fort Madison, Iowa, on their way to their new home in Missouri:

"On the streets of Fort Madison, Walt found a pocket knife. He was five years old, and I was thirteen. I said, 'Look, you can't trust yourself with a knife, you'll cut yourself.' And I took the knife away from him.

"Within the last two or three years, somethin' came up. He accused me of bullying him and throwing my weight around, and he says, 'You've been doin' that since I was born. I remember you took that knife away from me in Fort Madison.'

"That was sixty years later. Talk about an elephant!"

Roy Disney often enjoyed telling this story to studio associates and visitors, always with a wink and great affection:

"When Walt and I were on the farm in Marceline, we had to sleep in the same bed. Now Walt was just a little guy, and he was always wetting the bed. And he's been peeing on me ever since."

Roy sometimes added the lighthearted observation: "I can say I'm the only man in the world who has been peed on by a genius."

TO PAT WITH LOVE

ONE

❧

To film industry leaders, the Disney brothers were a curiosity, their studio an enclave in the parched flatness of the San Fernando Valley, their heritage derived from the American heartland rather than New York City's East Side and the ghettos of eastern Europe. The Disneys' counterparts at other studios admired but did not understand Walt's accomplishment in raising cartoons to a genuine art. Nor did they understand the inner workings of the studio and the unique partnership of the two brothers.

Long before Walt produced his first movie cartoon, he looked to Roy for counsel and sympathy. As business partners, Walt was the inventive dreamer, Roy the financial wizard. This inevitably led to disputes, as Walt's dreams exceeded what Roy believed to be financially practical. Often Walt remained so persistent that Roy, who was in awe of his brother's creativity, capitulated. Sometimes Roy remained firm, impressing Walt with the financial realities. Rarely was there acrimony between the pair, though there were periods of estrangement. During one basic disagreement late in their lives, they did not speak to each other for more than two years, communicating only through emissaries. The Disney family was Irish and subject to stubborn temperament.

Roy and Walt Disney resembled each other in appearance and their Midwest manner of speaking, but not in personality. Some of their longtime employees cite the differences.

John Hench, who started at the studio in 1938 as a storyboard developer and rose through various departments to become a chief planner and resident philosopher: "Roy was very different from Walt. Walt was prone to take risks; his security was the fact that he really thought the ideas that kept popping up—his own especially—were good and valid. Roy had a much more conservative approach to things."

Marc Davis, animator: "Roy wasn't the gambler that Walt was."

Jack Lindquist, who became the first advertising manager of Disneyland and later served as president of Disneyland and vice president of Walt Disney World: "Roy had the final word on everything that went into Florida, just as Walt always had the final word with Disneyland. Roy had a different way of how he judged things to make a decision. Walt always knew what he wanted, and that's what he wanted you to do. If you did it the way he wanted it, then it was right. Roy, not coming from that discipline, wanted to hear from everybody, wanted to know why. You had to prove to Roy what the rationale was for something to be done that way."

Neal McClure, a member of the law department and one of Roy's Boys: "Walt was the front man, and Roy was in the background. In his way, he was as much of a genius as Walt was. They shoved their last chips in the pot a couple of times. Roy always saved the day."

Ollie Johnston, animator: "Roy had always been so damned good to Walt when he was growing up; there was a real bond there even though they had their arguments. Roy was friendly with the animators. He'd walk in and kid and put his arm around your shoulder."

Frank Thomas, animator: "You could put your arm around Roy's shoulder, too, and did. Not with Walt."

Bill Cottrell, who began at the studio in 1929 and in later years headed Walt's subsidiary, WED: "In my observation over the years, Roy was a very calm, considerate executive. I liked him very much. As time went on, Walt grew more serious; he might have been feeling more responsibility. I don't think Walt was having as much fun as he should have had. Maybe he had too much on his mind. As Roy grew older, he seemed to be more easygoing."

John Tobin, consulting attorney: "There were tensions between the two brothers, but from my perspective, Roy Disney did whatever in the world he could to make life better, nicer, sweeter, etc., for his younger brother."

Harrison (Buzz) Price, who researched scores of projects for the Disneys: "The differences? Different temperaments. *Tremendous* mutual rapport and respect and closeness. Different styles. Walt was relentlessly creating stuff, and Roy was bird-dogging it like a consummate businessman. Walt was more intense. Roy was more laid back.

"I felt tremendously at home with Roy. You could tell him exactly what you thought. You didn't have to fart around or play politics or try to manage information; you could say anything. It was like that with Walt, too . . . They were like two brothers who were very close but very different."

· · ·

One of the rare times Walt spoke publicly about his older brother occurred when his boyhood vaudeville partner, Walt Pfeiffer, was honored in 1957 by the Los Angeles chapter of the Big Brothers of America at a benefit dinner in Beverly Hills. The event was chaired by Meredith Willson and attended by many film industry and civic dignitaries, including Los Angeles police chief William H. Parker. It had been a festive evening, and Walt glowed with sentiment when he was called upon to speak.

Walt began by praising the Big Brother organization, then he reminisced about his own family. He had three older brothers, he said, one he was close to despite the difference in their ages.

"I had a wonderful mother and father, but they were very strict," he remarked. "It reached the point that to tell the truth to my father got me a licking. I could always get out of things by telling a nice little lie . . .

"At the same time I had this brother eight and a half years older. I could go and talk to him and tell him things I could never tell my dad. Well, my mother was sweet and all that, but gosh! she couldn't keep it from dad if I told her . . .

"My father was reaching fifty when I was born; he had troubles and problems. He never understood me. He thought I was the black sheep. This nonsense of drawing pictures! He said, 'Walter, you're not going to make a career of that, are you? I have a good job for you in the jelly factory. It pays twenty-five dollars a week.' I said, 'Dad, I don't want to work in a jelly factory.' He said, 'What are you going to do?' I said, 'I'm going to be an artist.'

"He couldn't see it. Another thing he couldn't see was that I went into debt. I had to buy things, buy equipment. My father was one who paid for everything on the line. He didn't believe in [buying on credit].

"But my big brother would say, 'Kid, go ahead!' He said, 'Kid, I'm for you.' He encouraged me. When he was away—he was in a veterans hospital for a time—we wrote letters. I could tell him what I was going to do, and he'd write back: 'Go ahead, kid. Good for you, kid.'

"I was fortunate. I had a big brother. And he's still with me. And I still love him. I argue with him. Sometimes I think he's the stubbornest so-and-so I ever met in my life. But I don't know what the hell I'd do without him. He's the president of the company now . . ."

A voice from the darkness corrected: "I'm chairman of the board."

Amid laughter, Walt continued: "I'll tell you, Chief Parker, we started in the business here in 1923, and if it hadn't been for my big brother, I swear I'd've been in jail several times for checks bouncing. I never knew what was in the bank. He kept me on the straight and narrow."

TWO

❦

"T hat was a period of moving, from 1880 to 1930, moving, moving, back and forth in this grand big country," Roy O. Disney said to an interviewer in 1968, explaining his forebears' wanderlust. "People would try it in one place, then try something else, like the Oklahoma Land Rush. They were men of the soil trying to find a better homestead, or land, or climate.

"My folks went out to Kansas. They lived in a sod hut cut into the bank of a river until they quarried the native rock and built a stone house that still stands out there. They were good men, and they had good women. My mother remembers that her chore was to pick up fuel for the fire. The fuel was buffalo chips—buffalo manure. That was what kids picked up and stored. There wasn't much timber out in that country.

"Pioneering this country: that was a moving thing, shuffling around, finding out what was better, where they might improve their lives. That kind of man is always curious, wondering what's over the hill or around the corner."

Elias Disney was such a man. He spent his lifetime in a futile search for the bounty that America promised. Perhaps seeing their father fail in one enterprise after another helped provide the impetus for two of his sons to create a worldwide entertainment empire of a kind that had never been seen before.

The family can be traced to Isigny-sur-Mer, a small town in Normandy that dated to Roman times. Hughes d'Isigny joined William the Conqueror in the invasion of England in 1066. He remained in England, and as his descendants established themselves in Lincolnshire, the family shortened the name to Disney. In the 1660s, a branch of the family shifted to County Louth in Ireland.

Weary of the grim prospects of life in Ireland, Arundel Elias Disney and his brother Robert and their families set sail from Liverpool in 1834. Destination: New York.

"That makes me feel that the Disneys had foresight," Walt Disney remarked in 1965, "because it was in the 1840s when they had the Potato Famine in Ireland."

Elias Disney had been attracted to the Goderich township in Huron County, Ontario, by promises by the Canada Company of cheap and fertile farmland and full facilities. He and other settlers arrived to discover a primitive wilderness without roads, schools, churches, or cleared flatland. The buyers protested to the company and the Canadian government to no avail. Some shouldered their losses and departed. Elias Disney remained.

"He bought a tract of land close to and along the banks of the Maitland River and built a saw and grist mill that was patronized by the community for a number of years," wrote his grandson, Elias Disney, father of Roy and Walt, in a brief history in 1939.

"This country was heavily timbered, and there was plenty of wild fruit, grapes, plums, etc., along the banks of the river, and good fishing and wild game of different kinds. Wolves were numerous and a cause of much annoyance to the settlers, with their young stock, and many a time I have sat and listened in amazement to the stories my father and others would tell of personal encounters."

His grandfather Elias had married Maria Swan in Ireland, where their first child, Kepple, had been born in 1832. Another child had died during the Atlantic crossing. Maria gave birth to a total of sixteen children, eight girls, eight boys.

Kepple Disney matured into a rugged young man, a muscular six feet, with jet-black hair and an imposing beard. He married Mary Richardson, daughter of another immigrant Irish family, and they settled in the Ontario village of Bluevale, in the township of Turberry. Kepple bought 100 acres of virgin land, which he cleared for farming and for the family house. Elias Disney, first of eleven children, was born at Bluevale in 1859.

An ambitious man, Kepple engaged in many enterprises during his twenty years in Bluevale. He had been convinced that oil lay beneath the farm's soil, and he began sinking a well. After weeks of drilling, the well produced—salt. Kepple recovered his investment by engaging in the salt-supply business.

"We received our education in the public school of Bluevale and attended Wesleyan Methodist Church and Sunday School," Elias Disney recalled in 1939. "Our life and work were such as comes to boys and girls brought up on the farm—a pure and wholesome atmosphere, both physically and morally."

Kepple and Mary Disney followed Methodist principles with

utter strictness, and they reared their children accordingly. In 1967, Roy Disney recalled a story about his father:

"He came out of a period when they were very strict and stern. When the family was living in Canada, my dad learned to play the fiddle, and he had to go back in the woods to practice so the folks wouldn't know. Then he'd sneak off and play for dances. My grandparents got wind of it, and they went to one of those dance halls one night. They found their son playing the fiddle, and Grandma went up to him and grabbed it away and busted it all to hell over his head, took him by the ear, and marched him home.

"The devil was in the fiddle, to their notion. Dancing was just evil. Hard for us to imagine those attitudes today."

After twenty years of brutal winters and exhausting labor with meager reward, Kepple Disney resolved to seek a more agreeable climate and work with greater promise. Accompanied by his oldest sons, Elias and Robert, he set out for the gold fields of California in 1878, unconcerned that the rush for gold had occurred thirty years before.

The Disney men traveled as far as western Kansas. Pausing in the town of Ellis, Kepple was approached by an agent for the Union Pacific railroad. As a reward for routing the new transcontinental railroad, the Union Pacific had been given hundreds of thousands of acres of land by grateful counties, states, and territories. Kepple, who could not homestead because he was not an American citizen, was offered a half-section, 200 acres, at an excellent price. He sold the Bluevale farm and sent for the rest of his family. In 1879 he filed for naturalization.

Because the railroad exacted a high price for lumber, Kepple built his house of sod, the place half buried to ward off the summer heat and winter cold. Later he built the house of quarried stone. With the help of his sons, he planted acres of wheat and raised a herd of cattle.

For the eldest son, Elias, life in Kansas seemed little different from what he had known in Canada. He toiled on the farm from sunrise to dark. The snowy wind that swept across the prairie in wintertime could chill the bones just as readily as a Canadian freeze. He couldn't forget the exciting possibility of gold mining in California; now his life was drab and wearying and futureless.

Against his father's wishes, Elias decided to leave the farm to work as a machine-shop mechanic for the Union Pacific. Restless to see more of the country, Elias joined the railroad crews that were building the route to the west. He hired on as apprentice carpenter. The work ended when the railroad reached Denver. Elias tried to support himself by playing the fiddle outside saloons. Contributions were few. Unable to find work in Denver, Elias retreated to Ellis.

For a time Elias taught school, and among his students was his younger brother Will. Will's duty was to watch Kepple's cows, and he thought he could do it by looking out the school window. His father objected and ordered Elias to bar Will from school. Will's education ended at the third grade, and in later years he nursed a grudge against his older brother.

Among the reasons Elias was interested in teaching school was his desire to be near another teacher, Flora Call. She was scarcely older than her pupils, but her bright intelligence gave her an air of maturity. For the first time in his life, Elias believed he was in love.

Kepple Disney had tired of the Kansas winters, and he was intrigued when Flora's father, Charles Call, announced his plan to sell his farm and travel to Florida to seek land in a more favorable climate. Kepple decided to accompany him, and Elias eagerly volunteered to go along so he could be near Flora.

Charles Call settled in Akron, Florida, but Kepple Disney decided to return to Ellis. His son did not. He bought eighty acres of land at Kismet and continued his courtship of Flora Call, who was teaching grammar school. They were married on New Year's Day, 1888, at her parents' house in Akron. The bride was nineteen, her new husband one month shy of twenty-nine.

The earliest record of the Call family dates to the eighth century, when three brothers left Saxony for Norfolk in England. Flora's ancestors settled in Norfolk. The Calls were among the earliest settlers in the American colonies, arriving in Boston in 1636. They remained in Massachusetts until Eber Call decided in 1825 to move his wife and three children to Steuben, Ohio, then a wilderness. Eber cleared the land and created a productive farm. His son Charles returned from Oberlin College excited by stories of the gold rush in California. He and a friend left Ohio with one donkey to carry their belongings. Their long walk produced no fortune, and Charles returned to Steuben.

In 1879, Charles Call traveled to Ellis, Kansas, with his wife and ten children. Among them was the seventh child, Flora, born in Steuben on April 22, 1868. After a three-day blizzard, during which furniture was pushed into the stove to keep the house from freezing, Charles Call decided to take his family to Florida.

For the newlyweds, Elias and Flora Disney, Florida seemed like paradise. No more rising before dawn to face a fierce, bone-numbing winter. All around them was luxuriant greenery they had never seen before: palms, ferns, orange groves, grass that remained green the year 'round. They spent their honeymoon at Daytona Beach, and they marveled at the warm, flat, limitless expanse of the Atlantic. They stayed on in Daytona and managed the Halifax Hotel. When northern tourists stopped coming to Florida during an economic slump, they were out of work.

For a time, Elias delivered mail on a rural route, and Flora returned to teaching. He saw the prosperous orange growers on his route, and decided to buy a small grove; it was time to put down roots. Flora and Elias welcomed their first child, Herbert Arthur, on December 8, 1888.

Walt once told a story that illustrated his father's dogged independence. After Elias had become an orange grower, the United States became alarmed at warlike moves by the Spanish in Cuba. A militia was organized, and Elias was conscripted, despite his protests of having a young family and a crop to worry about. He was sent to the militia camp, and soon the emergency abated. Still the militia was not dismissed.

"My dad just picked up and went home," Walt related. "Finally the army came around and said he had deserted. He said, 'No, I didn't desert; there isn't any war. I had to take care of my orange crop.' They said, 'Well, you must give back your uniform.' He said, 'No, I didn't get any pay, so I'm keeping the uniform.' And he did."

That winter Florida experienced uncommonly cold weather, and a freeze destroyed Elias's entire crop. Disconsolately, Elias admitted that despite Florida's eye-filling landscapes, the tropical weather made growing crops too hazardous. An attack of malaria helped convince him that he was not meant for the sultry climate. He announced to Flora that they were moving to Chicago, where reports had indicated ready work for able-bodied, ambitious men.

When he first went to Chicago, my father worked as a carpenter," Walt Disney said. "He worked as a carpenter on the World's Fair buildings. He was paid one dollar a day, and out of that he and my mother saved enough money to go in business. I don't know how he did it."

Flora and Elias Disney had known frugality from their beginnings. They considered it more important than ever as they entered a new phase of their lives. Chicago, emerging as a metropolis of a million people, bewildered them at first. In their earlier lives they had known only the desolation of the hill land and the prairie. In those circumstances, neighbors were cherished, depended on. Chicago was loud, teeming with people, many of them speaking languages the Disneys could not understand. These people were suspicious of strangers, even hostile. Flora and Elias became more protective of their growing family. Two more sons arrived: Raymond Arnold on December 30, 1890, and Roy Oliver on June 24, 1893.

Decades later, Flora explained: "We had Roy as a name and we wanted to get a middle name or just a letter. We couldn't think of any name until one day there was a big load of lumber going by. It said on the side of it, OLIVER LUMBER COMPANY. We said, 'There's a name—Oliver—to go with Roy.' So we called him Roy Oliver Disney. I don't think Roy liked the name. He didn't like being named after a lumber company."

Unlike his brothers, Roy was a sickly baby. For some reason he couldn't digest his milk, and he grew thin and listless. Without nutrition he was barely holding onto life, and Flora and Elias feared they would lose him, a common tragedy in those times. Roy's aunt Margaret, wife of Robert Disney, saved his life. She recognized the problem and wrote to a Boston doctor whose patient she had been. He responded with a special milk formula. Soon Roy became a robust, healthy baby.

Elias, who had learned carpentry during his work for the Union Pacific, earned enough money from the World's Columbian Exposition and other jobs to establish himself as a contractor. He purchased lots, Flora drew up the plans, and he erected the small, wooden houses that were much needed by Chicago's everexpanding population. Elias also built a house for his own family in what was called Northwesttown. Tripp and Keeler Avenues offered the only paved roads in the area, and Elias constructed a compact, white house at 1249 Tripp, following Flora's specifications.

Walter Elias Disney was born upstairs in the house on Sunday, December 5, 1901.

"There were three boys, exactly two years apart," Walt said in an interview. "There was an eight-and-a-half-year gap, and here I came. I think my parents were trying for a girl . . .

"Roy was eight and a half years old when I was still a baby. It was Roy's chore to push me around. He started to do it, and he's been doing it ever since (laugh). Roy was always the one brother I remembered. He was always close. He always seemed like a brother. The others went away from home so they were more or less strangers to me all my life."

Roy remembered: "Walt would get a chair between him and Dad and just argue the dickens out of Dad. Dad couldn't get ahold of him. It was all kind of a mixture of fun and provoked attitude. We had a wonderful mother that could kid the life out of my dad when he was in his peevishness."

Elias also built the small Congregational church where the Disneys worshiped. It was in the late 1890s, and Roy had a faint memory of the entire congregation pulling an old-fashioned plow to break ground for the building.

In his late years, Roy Disney was concerned about Walt's portrayals of their father as aloof and punishing.

"We had a strict father; he was a fellow who could take his place in the pulpit when the pastor was on vacation," Roy remarked. "He was a strict, hard guy with a great sense of honesty and decency. He never drank. I rarely saw him smoke. He was a strict dad but a good dad.

"I don't like him put in the light of being a brutal or a mean dad. That he was not. But when you lose your temper and you hit a kid with the back of your hand, that's impulse, that's temper. But he came to switching us. I remember in Chicago we had an apple tree in the back yard. He'd send me to my room where I could see down into the backyard. He'd wait a half-hour, then he'd casually walk out there and eye the tree and go over to it—making an impression on me—select a switch and cut it off, feel it, test it out like a little whip. All the time I'm in torture up there thinking about my licking.

"When he came up to my room, he'd have this little switch, and the biggest part was no bigger than your finger. You had to take your pants down and get a switching. That was Dad. He'd give us impulsive whacks. He never took a club to anybody. He never took a strap to anybody. He wasn't a mean man at all."

From all accounts, Elias Disney was single-mindedly focused on making a living for his family. The discipline he applied to his sons was no different from what he had known as a boy, and he believed that his father's sternness had conditioned him to a sense of rectitude. He wanted his sons to grow up with the same set of values he had learned, particularly since they now were exposed to the temptations of a big city.

Elias had a lighter side. He delighted in taking up the fiddle and sawing off folk tunes at the end of a hard day. At church socials he was called upon to play hoedowns for square dances.

Seemingly out of character was Elias's lifelong belief in socialism. For a man committed to individualism, it seemed paradoxical. Yet his favorite nighttime reading was socialist tracts.

The Disneys' fifth child was a girl, Ruth Flora, born December 9, 1903. (By happenstance or design, the initials of the Disney sons spelled words: HAD, RAD, ROD, WED. Even RFD had a connotation.) By that time Elias was again feeling the need to move on. The house-building business proved unreliable, subject to the downturns in Chicago's economy. He was convinced that the big city was not a wholesome place to raise children. He remembered his own childhood, growing up on a farm amid nature, absorbing the solid values of diligence and hard work. Yes, he decided, they would return to the soil. Flora concurred. If she had any misgivings, she didn't express them. It was her duty to support her husband.

THREE

꧂

T his time Father didn't just jump into the deal," Roy commented. "He and Mother studied two or three places. He investigated real estate in a little town of Citronella in Alabama; he also thought of Steamboat Springs in Colorado."

Then Elias journeyed to the small town of Marceline in Lynn County, Missouri, about 120 miles northeast of Kansas City. His brother Robert owned almost 500 acres of farmland there, and Elias found the area ideal. In the spring of 1906, Elias bought a house and forty-five acres from the estate of William Crane, a Civil War veteran. The price was $125 an acre, and Elias paid in installments as he received payments for property he had sold in Chicago.

Marceline was conceived in the Boston headquarters of Santa Fe as the railroad planned its ambitious route from Chicago to Kansas City. The company's agents descended on the Marceline area seeking to buy acreage from farmers at bargain prices. When word spread of the railroad's intentions, prices skyrocketed. The railroad responded by seeking options for farmland in a nearby area, creating the notion it planned to build there instead. The Marceline farmers gave in.

Elias sent Flora and the three younger children to their new home first, then he followed with Herb and Ray in a boxcar he had chartered. It contained the family's furniture and belongings as well as a team of horses Elias had purchased in the Chicago stockyards.

Flora and the three children arrived at the Marceline train station, crossed the tracks, and waited in the shade of a grain elevator, just as they had been instructed. Finally a neighbor came, and the Disneys loaded their bags into his wagon. The journey past the one- and two-story stores and banks of Main Street and into the gentle green hills of the farmland held wonders for the children. They had known only the crowded blocks and the constant clatter of Chicago. Now they saw an occasional house with a wide yard, and the only sounds were the horse's clop-clop-clop, bird songs, and calls from the barnyards. At last the wagon stopped before a square white house surrounded by a grassy yard.

Roy, who was twelve when the family arrived in Missouri, remembered the farm with fondness: "It was a very cute, sweet little farm, if you could describe a farm that way. Forty-five acres, and five of it in wonderful apples, peaches, plums. And plenty of grapes and berries and little pasture plots. We had about a four-acre place where we raised hogs. And, of course, we had chickens. We had our pets and about four to six horses all the time and a few milk cows. It was just heaven for city kids."

The Disneys' new residence was roomier than what they had known in Chicago. The single story contained a parlor/living room, a dining room, a large kitchen with plenty of storage space for home canning, and three bedrooms. The shingled roof was shaded against the midsummer sun by towering elm trees. William Crane had dug two wells that provided cool sweet water.

Roy spent the summer of 1906 at his farm chores, which he later described as "slopping the pigs or mending the fence from the rascals who were trying to root out, feeding the chickens, that sort of thing." He also had time for his little brother. Roy and Walt explored the nearby woods, walked to the Santa Fe tracks to watch the trains go by. If they were lucky, they'd get a wave from their uncle Mike Martin, who engineered the local train from Fort Madison to Marceline. On hot days the two boys skinny-dipped in Yellow Creek.

Roy once related the incident that became part of Disney family legend: "We used to catch the rain water off the roof, at the eaves. Water was always a problem. Missouri had its droughts, and maybe your well would get low, so you always saved rain water. Dad used to get barrels in those days, and to make them keep their shape, he'd tar them on the inside. So there was a tarred barrel sittin' in every place where the eaves emptied from the roof.

"In hot weather, the tar'd get soft. That was a source for Walt to get something to draw with. Our house was a white house with green trim. So Walt with his source of soft tar was drawing pictures on the house, his idea of animals and so on. Well, he couldn't wash it off."

Ruth Disney in later years remembered that she helped Walt do the painting, and their father was so angry that he didn't try to remove the tar. It remained on the side of the white house when the family moved away.

The house-tarring story was told and retold by members of the family over the years, in differing versions. After Mickey Mouse made Walt world-famous, his parents, then retired in Portland, Oregon, gave a few press interviews about their son's early life. In a 1932 story for the fan magazine *Silver Screen*, Elias put a benign spin on Walt's prank: "That was just like Walter. Whatever he wanted to do he did without ever thinking of the harm. He would always go ahead with any of his ideas whether he had the means or not. He never asked questions. I think that is the basis of his success. He has the courage of his convictions."

Roy was amused by his father's revisionism. On October 20, 1932, he wrote to his parents and Ruth: "I see you have been continuing your publicity work—a copy of *Silver Screen* for November having just come to hand. My, wasn't that a cute little son you had, with all of his dear darling painting work on the farm! The way I remember it, you didn't get such a kick out of it in those days.

"You're just like the rest of the public—nothing succeeds like success and now all the little devilish things that Walt did look awfully sweet and cute! I think Herb, Ray, Ruth, and I will have to band together and try to do something to achieve publicity or notoriety so that you can point to our early days with questionable pride!

"Don't you remember the cute little things the rest of us did? It seems to me I was always in trouble. Ruth was the angel, and I remember Herb cutting his initials in the church seat. At least, he got the credit for it and the licking that went with it! I can also vividly see Ray cutting across the cornfields about forty miles an hour! Wasn't that just darling? Then, too, Ray's mischievous pranks, like stealing the transfers from the street-car conductors on his way to school, were just too cute for anything!"

•   •   •

20

The Disney farm at Marceline seemed as idyllic as any in a Hollywood movie, and indeed, Walt Disney borrowed from his boyhood experiences for the films he later created. Not far from the place of Mark Twain's youth, the farm provided flatland planted with gold-tassled corn and tall sorghum cane. Beyond were gentle green hills clustered with nut trees and wild fruits. Sweetwater creeks ran through the property and nearby, offering sunfish, crappie, perch, and bullheads for the diligent fisherman.

Like all other houses in the vicinity, the Disneys' had no electricity or running water. When Flora needed water for cooking and cleaning, she drew it from a pump in the kitchen. The outhouse stood a respectful distance from the house. There was also a smokehouse for curing pork and other meats. Coal from the nearby mine was cheap, and the local residents used it as fuel for their stoves. Black smoke hovered over the farms and the town during cold snaps, and on winter mornings the snow was black with soot.

At Christmas time, the younger children helped Elias find the perfect pine tree in a nearby grove. He sawed it and brought it to the house for the children to decorate with their mother's help. She sewed popcorn onto a long thread and did the same with wild berries Walt and Ruth had gathered. The two youngsters festooned the tree with the strings.

When Elias had a bumper crop of apples one year, he decided against putting them on the market at low summer prices. He remembered a trick from his Kansas youth. He and the boys placed a layer of wheat straw on the ground between the trees. They built pyramids of apples, carefully laid so the fruit would not bruise. They placed more straw on the piles, then covered it all with earth. When winter came and fruit was scarce, they dismantled the snow-covered mounds and found the apples as perfect as when they were picked from the tree.

21

"I remember that my dad and mother and Roy and I went to town with a wagon," Walt said. "We all went from door to door selling apples to try to turn some cash."

Business was good for the Disney apples. Also for Flora's butter, which she and the boys sold to the folks in town. Her butter was prized, since it was assuredly fresh. Clem Flickinger, a boyhood friend of Walt's, recalled in 1987 what may have been Roy's first venture into capitalism. He planted an acre of popcorn. When the ears ripened, he shucked them, dried them in the sun, and shelled the kernels. He packed the popcorn into candy sacks and sold them in Marceline.

Elias and his older sons labored from dawn to sunset to produce a bounty from the land. Corn, sorghum, wheat, apples. Cattle, milk cows, hogs, chickens to feed the family. Potatoes, rutabagas, carrots, turnips for Flora's stews. And she filled the kitchen storage closets with sausages, smoked meats, eggs, canned fruits, and preserves for the winters ahead.

In September, Roy enrolled at Marceline's combination grade and high school, entering the ninth grade. It was a small school of 200 students. Roy's class had only eight students; he and Elmer Love were the only boys. Roy and Elmer became close friends, and they befriended Thelma Simpson. The trio walked to school together and often went to Thelma's house for refreshments after classes.

His new neighbors considered Elias Disney something of a curiosity. They criticized his radical political leanings and declined his offers to join the American Society of Equity and form a united front against the high-handedness of the railroad and the food processors. Elias's skills as a farmer were deplored. He refused to apply fertilizer to his crops until its effectiveness was demonstrated to him. Visitors noted that the Disney boys drew water from the well in mid-morning to refresh the horses; any farmer would know that the horses needed to be watered morning, noon, and night. Elias's tightness with money was often commented on.

Gradually the Disney family was embraced by the community. For all his gruffness, Elias exposed another side on Sunday afternoons when he and Flora and the two youngest children would go to neighbors' houses and join with other musicians in an impromptu concert of down-home favorites. Elias played his fiddle in country style and sang in a melodic tenor voice.

Everyone was genuinely fond of Flora Disney. She baked delicious pies, cakes, and breads for the hog killings and the sorghum harvests. She always contributed help and sympathy to those in need, and her homespun humor was infectious.

On the farm Elias drove his older sons relentlessly. When they failed him, they could expect a tongue-lashing. "My father was a great cusser," Roy recalled. " 'Consarnit!' 'Great Scott!' 'Land o'livin'!' 'Land o' Goshen!' All those old corny expressions, which gave us just as much fun and emphasis as people do today with these dirty words."

Despite his heavy labors on the farm, Roy Disney enjoyed his life in Marceline. He cherished Sundays when he and his school chums picnicked in the park and listened to a band play Sousa marches in the gazebo. Strangely, in view of their devoted churchgoing in Chicago, the Disney parents rarely attended church in Marceline. Partly that was because there was no Congregationalist church. Flora and Elias occasionally visited the Baptist or Methodist church. But, as Roy once explained, "We just sort of got out of the church habit."

Unlike most older brothers, Roy didn't mind having his little brother and sister tag along. He coddled Ruth, though he didn't mind scaring her at times. When he came across a garter snake on the farm, he put it in his pocket and brought it out to evoke a scream from Ruth.

The bond that had formed when Roy pushed Walt in his carriage on the streets of Chicago remained steadfast on the farm. They slept together, went off on adventures together, even though Roy was already in high school and Walt hadn't started the first grade. Walt grumbled about having to stay home with his little sister; his parents thought it more convenient if the two youngest began school together.

Having three older brothers, Walt was mature for a seven year old, and Roy treated him as a companion, rather than a pesky little brother, and took him along on chores. One day Roy told Walt, "C'mon downtown with me, I got a job washing the undertaker's hearse." While Roy did his washing, Walt lay motionless inside the hearse, posing as a cadaver.

Older brothers Herb and Ray yearned to become independent of their father's commanding ways and occasional switchings. The two boys planted crops on land Elias had leased from his brother Robert, and by the end of the summer of 1907 they had earned almost $170. They marched downtown, and each bought a gold watch and chain. Elias was appalled at such profligacy.

One night at supper, Elias asked the boys what they planned to do with the rest of the money. They said they might buy a pony and a heifer. No, their father decreed, the money would be used to help him pay off the farm's indebtedness.

In their bedroom after supper, Herb and Ray plotted their escape. During the noon break from chores, Herb raced the horse to the town banks and withdrew the money he and Ray had earned. Claiming to be weary, they retired early, and they quietly packed their belongings. As soon as the house was quiet, they climbed out the bedroom window and hustled into town, where they boarded the night train for Chicago. After working there, they moved in 1908 to Kansas City, and Uncle Robert found them jobs—Herb at the Pioneer Trust Company and Ray at Commerce Trust Company.

The departure of Herb and Ray dealt a devastating blow to Elias. He had counted on his two strapping sons to help make the farm a prosperous enterprise. Now he was left with only himself and his sixteen-year-old son Roy to maintain the forty-five acres of field crops, orchard fruits, and farm animals. He had no money to hire farm hands.

Elias pushed his physical strength to the limit and inevitably exhausted himself; he was in his late forties and lacked the stamina of his younger years. His weakened condition probably contributed to an attack of diphtheria. He was totally immobilized, dependent on Flora's expert care.

To Roy befell the responsibility of maintaining the farm. It was too much to ask of a sixteen-year-old boy who was also attending high school. Elias and Flora conferred, and he finally agreed to a sad conclusion: The farm, in which they had invested four years of intense and loving labor, would have to be sacrificed. They could expect no more than what they had paid for it.

Roy and Walt assumed the melancholy chore of posting auction signs throughout the county. The day of the auction arrived, and the two boys watched tearfully as their favorite horses and pigs and other animals were claimed by farming neighbors.

Roy remembered: "We had this little six-month-old colt that we had tamed and broken in. The colt was sold and tied to a buggy and taken away. Walt and I both cried. Later on that day, that was Saturday, we were down in town, and here was this farmer with his rig hitched up to the rigging rack and our little colt was tied on behind, standin' there all that time. That damn little colt saw us across the street, and he whinnied and whinnied and reared back on his tie-down. We went over and hugged him and cried over him and that was the last we ever saw of him. I went out to see that colt later and he was grown and he didn't know me at all. I was brokenhearted."

Walt recalled another happening: "We sold everything but our one old buggy horse, Charlie. We still had some hay to sell, so one day Roy borrowed another horse to make a team . . . We loaded the wagon with hay and went into town and sold it.

"Charlie was a calm old thing; you could crawl all over his back and walk right under his belly and hang onto his tail and he wouldn't do anything. Something happened under one of the traces or something, and the borrowed horse panicked and started to run. I think the tongue came down and was going along the road, and Charlie started to run, too. My brother was up there and we had a runaway.

"We were coming into town and the horses were running and my brother was pulling. We had no brakes on the wagon, and he was pulling and he said, 'Jump, kid, jump.' I wouldn't have jumped for anything. I said, 'No,' and he said, 'All right.'

"We were coming to a big hill, but there was a turnoff. He said, 'All right,' and he gave me the right rein. He kept holding the left rein, and he turned those horses around and ran them right into a tree. The neighbors were out all around there . . . and the talk was what a wonderful thing that he'd pulled them into those trees. They said if he hadn't done that, we would have been killed goin' down that hill. I was thrilled to death."

Partly because of Elias's ill health and partly because Flora wanted the three children to finish school, the family rented a house in town at 508 North Kansas Avenue. It was a solemn time for the Disneys. Elias lay in bed, weakened by diphtheria and pneumonia and despondent over the failure of his dream of a fruitful, profitable farm. Flora spent her days and evenings ministering to her husband, cooking meals, mending clothes for the three children, packing their lunches for school, and attending to the myriad of household duties.

After serious consideration, Elias and Flora decided the family would move back to a big city. He had learned of an opportunity to buy a delivery dealership from the *Kansas City Star*. It was something entirely new for him, but with two boys to help him on deliveries, it seemed like a promising enterprise. As soon as the school year ended and Elias had regained his health, they would make the move.

Despite the somber atmosphere at home, the winter and spring of 1909-1910 was a happy time for Roy. As he approached manhood, his face had taken on the Disney family look: long, straight nose, narrow chin, high, wide brow, penetrating blue eyes. Girls considered him handsome, and in later years many of them claimed to have dated him. There was plenty for teenagers to do at Marceline: skating till midnight on pasture ponds, sleigh rides through moonlit country roads, dancing at church socials. A few of the well-off families had acquired automobiles, and rides through the town and into the countryside were a thrilling novelty. So was the movie house that had opened on Main Street. It was there that Roy and Walt saw for the first time the flickering images of adventures they had only dreamed of.

After four years of physical exertion on the farm, Roy had developed a lean and wiry frame that allowed him to excel on the school's athletic teams. He performed well in his classes, especially mathematics. With his afternoons free, he could take part in school activities, including his only recorded entry into dramatics.

Ruth Disney Beecher recalled that Roy had acted in a play adapted from Longfellow's *Evangeline*: "He told me he was playing the part of Bellefontaine, and he was supposed to die in the play. I questioned him about that dying quite a bit. It kinda bothered me, so finally I would tell people that my brother died in this play—but not really."

There was an air of sadness among Roy's fellow students at Park High School in the spring of 1910 as they realized he would not join them for the senior year. The loss was especially severe since he was one of only two boys in the class. Roy himself tried to hide his own regret as he attended the round of end-of-semester parties, vowing he would return from Kansas City to visit the friends he had made during his high school years. He never came back.

FOUR

❧

It was Kansas City, Missouri. Fall, 1910. Oldtimers could still recall when the Santa Fe Trail cut through the town, when the overlanders embarked across the Missouri River to join up with the Oregon Trail. It had grown into a city, the hub of railroads that shipped cattle and wheat to all parts of the nation. Kansas City now thrived with boosterism and shady politics, as well as movie theaters, amusement parks, and other attractions to delight two boys just off the farm. And they were near their older brothers Herb and Ray again.

The Disney family settled into a small house with an outdoor toilet at 2706 East 31 Street. Elias could afford nothing bigger after paying the *Kansas City Star* $2,100 for a delivery list of 700 subscribers. At fifty-one, he had been a railroad worker, schoolteacher, hotel manager, orange grower, carpenter, contractor, and farmer with scant success. He was determined to succeed as a newspaper distributor.

Roy enrolled for his senior year at Manual Training High School; Walt and Ruth entered Benton Grammar School. Both boys had little time for school activities. They rose before dawn to deliver the morning paper, the *Times*, barely making it to school before the bell rang for classes. After school was dismissed, the boys collected their copies of the afternoon *Star*, delivered them, and returned home in time for dinner. On Sundays it was the same morning routine, except that the Sunday *Star* had to be delivered from a wagon because it was so thick.

Walt once explained the delivery routine: "[The *Star* people] were a little reluctant to sell to my father because he was a little older than they liked to have their route men, and they didn't know my dad. They finally gave in and let him have it; they were very particular, you know . . .

"My father was so conscientious. He was so concerned the *Star* would feel he wasn't doing a good job. And also he was just that way with his customers that he wouldn't allow the boys to roll the papers and throw them from the street. We had to take the papers [to the door], and if there was any wind, the paper had to be carefully put under a brick. If there was any storm . . . you had to go up those steps and go in and put them behind the storm door. No throwing them. So he wouldn't allow us to work from bicycles."

At first, Walt related, the *Star* delivered the papers to a distribution point by horse and wagon. The Disney boys had to collect their papers at 4:30 A.M. Then the company added electric trucks, and the delivery came at 2:30 A.M. That didn't last long because of newsboys' complaints. Roy and Walt loaded the papers onto pushcarts and went to their routes. They delivered to almost every door; it seemed that everyone in Kansas City subscribed to the *Star* and *Times*—except the Democrats, who wouldn't read the papers. The boys were out in the early morning streets in rain-

storms and blizzards, sometimes plunging up to their chests in snowdrifts.

Neither Roy nor Walt was paid for his services. Their father gave them allowances of $3 for Roy and 50 cents for Walt. Elias decreed they would get no salaries because they were merely earning their room and board. Both boys considered that unfair. Walt didn't complain to his father. Roy did.

"My dad was pretty tough on him," Walt said. "You could never argue with my father. He would get mad. He had a violent temper. Yet he was the kindest fellow, and he thought of nothing but his family. But he couldn't control his temper . . . Roy couldn't help but be impudent. So my father would get angry. Roy would always get away, get away. He didn't want to tangle with Dad."

One day when Roy was in his mid-teens, he was unable to elude his father's wrath. Elias was about to thrash him when Roy grabbed both his arms in a strong grip. Unable to escape, Elias lowered his arms and walked away dejectedly. He could no longer discipline his third son.

The two brothers shared their grievances in private. Roy was repeatedly amused and sometimes astonished by his kid brother's ingenuity. Walt was beguiled by the show world. When the circus came to Kansas City, he followed the parade all the way to the show grounds. Then he organized the neighborhood kids into a pint-size circus parade, with pull-wagons decorated as floats and dogs and cats masquerading as wild animals.

Ruth Disney Beecher recalled, "One time Roy got wind that Walt was going to be in an amateur night somewhere; Walt never told us. So we all hurried and got down to the theater a little ways away, and sure enough, he was acting as Charlie Chaplin. According to us, he was the best, but he didn't win the prize."

Ruth commented: "We all had a wonderful relationship with

Roy, who was the only [older brother] at home. He was always looking out for us—for Walt and me. He was full of fun and always doing something for the family. He'd come home and he'd have some kind of candy—a box of chocolate-covered cherries I remember so well."

She said that Roy was the one who said, "Let's go to the movies." The three Disney children played pinochle. They also played horseshoes in the backyard. Roy and Herb had taken up tennis, and they had matches every Sunday. Roy had joined a club a block from the Disney house. A vacant lot had been converted into a tennis court

Walt and Roy remained as close in Kansas City as they had been on the farm. "We were great pals, and anything that happened I'd tell him," Walt said in 1956. "I never kept anything from Roy. And we used to have fights.

"He had all these pretty ties, and he used to step out with the girls. He had to go to work early. I would always be back [from delivering newspapers] until around nine, so . . . if Roy had a brand-new tie, I'd wear it that day to school. And I'd usually end up with chili and beans on it. Then I'd sneak home and take the tie off and hang it up. When Roy'd put it on to go out with his girl, he'd see the chili beans right on there. He used to get mad at me.

"But it was funny. We'd argue and fight, but we'd crawl in bed, and we'd usually tell each other the latest stories we'd heard about Pat and Mike or something like that."

Her name was Edna Francis and she was born in Reese, Kansas, on January 16, 1890, though her driver's license fudged the date in later years. Like the Disneys, her family had lived in several locations. Her father was a railroad man, and he and his wife and their six children moved to Pittsburgh and Bartley, also in Kansas, then settled in Kansas City. Her father died in 1917. He had abandoned the family just before the youngest son was born. Her mother was almost totally deaf. Unable to find work, the mother stayed home to care for the younger children, and the three oldest girls sought employment.

Edna's younger brother Mitch worked as a teller at the First National Bank of Kansas City. He had struck a friendship with another young employee, Roy Disney. Following high school, Roy had never entertained any thought of attending college; no one in his family had ever gone beyond high school. He worked harvesting crops and selling goods on trains, but then decided to find a job that might afford opportunity for a future. Banking seemed a likely choice.

Roy and Mitch became best friends, and would remain so to the end of their lives. During a vacation period they took a canoe ride down the Mississippi together, playing latter-day roles of Huck and Tom.

One day at work, Mitch said to Roy, "I've got tickets to a dance given by a club I belong to. How about coming home with me, and we can take my two sisters to the dance?" Even though Roy claimed to be a poor dancer, he agreed to the proposal.

Roy was paired off with Mitch's sister Edna, who was working for the Kansas City *Star* and *Times*. Roy had taken two dance lessons, and they didn't help. But if he danced clumsily, Edna didn't notice. She was impressed by the slender eighteen-year-old. He wasn't handsome, but he had strong features and was athletic and humorous and well-mannered. No matter that she was four years older.

Edna remembered meeting Roy's little brother: "I thought he was a very cute youngster. So good-looking—he had such big brown eyes—so interested in what he was doing. Roy and I were just going together, and we'd been out to play tennis. We stopped at a drugstore to get a soda, and Walt came to see Roy because he wanted a quarter or a half-dollar for paper to draw on. That was always the story: Roy provided the money for Walt's artistic endeavors."

After five years of steady companionship, Roy and Edna decided to get married. But it was 1917, and Roy faced service in the war. Eight years would pass before their wedding.

I wrote a story of my period in the navy after spending over a year on the Atlantic during the 1918 war," Roy Disney remarked to an interviewer fifty years after the war.

"We were loaded up with coal and sent around to Bremerton, Washington, a thirty-day trip on our tub. So at that time I wrote a story of my naval experience for posterity. It was all in longhand, and my sister typed it up and copies were around the house for long periods of time . . .

"Many years later, I picked up one of those copies and read it over again. I found I had been telling the biggest whoppers ever. Everything gets embellished."

Alas for the biographer, whether Roy destroyed the copies or they simply were lost in the Disney family's many moves, Roy's navy memoir cannot be found. His rejection of it was emblematic of his nature: He lacked Walt's genius for self-promotion, preferring the role of the older brother, self-effacing but firm, uncompromising in his principles.

Roy had closely followed newspaper accounts of the events of 1917 in Europe and Washington. After the reelection of President Wilson, it seemed apparent that America would enter the war, especially with the increasing provocations of the German U-boats. Roy and Mitch Francis often discussed the latest news and deliberated on what they would do if war came. Both were in their mid-twenties and enjoyed good health, certain to be drafted.

By the time the United States entered the war in April of 1917, the two young men had concluded they would enlist in the navy together.

Roy Oliver Disney was sworn into the navy in Kansas City on June 22, 1917, two days before his twenty-fourth birthday. He was listed at 5 feet, seven inches, 124 pounds, with blue eyes, brown hair and ruddy complexion. A few scars from his farm days were itemized: forehead, right cheek, back of neck, fingers of right hand. Mitch took the oath for a four-year term beside Roy, and they and other recruits were loaded onto a train destined for the Great Lakes Naval Training Station in Chicago.

After training, the two friends were separated, Roy being assigned to the navy yard at Charleston, South Carolina. Roy rarely talked about his navy experience, perhaps abashed at the "whoppers" he had related in his memoir. A few fragments have survived in letters and tales he told his son Roy.

In 1969, Roy, who never neglected to respond to letters from old Kansas City friends or their families, dictated a letter to a friend's son who was serving in the navy in San Diego:

". . . Edna and I were glad to hear from you again and to know that the wheels of the navy are turning and you are somewhat established—temporarily, I suppose. I am glad you like it. There's a lot of good to be gained from experience in the service, if one really looks for it and tries, and a lot of that 'new vocabulary' you mention you can easily forget!

"Did I ever tell you that I was in the navy in 1917-1919 in the 'war to end all wars'? I got assigned to the scullery one time for some offense or other (I think I punched the captain or my petty officer in the nose, or something equally trivial). I am just kidding, of course, but I actually wound up in the scullery and developed blisters on my feet to such an extent that I was hospitalized for a couple of weeks. Believe me, I never appreciated *sore feet* so much in my life, for that scullery job was just not to my liking. But I guess that just proves there is some good in anything that happens to us."

At Charleston, Roy was assigned as a seaman aboard the USS *Adonis*, which was part of the convoy fleet. It was perilous duty, though Roy made no mention of the dangers in his letters to Edna and his family. German U-boats virtually ruled the Atlantic in 1917. In January, Germany announced it would sink any vessel going in or out of an Allied port. The torpedoing of many U.S. merchant ships helped bring America into the war. The United States responded by sending troop and supply ships under convoy of navy vessels. Even under such protection, the Germans were able to inflict heavy losses.

For a Midwesterner who had never seen an ocean much less sailed on one, the Atlantic crossings were a rare adventure. Crews remained on a nervous alert at all times, scanning the horizon for any hint of a periscope. Terror struck when the men heard a muffled boom far ahead of the convoy and saw a pillar of black smoke begin to blot the sky. Alarm bells clanged, and all hands reported to their stations as the ships began their zigzag course to escape the marauder. More often than not, the tactic failed, and more ships were lost.

In his three crossings on the *Adonis* and the USS *Houston*, Roy saw a great deal of danger. His son remembers one story concerning another danger—Atlantic storms: "His duty was on the bridge, and I guess it was a fairly stormy crossing. He said he was on a steel-hulled ship, and steel-hulled ships have the compass in a binnacle with great big iron corrector balls to compensate for the magnetism of the ship's hull. Apparently in a very stormy sea, one of the big balls broke off and started traveling back and forth across the bridge.

"Every time the ship would roll this way, the ball would, too. Dad said there was no getting in front of it to stop it. He described it as fifty-seventy pounds of solid iron. Everybody was dodging, trying to get out of the way of this damned ball. Finally it went hippity-hop and took a big jump and went out a window and over the side.

"He did see ships blown up around him. He said it was really scary; he was impressed with the terror of it all. A convoy is only as fast as the slowest ship in the fleet. And that was pretty slow in those days, probably ten or twelve knots. It takes a long time to get across the Atlantic at that rate."

The convoy landed at Le Havre, and Roy and the rest of the seamen were allowed liberty to explore the sights of the seaport city. It was a heady experience for the onetime farmboy and recent bank clerk, seeing buildings that seemed ancient and hearing a language that was incomprehensible to him, as well as the dialects of the English, Australians, and other members of the Allied forces. Roy had little time to explore, since his ship had to turn around and help lead the empty vessels back across the Atlantic in time to reload troops and materiel much needed for the Allied drive to end the war.

In 1917, Elias had grown restless again. Newspaper delivery had not proved the bonanza he had hoped, and he planned to move on, again with Flora's dutiful acquiescence. He found a promising opportunity: investing in a Chicago jelly factory and soft drink factory, where he would be head of plant construction. The Disney parents and Ruth moved back to Chicago and a home at 1523 Ogden Avenue.

Walt had stayed in Kansas City to finish his final year at Benton School and to help the new owner of the *Star* and *Times* dealership. He rejoined his family in Chicago and entered William McKinley High School in the fall of 1917 and became a staff cartoonist for the school's monthly magazine. At night he attended art classes at the Chicago Museum of Art. That summer he delivered mail in downtown Chicago.

The news from the battlefields of France excited Walt, and he yearned to follow the course of Roy and also Ray, who was serving in the army. But Walt was sixteen, and none of the services would accept him. Finally, by convincing his mother to let him falsify his age, he was accepted by the American Ambulance Service, a branch of the Red Cross. To Walt's profound disappointment, he was unable to reach France before the Armistice.

After his three Atlantic crossings, the Armistice was declared, and Roy made his final voyage to the naval base at Bremington, Washington. He had more than two years left under his enlistment, but with the war over, the navy was reducing its force, and early departures were encouraged. Eager to return to Kansas City and Edna Francis, Roy requested a discharge. On February 14, 1919, he was severed from the service at the same Great Lakes Training Station where he had trained as a seaman.

At twenty-five Roy returned to Kansas City a changed man, stronger, more mature, wiser in the ways of the world. His family had changed, too. His parents had returned to Chicago with Ruth. Herb Disney and his wife Louise and daughter Dorothy now resided in the Disney house on Bellefontaine. And Walt, barely eighteen, was driving an ambulance in France.

The bond between Roy and Edna proved even stronger after his absence of almost two years, and they renewed their vow to be married. But not yet. Edna, who now worked for an insurance company, remained the sole support of her deaf mother. Roy returned to his job as teller at the First National Bank, but his $90-a-month income was not enough to maintain his own lodging, much less support a wife. He and Edna resolved prudently to defer any hope of marriage until his fortunes had improved. Their plans seemed distant, since promotion at the bank appeared impossible.

Walt returned to Kansas City in late 1919, full of tales of his adventures in France. Roy had a few of his own, and they exchanged stories far into the night. After his return from France, Walt had first gone to Chicago, where he decided not to return to school. Elias had tried to interest him in a job at the jelly factory at $25 a week. Walt astounded his father by declining the opportunity and announcing that he intended to earn his living as an artist. "I had two ambitions: to be an actor or an artist," he said in later years. "It seemed easier to get a job as an artist than as an actor, so I decided on the former."

Walt offered his cartooning talent to the Kansas City *Star*, which declined to hire him. The Kansas City *Journal* admired his work but had no openings. At night Walt explained his frustrations to Roy. One day Roy was telling another bank employee of his kid brother's difficulty. "I know a couple of commercial artists, Louis Pesmen and Bill Rubin," the man said. "They say they're looking for an apprentice." Walt was accepted for the job, and his career as an artist began.

Again, defeat for Elias Disney. The president of the jelly company, in whom he had placed so much trust, proved to be a crook, and Elias lost his entire investment. He retreated to Kansas City and sought work as a carpenter. Now, except for Ray, the entire family was united under one roof: Elias, Flora, Ruth, Herb and his family, Roy, and Walt. It was different now. All three sons were grown and employed. Their father, again the victim of misfortune, held no sway over them. Flora resumed her old role, cooking hearty meals for the working men, mending their clothes, filling the house with her undaunted cheerfulness.

Roy had not been well since his return from the navy. Edna told me in 1973: "Roy had the flu a couple of times, and in 1920, many people were dying [in the postwar epidemic]. His doctor told him he should have his tonsils out. His brother Herb knew of a doctor who could remove Roy's tonsils on his lunch hour, so he wouldn't have to lose any work. Herb talked him into it, and the doctor was a quack. After Roy left the office, he had a hemorrhage on the street. My brother Mitch rushed him home, and then he was taken to a hospital."

An X ray revealed a spot on Roy's lung. Tuberculosis. Apparently he had acquired the disease while in the navy. Treatment at that time called for isolation in a dry climate. The government assigned him to a hospital at Santa Fe, New Mexico. Another tearful parting for Roy and Edna.

Santa Fe did not agree with Roy. It was too cold, the hospital too austere. He found other patients who were equally dissatisfied, and they walked out as a group. Roy traveled to another veterans' hospital in Tucson, Arizona, which accepted him despite his Santa Fe desertion. But Tucson in summer turned out to be blistering and desolate. Roy wearied of resting in bed with little to do but write letters to Edna and his parents. He was twenty-seven, an age when he should have been establishing himself in business. Despite what the doctors said, he felt well enough to leave the hospital. He decided he would not return to the bank in Kansas City, where years would pass before he achieved any real advancement. Instead, he headed for California.

Glendale was a quiet, church-filled town a few miles north of Los Angeles. Roy found a room there, and he began his hunt for a job. With millions of servicemen back in civilian life and America's economy in a postwar slump, work was scarce. All Roy could find was selling vacuum cleaners door to door. In 1971, Roy told Dave Smith of the Disney Archives about his first experience as a salesman. For days, Roy worked one neighborhood after another, greeted by angry housewives and slammed doors.

"One day I got fed up," Roy said. "I left the sample vacuum cleaner on the curb and caught a bus home. I called the company and told them where their vacuum was. When they went to get it, it was still there."

Roy suffered a relapse with his TB and was forced to enter the veterans' hospital at Sawtelle in west Los Angeles, adjacent to what is now Westwood Village and UCLA. Sawtelle was surrounded by open fields, some under cultivation. The only landmark was the veterans' cemetery, the rows of white crosses now growing in number.

News from home brightened Roy's dreary hours. Ray was working as a teller for the National Bank of Commerce and lived alone, as he would for the rest of his life. Herb had found his work at the Pioneer Trust Company too confining, and he took a job as a mail carrier for the postal service. In 1920 he applied for a transfer to California or Portland, Oregon. When the opening in Portland came through, he took it, despite the city's reputation for being rainy. Herb sent a postcard to his family every day, reporting, "Hasn't rained yet!"

After only a year in Kansas City, Elias decided to move on. He and Flora and Ruth joined Herb and his family in Portland. Walt came to the train station to see them off. Ruth recalled that Walt appeared upset by their departure: "I saw the tears in his eyes, and he suddenly left—real quick."

Alone in Kansas City for the first time, Walt moved into a rooming house. He became a frequent visitor to the home of Edna Francis. "He used to come over to my house and talk and talk till almost midnight," Edna recalled. "He was having kind of a struggle, and when he'd get hungry, he'd come over to our house and we'd feed him a good meal. He'd just talk and talk. I always was a good listener and would just let him talk."

Walt sent letters to Roy regularly, relating his plans for going into business. Roy responded promptly with words of advice. He often enclosed a $20 bill, which he knew Walt sorely needed.

The letters from Walt brimmed with enthusiasm for his new enterprise. After a few months at Pesmen-Rubin, he had been laid off, and he delivered mail during the Christmas season. Then he found work at the Kansas City Slide Company, later named Film Ad, which made advertising shorts for theaters. The company was run by a man named A. Vern Cauger. Another employee was a young artist with the odd Dutch name of Ubbe Iwwerks. (He later shortened his name to Ub Iwerks.)

"Walt and Ubbe made a great team together," Roy said, "because Ubbe was not only a good artist but a kind of mechanical genius, too. They just worked it out together, and . . . they upgraded the old man's business with new methods, better methods and came up with better stuff. That's why the old man liked them very much."

Walt worked all day at Film Ad and at night, in a primitive studio Roy had helped him set up, created brief cartoons for the Newman chain of three theaters. Walt wrote Roy that the one-minute cartoons had proved so popular that he had been encouraged to make regular cartoons for theaters. Walt resigned from Film Ad and incorporated Laugh-O-Gram Films with $15,000 borrowed from businessmen, relatives, and friends. Walt had convinced Film Ad to hire his friend, Ubbe Iwwerks, and now he enlisted Ubbe for Laugh-O-Gram. Walt realized that Ubbe was a far better cartoonist than himself and a prodigious worker.

Walt's letters to Roy became more jubilant as Laugh-O-Gram

progressed. The twenty-year-old president of the company had hired more artists of equal youth, and under Ubbe's leadership they had produced a cartoon, *Little Red Riding Hood*. A New York company offered $11,000 for six cartoons, and Walt put five more into production.

But the New York company went broke and paid no more than the $100 advance. Walt had overextended Laugh-O-Gram, and little income was flowing in. Desperately, Walt launched a new series, Alice Comedies, which would combine a live-action girl with cartoon characters. A New York distributor, M.J. Winkler, encouraged him, and he completed half of the film before he ran totally out of money.

Walt explained his situation in a despairing letter to Roy. The response: "Kid, I think you should get out of there. I don't think you can do any more for it."

Laugh-O-Gram went bankrupt. Walt paid a last visit to Edna Francis's house, enjoyed a good meal, and poured out his frustration and disappointment about his business failure. The next morning he boarded a train to join his brother in California.

Reviewing Walt's business venture, Roy remarked in 1968: "I really believe, knowing there are things like that in life, that Walt would have gotten mired down with crooks. That was his problem in Kansas City. He made some nice little pictures. They were sold . . . on a silly thing of a six-month trade acceptance . . . It was stupid. So in six months time he delivered the pictures, and when the first one came due, the damn [releasing] company went into bankruptcy . . . They ultimately paid off, and the $28,000 came back into Walt's company and paid all his debts. And even his stockholders got part of their money back.

"So it was a pathetic, interesting little story. If Walt had gone on like that in life, he never would have gone anyplace. Because there are always slickers to take you."

FIVE

❧

R oy Disney once related the beginning of the Disney company: "That was when Walt came to Hollywood. He came
out here in June of '23 [actually July]. I was in the hospital at
Sawtelle. By correspondence he sold somebody in New York on
a series of pictures. One night he found his way to my bed, which
was on a row of beds on a screened porch. It was eleven or twelve
o'clock at night, and he shaked [sic] me awake and showed me
a telegram of acceptance of his offers. He said, 'What can I do
now? Can you come out of here and help me to get this started?'
So I left the hospital the next day, and I've never been back since."
He was officially discharged from the hospital on December 2,
1923, with the notation "Against Medical Advice."

Hollywood in 1923 bore some resemblance to a gold-rush
town. Financial control of the film companies remained in New
York, but production had shifted predominately to California,
with its year-round sun and scenic locations. Studios sprouted up

all over Los Angeles County, in Culver City, the San Fernando Valley, even as far away as Santa Barbara. Hollywood itself was home to a score of studios. Big ones like Fox and Famous Players-Lasky (later Paramount). Tiny ones like those along Beachwood Drive, known as Poverty Row. Almost daily, the Keystone Kops, Buster Keaton, or Harold Lloyd could be seen staging their chases on Larchmont Boulevard or Hollywood Boulevard, weaving perilously around the streetcars.

Walt had not intended to reenter the cartoon business. He had been disillusioned and disheartened by the duplicity of the New York distributor. He reasoned that his experience in making the Kansas City films and in photographing news events for newsreel companies qualified him to be a director. But the studios rejected the twenty-one-year-old tyro from the Midwest.

On arrival in Los Angeles, Walt had moved in with his Uncle Robert, the same Uncle Robert who grew up with Elias in Ontario and Kansas and owned a farm near Marceline, which had attracted Elias there. Stone broke, Walt seldom could afford the $5 weekly rent payment. Roy loaned him the money.

Roy worried about his brother. He recalled, "He was skinny as a rail from his harrowing experience in Kansas City where he spent everything on the shop and nothing on himself. He looked like the devil. I remember he had a hacking cough, and I used to tell him, 'For Christ's sake, don't *you* get TB!' "

Roy remarked about Walt during his first weeks in Hollywood: "Tomorrow was always going to be the answer to all his problems . . . During the period before he got his [cartoon] contract, he was hangin' around this town and I kept saying to him, 'Why don't you get a job?' And he could have got a job, I'm sure, but he didn't want a job.

"He'd get into Universal, for example, on the strength of applying for a job. Then when he'd get out of the office, he'd just hang around the studio all day and go over on some sets and see what was going on. MGM was another favorite spot where he could work that gag . . . But he had a persistency, an optimism about him, all the time. A drive."

Finally Roy counseled him to go back into the cartoon business. Walt protested that he was too late; he could never compete with the New York cartoon factories now. But inevitably he retreated to cartoons out of frustration and the pressure of Uncle Robert's nagging about his not having a job. He built a stand for an animation camera in his uncle's garage.

"He had made a picture [*Alice's Wonderland*] in Kansas City that he didn't own but he used it as a selling example with the sheriff's permission," Roy said. "They let him have this print. Sending that as an example of the work he could do, he proposed a new series. This was a series where you'd have a little combination live action–cartoon. We had a pretty little girl, and she'd be playing with some animals, and something would happen. She'd get hit on the head and while she was asleep the cartoon would come on."

The offer from Margaret Winkler exceeded Walt's hopes: $1,500 per film, payable on receipt of the negative. Now the brothers needed to find seed money to start their little company. Roy had been saving his $80 a month disability pension, and he contributed the first $200. No bank would agree to lend money for such a shaky enterprise as movie cartoons. The Disneys' only recourse was Uncle Robert. He had little regard for Walt, whom he considered an irresponsible dreamer. But Robert Disney recognized the levelheadedness of the older brother, and Roy was able to persuade him to advance his nephews $500.

"When we were just getting started down here," Roy once related, "our folks put a mortgage on their house in Portland and loaned us $2,500. In our family we all helped each other."

Roy's motivation for entering the chancy cartoon business went beyond his desire to help his talented kid brother. Roy at thirty felt the overwhelming need to find an occupation so he could settle down and marry his Kansas City sweetheart. He couldn't return to banking, or any other office work. The stigma of tuberculosis would preclude his being hired. Starting an enterprise with his brother provided an ideal solution.

Miss Winkler had specified that Alice Comedies, as they were called, would have to feature the winsome little Kansas City girl who appeared in Walt's first film. Walt convinced Virginia Davis's parents to move to California and promised to pay the girl $100 a month. Roy learned to operate the secondhand camera Walt had bought for $200. They went out into the neighborhood and found some youngsters who would play in scenes with Virginia. Walt directed the action, and Roy cranked the camera. Years later, one of the girls was grown up and working at the studio. Walt reminisced about how he used to pay the girl 50 cents to act in the Alice Comedies. "No, Walt, you paid us a quarter," she corrected. "Humph," Walt replied. "That must have been Roy. He always was a cheapskate."

The live action with Virginia and the children completed, Walt added all the animation himself, working in a back room of a real estate office he had rented for $10 a month. He and Roy hired two young women to do the inking and painting of the celluloids at $15 a week. The completed *Alice's Day at Sea* was dispatched to New York, and M.J. Winkler responded with immediate payment.

The Disney brothers were jubilant. Just two months after Walt had awakened Roy in the hospital ward and enlisted his support on a new enterprise, they had their first paycheck. Walt immediately made plans for expansion. He rented a vacant lot on Hollywood Boulevard at $10 a month to be used as a location for Virginia and her playmates. He hired his first animator and moved the studio from the real estate office to a small store on Kingswell Avenue. A sign appeared in the store window: DISNEY BROS. STUDIO.

A snapshot taken outside the storefront studio shows how unprepossessing the two partners were. Both wear caps, white shirts, and slacks, both are slim and have the prominent nose and narrowing chin line that were Disney characteristics. Roy glances at the camera with a bemused smile. Walt, slightly taller, stares scowlingly, as if eager to return to work.

Walt continued expanding as the checks from Winkler came in. Roy cautioned him that the profit on each of the Alice Comedies was shrinking. "Then we need to get more money," Walt replied. He suggested asking Edna for a loan. Roy absolutely refused. Walt wrote her a pleading letter anyway, and Edna responded by sending $25. Walt also exacted $275 from Carl Stallings, a Kansas City theater organist who had bought a song reel from Laugh-O-Gram.

Roy kept his accounts in a small Standard School Series notebook, penning the entries in a tiny, meticulous script. In Ledger #1 he noted receipt of five installments of loans by Robert S. Disney, from Nov. 14 to Dec. 14, 1923. With receipt of the first payment from Winkler the entire loan was repaid with interest on Jan. 12, 1924: $528.66. Also entered was a loan from Edna Francis on January 2, 1924: $25.

Among the expense entries:

Rent on 4651 Kingswell	$15.00
Film	$49.53
Examiner ad	$1.65
Light bill	$4.20

Camera	$200.00
Lumber, tools, brushes	$30.00
Desk	$2.00
Light cord	$1.17
Western Costume [Company]	$5.00

Walt understood his limitations as an animator, and he realized that if the Alice Comedies were to improve, he needed a facile draftsman at the studio. Someone like Ubbe Iwwerks. He asked Ubbe to join him in California. His former partner was hesitant. The Disneys offered him a salary of $40 a week; he was already earning $50 a week from Film Ad. But in the end Ubbe succumbed to Walt's persuasion. He joined the Disneys and shortened his name to Ub Iwerks.

Walt was relieved to have Ub take over the animation. His perception of other people's talents, which would sustain him throughout his career, extended to self-analysis as well. He knew that his strength was story and gags. "Walt was never a good artist in execution," Roy reflected in later years. "He was a Rube Goldberg type of an artist. Walt always put a meaning in his pictures, but the technique was not [as good] . . . He was always conscious of it and would certainly turn to a better artist if he had one around."

The addition of Ub Iwerks helped improve the quality of the Alice Comedies, and the distributor seemed pleased with the product. In June of 1924, Roy entered the leading salaries into his ledger: Walt, $75 (a raise from $50); Ub, $60 (a raise from $55); Roy, $50. The honeymoon with the distributor soon ended. Walt's savior, Margaret Winkler, had married Charles Mintz and retired. Mintz took over the enterprise, and he proved to be tightfisted and arbitrary. He complained about the quality of the comedies and reduced his payment. Walt protested that he couldn't make a profit at $900 per picture. In December, with the Alice Comedies earning praise in the trade press and becoming more popular, Mintz finally relented and offered a new contract at $1,800 per picture as well as a percentage of the theater rentals.

With the company on a more stable footing, Roy and Walt seemed ready for a change in their lives. Roy described how it happened: "Walt and I were living in an apartment nearby [the studio]. First, we had just a single room in a house, then later on we got an apartment. I used to go home in the afternoon and take a sleep because I was still convalescing.

"It came to the point where Walt didn't like my cooking. As I say, I used to go home early to take a nap in the afternoon and then come back to the studio and work a couple of hours. Then I would go home and prepare something for dinner. Well, he just walked out on my meal one night, and I said, 'Okay, to hell with you. If you don't like my cooking, let's quit this business [of living together].' So I wrote my girl in Kansas City [a telegram] and suggested she come out and we get married, which she did."

Edna remembered receiving the wire and responding immediately with an enthusiastic yes. "My brother Mitch had just gone off to get married, and that left just Mother and me at home. We got [to Los Angeles] on April 7, and Roy and I were married on April 11 at Uncle Robert's house. Mother, Father, and Herb came down from Portland. Walt was the best man, and Lilly was maid of honor."

The home movie made of the wedding shows the bride and groom emerging from Uncle Robert's house and being showered with rice. Roy shakes the minister's hand heartily. Walt clowns for the camera, and he gives the maid of honor a lengthy kiss. The newlyweds drive off in a Model-T Ford with tin cans dragging behind, no doubt the work of Roy's younger brother.

Roy and Edna spent their honeymoon at the Hotel Del Coronado, across the bay from San Diego—with Mrs. Francis. Edna's daughter-in-law, Patty Disney, once asked incredulously, "Is it true your mother went on your honeymoon?" "Certainly," Edna replied. "It worked out okay. Mother was deaf."

Edna's maid of honor was Lillian Bounds, who had come to Los Angeles from her home in Lewiston, Idaho, in 1923 to visit her sister.

"A friend of mine worked in a tiny office where they made cartoons," Lilly told me in 1973. "She said they were going to hire another girl to do the inking and painting. Since it was within walking distance from where I lived, I applied for the job. That's when I met Walt. He was wearing a brown coat, sweater, raincoat, and pants. I went to work right away.

"Walt would take the girls home in his Ford runabout after work. One day when he dropped me off, he said, 'I'm going to get a new suit. When I get it, would it be all right if I called on you?' I said it would.

"Roy and Walt both went to Foreman and Clark's downtown. Walt bought a two-pants suit, Roy's had one pair of pants. Our first big date was to go see *No, No, Nanette*. When he came to my house he said, 'How do you like my new suit?' It was gray-green and double-breasted, and he looked very handsome."

They began dating steadily; often he drove his racy, secondhand Moon roadster to outlying towns on the weekend. Many nights he took Lilly to local theaters, where he looked at competitors' cartoons while she waited in the car.

"I was not very artistic at all and I was never very good at inking and painting," Lilly admitted. "Later Walt made me his secretary, but I made too many mistakes when he was dictating. He always said I was so bad he had to marry me."

Three months after the wedding of Roy and Edna, Walt and Lilly were married in her hometown of Lewiston.

"Lilly was the kind of girl who let Walt have his way," Roy once observed. "Walt was a dominating person. And she was the kind that just went along with him in what he did. She worshipped him, and anything he wanted to do was all right with her. She had a lot of patience with him, and they used to fuss at each other in their own kind of kidding way."

N ow that they were married, the Disney brothers had even more incentive to make their enterprise profitable. Walt was always seeking ways to expand and to make the Alice Comedies more polished. He brought two more of his former employees from Kansas City, Hugh Harman and Rudy Ising. He was able to deliver the comedies faster, and Charles Mintz complained they were arriving too often. Walt countered that the payment checks were arriving too slowly. Mintz replied that his company was "a great distance from breaking even" on the comedies and claimed "the independent market has gone to smash."

Mintz made the offer of a new series of comedies at $1,500 per picture, a $300 drop from the previous contract. He added a 50-50 split of the profits after he had recovered $3,000 in rentals. For two months, Mintz and Walt argued back and forth until Walt finally threatened to end their association entirely. Mintz acquiesced.

The new contract bore the mark of Roy's farsightedness. It called for a 50-50 split if the Alice Comedies should be exploited in such areas as toys, novelties, comic strips, etc.

Both Roy and Walt agreed that their company could not continue in their cramped Kingswell Avenue quarters. In July of 1925 they put a $400 down payment on a 60x40-foot lot and a one-story white stucco building at 2719 Hyperion Avenue in the Silver Lake district two miles from downtown Los Angeles. Nearby was Mack Sennett's comedy factory.

When the Disneys moved into the Hyperion studio in January 1926, a significant change had taken place. The sign on the two-story wooden building read: WALT DISNEY STUDIO.

Was this an ego trip on the part of the younger brother? Apparently not. In his last year Roy told Disney archivist Dave Smith: "It was my idea. Walt was the creative member of the team. His name deserved to be on the pictures." As future events would prove, it was a brilliant move on both their parts.

With Roy's approval, Walt soon filled the studio offices, mostly with his young pals from Kansas City. He spent long hours working on stories, figuring out gags, reviewing rough animation, checking over the finished product. Thus he established the pattern that would occupy the rest of his life.

"He knew every nook and cranny of the studio," Roy said. "He knew everybody's work. He had practically done the type of work that everybody was doing. He spent many, many evenings at the studio, going from desk to desk of the animators, looking over the work they'd done in the daytime. He used to aggravate a lot of the boys because some of 'em, of course, looked on it as snooping. But Walt was just too busy to do it in the daytime, and so he took this way of keeping up with the animation that was happening on a picture. The next day he would either [have left] notes with them or would call 'em in and talk their sequence over . . .

"The creative [people]—the artists—were always the fair-haired boys. Walt always looked at bookkeepers and lawyers and bankers like cement you had put in a foundation of a building— necessary, he guessed, but you couldn't peddle it. It was part of the drag of doin' business."

Significantly perhaps, the animation department at Hyperion occupied the second floor, the business end the lower floor. Roy once told his sister Ruth: "I have my office on the main floor and Walt has his on the upper floor. He said I have mine on the main floor so I can keep my feet on the ground."

If Walt didn't work late, he and Roy often left the studio together, and the two husbands and their wives dined together in one or the other's home. They were now next-door neighbors.

"In '26, we bought this lot, about 50 by 150 feet, on Lyric Avenue near St. George Street; it was on a side street," Roy said. "We built two houses. They were the ready-cut type of houses. The lot and the houses cost us $16,000. And today [1968] one of those houses sold for $31,000 a year or so ago. That's what you call inflation."

The two wives spent much time together while their husbands worked at the studio, and they compared notes about the brothers. Edna once remarked, "That's what we always kidded about, Lilly and I: the Disney disposition. They could flare up very easily, both of them, and maybe hurt each other for a few minutes. Then they're always sorry and apologize."

Occasionally Edna and Lilly went to downtown Los Angeles to shop at May Company, Bullock's, Robinson's, and other stores. After work, Roy and Walt joined them, and the foursome had dinner at a cafeteria.

"Sometimes I went to the studio with Walt at night," Lilly recalled. "Walt concentrated on some work he was doing, and I slept on the davenport in his little office. I would wake up and ask, 'What time is it?' 'Not late,' he'd say. It would be three o'clock."

With their new wives and new homes and the checks coming regularly from Mintz, the Disney brothers started to feel confident. The production crew numbered ten, not counting the inkers and painters. Walt encouraged a collegial atmosphere, installing a baseball diamond and a badminton court on the lot. Animators used them at lunchtime to shake off the tedium of drawing all day. The few who owned cars drove to nearby Griffith Park at the noon hour for horseback rides in the hills. Everyone was on a first-name basis. Neither of the bosses was called "Mr. Disney." Always it was "Roy" and "Walt." Only two men wore ties at the studio: the paymaster, Mr. Keener, and Roy.

Charles Mintz occasionally praised the Alice Comedies as they were received, but he could dismiss Walt's effort as "just another picture and has nothing in it whatever that is outstanding." Walt himself realized that it had become increasingly difficult to energize his production crew with plots and gags they hadn't done before. Walt had an intense dislike, which continued throughout his career, for repeating himself. By the middle of 1927, he had produced fifty-six Alice Comedies, and he and his men had exhausted the series' possibilities.

During a squabble over the hiring of a new girl to portray Alice, Mintz mentioned in a letter that "a national organization" was considering a new cartoon character, possibly a rabbit. There were too many cats in cartoons (including Disney's Julius in the Alice Comedies), the organization had observed. Margaret Winkler Mintz, still loyal to Walt and Roy, suggested to her husband that the Disneys could produce the proposed cartoon.

Ever calculating, Mintz didn't mention to Walt that the inquiring party was Carl Laemmle, head of Universal Pictures. Mintz had found outlets for a number of cartoons, including the popular Felix the Cat. To win a contract with a major company like Universal would be a bonanza.

Roy and Walt agreed that the offer was a prime opportunity for their young company. Ub Iwerks produced sketches of a rabbit character to be called Oswald the Lucky Rabbit. They were approved by Universal. Only then did Mintz reveal the identity of the buyer.

After a slow beginning with the first Oswald, *Poor Papa*, the animators hit their stride. Oswald began to be noticed by the trade. *Film Daily* reported: "Oswald looks like a real contender. Walt Disney is doing this new series. Funny how the cartoon artists never hit on a rabbit before. Oswald with his long ears has a chance for a lot of new comedy gags and makes the most of them. Universal has been looking for a good animated subject for the past year. They've found it."

The newfound recognition stemmed from Walt's insistence on quality. He photographed rough animation and screened it to determine if it matched his standards. If not, animators went back to the drawing board. His meticulousness bothered Roy, who complained that the difference between the cost of production and the $2,250 Mintz paid per episode was ever-narrowing. Walt listened to his brother's lectures, and continued as before.

Roy found consolation in one factor: Mintz had arranged tie-ins for products bearing Oswald's likeness—a candy bar, a badge, and a stencil set. The manufacturers paid no royalty to the Disney company, but Roy could foresee a chance for income if Oswald became popular enough.

After a year of producing Oswalds, one every fortnight, the cost had outrun the income. In March of 1928, Roy and Walt conferred and decided that Walt would go to New York to present his case to Mintz for a larger payment per episode, at the least, $2,500. Walt received a hint of a cold reception, but he chose to ignore it.

Les Clark, who came out of high school in 1927 to work for the Disneys, told me in 1973 that before Walt left he had been approached to go to work for Universal. Ub told Clark he had been asked, too. When Ub told Walt about it, Walt couldn't believe that Universal would steal his staff.

Walt recalled: "These Oswald pictures were fairly successful. At the conclusion of our first year, because of the success they had attained, I was of course expecting to be allowed a little more money to build them to a still higher standard. But Winkler and I had a difference of opinion on that subject, and he decided he could get along very well without me. So, 'taking' a few of the men from my organization, he started his own studio and produced a second series of Oswald. This left me with two or three loyal men and nothing to do.

"The split with Winkler happened when I was in New York, and my brother Roy was temporarily running the studio. Not wanting to burden him with worries, I just kept quiet about the break with Winkler, and wired him that everything was all right and that I was on my way home. However, before coming home, I tried to create another character . . . and sell the idea to some distributor before I left, on the strength of the work that I had done on Oswald. I couldn't find anyone who was interested in the idea, so again I thought the best thing to do was make a picture. However it was quite a problem to decide what to use. [Cartoon makers] had used cats, dogs, rabbits. About the only thing they hadn't featured was the mouse.

"A mouse had always appealed to me. While working in Kansas City, I caught several in waste baskets around the studio. I kept them in a cage on my desk and enjoyed watching their antics. One of them was quite tame and would crawl all over my desk while I worked. He seemed to have a personality of his own, and I gave him a pet name. That is more or less what started the idea of Mickey Mouse."

Lilly told the rest of the story: "Walt showed me some of his sketches on the train coming home. They were cute little things; they could do anything. I asked him what he was going to call the character. 'Mortimer Mouse,' he said. I said, 'That doesn't sound very good,' and then I came up with 'Mickey Mouse.'

"Roy met us at the station, and he looked very worried. He asked Walt: 'Have you got something lined up?' Walt said, 'No, but I've got a wonderful idea.' Roy was deflated, and he seemed depressed all the way home."

At the studio, Walt presented his idea to Roy and Ub. Again, Walt was irresistible. Roy and Ub consented to the new venture.

"We all agreed that the best thing to do would be to take a chance with what little money we had saved and see what we could do alone," Walt related. "We all dug in and started making the first Mickey Mouse. We still had three or four subjects of Oswald to complete for Winkler, therefore it was necessary to keep quiet about the fact that we were making this new series of cartoons. So we decided to make the first Mickey in the garage at my home while we continued making the Oswalds at our studio."

Security was mandatory because the animators who had defected to Mintz would not be leaving for two months. Walt and Ub worked up a story line that would capitalize on the nation's craze for airplanes in the wake of Charles A. Lindbergh's historic flight across the Atlantic. Ub locked his door and whipped out animation at an astonishing rate, seven hundred drawings a day. Edna, Lilly, Lilly's sister, Hazel Sewell, and two other women inked and painted the cels in Walt and Lilly's garage.

I've been mad at people, but I could never carry a grudge for very long," Walt once said. He held no rancor against the men who defected to Universal: Rudolph Ising, Hugh and Walker Harman, Friz Freleng, whom he had broken into the animation business at Laugh-O-Gram and brought to Hollywood. Nor did he express anger at Charles Mintz. When they parted for the last time in New York, Walt told him: "These boys will do the same thing to you, Charlie. If they do it to me, they'll do it to you. Now watch out for them."

In April 1929, Universal announced that the Oswald cartoons would henceforth be produced by its own cartoon department, headed by Walter Lantz. Walt Disney's prediction had come to pass.

SIX

❦

P *lane Crazy* had its first public screening at a Hollywood theater on May 15, 1928. The audience laughed in the right
places, but the response was not as great as Walt had hoped. The
same was true at a screening for MGM executives. Walt realized
he needed to sell Mickey Mouse to the decision makers in New
York, and he hired a film dealer to show *Plane Crazy* to the major
distributors. Nice comments but no buyers. Undiscouraged, Walt
launched a second Mickey Mouse, *The Gallopin' Gaucho*. This
time he didn't need the cloak-and-dagger secrecy. The Oswald
defectors had departed.

The Disneys were trying to sell Walt's new character at the
worst possible time. Eight months before, Warner Bros. had given
the world a talking, singing Al Jolson in *The Jazz Singer*. The
reaction was volcanic. After thirty years of silence, the motion
picture screen had suddenly found its voice. Every film company,
every theater owner was in turmoil. Could they afford the im-

mense cost of converting to sound? If so, what system was best? And would the ticket-buying audience accept talking actors after years of pantomime and titles?

Walt instinctively seized upon sound as a new tool to add to the sophistication of the cartoon. He launched a third Mickey, *Steamboat Willie*, which he intended to synchronize to the old tunes "Steamboat Bill" and "Turkey in the Straw." But how? Wilfred Jackson, who had been hired two weeks before the Oswald exodus, suggested borrowing a metronome from his mother, a music teacher. By coordinating the beats of the metronome to the 24-frames-per-second speed of the camera, Walt could time the music.

But would the system work? And would audiences accept sound in a cartoon?

Roy recalled: "[*The Jazz Singer*] startled the whole industry, but it didn't startle anybody more than Walt. So we immediately, around the studio, began experimenting. We'd take our cartoon feature, throw it on the screen, where you could see the picture from the reverse side. Some of us fellows and some of the wives with the lighter voices would each take a character, and we would ad lib to that character.

"Then we'd get all the rest of the organization out in front to view the effect. Walt was quick to say, 'That's it. If it looks realistic, it'll be realistic. That's what we gotta do. Stop all those silent pictures. Let's go after sound.'

"So we started making sound pictures. We knew nothing about sound except the boys worked it out using a metronome as their guide. And the pictures were drawn to the musical tempo [since] music is mathematical in that sense. And Walt went back East to try to get this first picture scored in sound.

"Western Electric and RCA were too busy with the big companies [to bother with] us. They said, 'Leave your picture here, and we'll get at it some day and put sound to it.' Walt said, 'Oh no. You can't produce sound for pictures we make. That's pre-posterous.'

"We had been looking around, and there were some other little independent fellows making sound equipment. One of them was an Irishman named Pat Powers. He called [his system] Ci-nephone. So Walt signed up for Cinephone equipment on a ten-year deal that cost us quite a bit of money, guaranteed each year."

The cost, which Walt did not immediately reveal to his brother, was $26,000 a year, plus payment for the equipment. It was a huge outlay for the tiny company. Walt had been bamboo-zled by one of the great con men in the film business. A fellow Irishman, Pat Powers had been a blacksmith and a cop before entering the rough and tumble of the movie business. He became notorious for his shenanigans in the industry.

Walt later recalled his search for sound equipment in New York: "I kept hunting and hunting and I ran into this fellow who had what they called at that time, sort of an outlaw sound equip-ment. It was not properly licensed by RCA, say. He claimed he had patents, and they claimed they were no good.

"The fellow was named Powers, Pat Powers. He was a partner with Laemmle, and he helped found Universal with Laemmle. When he got in a bind with Laemmle and Laemmle wanted to look at the books, Powers threw them out a twelve-story window. He had a fellow with a truck pick the books up and take 'em over and hide 'em in Brooklyn somewhere."

Powers arranged a recording session, supplying an orchestra leader who insisted on doing it his way, not Walt's. The first at-tempt was a failure. Walt demanded his own instructions at the second session, and it was successful.

Back in California, Roy eagerly read Walt's letters detailing his travails in the big city. Walt had told Ub to make a fourth Mickey

Mouse, *The Barn Dance*. With the company's treasury dwindling, Roy was concerned about meeting the payroll. Walt was called upon to make a sacrifice.

"I had a beautiful Moon roadster that I was so proud of, a cabriolet with the top that went down," Walt remembered. "Red and green running lights on it, oh, it was the sportiest thing . . . By the time I got back, I didn't have my car. I had them send the pink slip to me. I signed it, I sent it back. They sold my car to meet payrolls before I ever got out of New York."

Pat Powers had promised to arrange for top company bosses to view *Steamboat Willie*. When Walt arrived at the offices of the major companies, he was usually told to wait. His film was finally reviewed by lesser officials, who laughed at the antics of Mickey and the villain Pete but responded with the customary put-off: "We'll get back to you." Walt's letters to Roy and Lilly reflected his growing disillusionment.

Harry Reichenbach, a legendary publicist and promoter, listened to Walt's laments and volunteered to show *Steamboat Willie* at the theater he was managing, the Colony on Broadway. Walt thought that public exposure would sour his chances of landing a distributor. Reichenbach argued otherwise, and he offered $1,000 for a two-week run. Walt knew Roy needed the money for the payroll, so he accepted.

Reichenbach's instincts proved correct. *Steamboat Willie* opened at the Colony on November 18, 1928, and it aroused a sensation beyond Walt's dreams. The trade paper reviewers raved, and even the *Times* called it "an ingenious piece of work with a good deal of fun." Walt stood at the back of the theater every night and gloried in the waves of laughter from the delighted audience.

Now the major distributors were eager to distribute Mickey Mouse—on their terms, which were to buy the cartoons and pay

Disney weekly. No thanks, Walt replied. After the debacle with Mintz, he refused to relinquish control of his product. Powers agreed. He convinced Walt to let him distribute Mickey Mouse state by state, offering to pay production expenses and take 10 percent of the gross returns.

Walt returned to California with $2,500 in cash, feeling like a conquering hero. Roy was less than thrilled.

"Did you read this contract?" Roy demanded.

"No, I didn't read it," Walt replied. "What the hell, I want the equipment."

The shipment from Pat Powers arrived, and Walt plunged into production, hiring more animators and bringing Carl Stallings from Kansas City to help with the music. At a recording session in New York, Carl Stallings suggested a cartoon with ghosts and skeletons dancing to the music of Grieg's *March of the Dwarfs*. Back at the studio, Walt and Ub fashioned a continuity for what Walt called the spook dance.

"Give 'er hell, Ubbe," Walt wrote in a cheerleading letter from New York. The result was *The Skeleton Dance*. Powers contended that theater operators didn't want it—"*More mice.*" Walt booked the cartoon into the prestigious Carthay Circle Theater in Los Angeles. Walt sent the glowing reviews to Powers, suggesting a booking at the huge Roxy Theater. The response was so good that Walt proceeded with his plans to launch a second cartoon series to be called Silly Symphonies.

Roy doubted the wisdom of undertaking an additional series at a time when the costs of the Mickey Mouse cartoons were mounting alarmingly. In small handwriting for his ledger book, he entered the amounts, which included production and prints:

Plane Crazy	$3,528.50
The Gallopin' Gaucho	4,249.73

Steamboat Willie	4,986.69
The Barn Dance	5,121.65
The Opry House	6,017.24
The Skeleton Dance	5,386.65

Roy found a way to help offset the costs. As part of the Pat Powers deal, the studio had acquired two sound trucks. Roy disliked seeing them idle, so he rented them out to the producers of five-day movies who couldn't afford the sound systems of Western Electric and other more established companies.

Mickey Mouse had become a national sensation, and the Silly Symphonies had been successfully launched. Yet weeks went by without any checks from Pat Powers. Roy suspected something was amiss, and in late 1929 he made a trip to New York to confront Powers. Powers responded with his customary blarney and double talk.

Roy remembered: "I had about only one thing at the time: honesty and love of Walt. So nothing was done that would ever hurt the business or would hurt Walt. I protected that with a fervor. That was the difference.

"I came back from New York, and I said, 'Walt, that Powers is a crook. He's a definite crook. He won't give me satisfaction. I can't find out what we've got coming to us. He makes us sign these notes.'

"He made us sign a note every time we delivered a picture. We owed him money. Walt was very upset with me, and he said I was a troublemaker, that I was suspicious, that I didn't believe in people, and so on. So I said, 'All right, you go back and find out for yourself.'

"Powers said [to Walt]: 'Sign this five-year contract, and we'll go on with the business. Walt said, 'No, I won't sign any contract. I want to know where we stand today.' Pat finally said, 'You sign this contract or I'll go into business myself.' Walt said, 'That's okay.' And Powers said, 'I've got your main man—Ub Iwerks.' "

Walt was stunned. Had he once more fallen sucker to a New York sharpie who stole the company's most valuable assets: its animators? Walt couldn't believe that Ub, after their long history together, would leave him. Beyond his personal feelings, Walt realized the loss of Ub would be serious; Ub had been the creative force that made Mickey a hit, and he had made *The Skeleton Dance* almost single-handedly. It was true that friction had arisen between the longtime partners. Ub had complained about Walt's interference with timing of the animation and Walt's insistence on spreading the work to younger animators. Walt didn't take Ub's complaints seriously.

After leaving Powers, Walt telephoned Roy with the bad news. Roy already knew. Ub had told him that same day that he wanted to be released from his contract, blaming his differences with Walt. He made no mention of the Powers connection.

As with the defections to Mintz, Walt and Roy held no rancor toward Ub. At the time, Ub was being paid $150 a week. Roy's salary was $50 and Walt's $75—but they never drew the full amount unless they urgently needed money. Ub also held a 20 percent interest in the company. Powers had offered Ub $300 a week. "Ub couldn't stand the pressure," Roy explained. "He had a wife and babies. There were no hard feelings."

When the partnership had been formed, Roy had stipulated that if any partner left he couldn't claim values that weren't on the books. Ub's share came to $2,920.

The Disney brothers agreed that they needed to rid themselves of Pat Powers, even if it meant failing to collect their share of the $17,000 per picture he was receiving. In January of 1930,

Roy sent Walt off to New York with the admonition: Whatever you do, bring back some money. Powers again stonewalled any attempt to see his books; "Sue me," he challenged. Walt exacted a $5,000 advance, which he dispatched to California. He and Roy debated whether to take Powers to court. They decided the litigation would be lengthy and would hamstring their company just as it was developing a head of steam.

Walt sought another distributor, and MGM expressed great interest, then backed off because of Powers's threat to sue any company that tried to do business with the Disney cartoons. Harry Cohn, the blustery boss of Columbia Pictures, did not scare easily. Upon the recommendation of his brilliant director, Frank Capra, Cohn proposed a $7,000 advance per cartoon and assured $25,000 to fight any Powers lawsuit.

Powers conceded defeat, but not before exacting his tribute. He demanded $100,000 for the rights to the first twenty-three Disney cartoons. Eager to move on with the company, Walt agreed to the ransom.

The year 1930 proved pivotal for the Disneys. They had learned a painful lesson from Mintz and Powers: never again would they relinquish control or ownership of their product. Walt would continue his role as the creative dynamo, ever seeking to extend the cartoon beyond its accepted limits. That meant more and more expense. To Roy fell the responsibility of finding the money to fulfill his brother's imagination. Cartoons had long languished as the stepchildren of the movie industry (even though many theaters now billed MICKEY MOUSE CARTOON above the feature attraction on their marquees). Most major companies lacked cartoon departments because the profit margin was too small.

.   .   .

R oy realized that the company could not exist on a boom-
or-bust economy, splurging when money poured in, near-
ing collapse when it did not. He needed a steady source of
financing, and that meant associating with a bank. This contra-
dicted family tradition. The avowed socialist Elias Disney dis-
trusted all banks and preached that belief to his sons. He nearly
always paid cash for his transactions. Running a burgeoning company obviously didn't allow that, Roy realized.

He approached A.P. Giannini, whose San Francisco-based
Bank of Italy (later Bank of America) was expanding aggressively
throughout California. Giannini had done some studio financing
and was intrigued by the movies, especially cartoons. Against the
wishes of his board, he agreed to lend money to the ambitious
young brothers from the Midwest. Thus began a thirty-year association, sometimes acrimonious, that kept the Disney company
afloat in treacherous times.

"A.P. used to travel a very great deal in those days," Roy commented. "I used to get postcards from him. From Rome, Milan,
Paris, London, New York. He'd say, 'I saw one of your pictures,
and it's a pretty good one.' Or then he'd say, 'This one wasn't so
good.' Or he'd say, 'It got a good audience reaction.' He was very
much attuned to the fact that people—audiences—had to like
pictures."

Around the same time, the Disneys discovered a source of
income that would help keep them solvent in good times and
bad: merchandising.

R ight after Mickey Mouse hit, I was in New York and we
needed money," Walt recalled. "A fellow kept hanging
around the hotel with three hundred dollars cash waving at me,

and I finally signed a deal to put Mickey Mouse on these big cheap [writing] tablet type of things. It was the first deal ever signed."

Roy realized that in order to profit from merchandise, it was imperative to protect the cartoon characters' names and likenesses from infringement. He cited the case of the producer of the cartoon series Aesop's Fables: "He was a very stubborn guy who first offered Walt a job and made him what was then a flattering offer. Walt, of course, refused. Then he offered to buy us out. Which we refused. Then he openly challenged us and said, 'Your copyright is no good; anybody can make a mouse.' So he went ahead and made several pictures with mice characters that pretty much looked like ours. So we sued him.

"It didn't take so long when we actually got down to it. We gave him enough rope until he actually kind of hung himself. We finally got down to court with big blowups of his characters and our characters right out of the film . . . We just stopped him; that's all we were out to do. We didn't ask any damages. We wanted to establish our right . . . To establish a copyright like that is a big thing and that's an important thing to do. A good case. Make it a judicial win that sticks."

The decision marked a crucial milestone in the history of the Disney studio. Roy launched a campaign to convince corporations to adorn their products with Mickey, Minnie, and other Disney characters. Roy signed the first contract with a New York company, George Borgfeldt, on February 3, 1930, for the making of toys and other objects with the likenesses of Mickey and Minnie Mouse.

On March 20, 1930, Roy sent a letter to the Buzza Company of Minneapolis, publishers of children's books, proposing a series of books about animals, featuring Mickey Mouse.

After bragging that Mickey "is probably one of the best-known characters ever seen on the screen," Roy noted that the Disney company had already made strides in merchandising: "Mickey Mouse is now being handled in newspaper comic strip form, through King Features Syndicate, who are rapidly placing the strip in many leading newspapers throughout the country.

"Borgfeldt & Co. of New York have taken the world rights to manufacture toys and novelties and are very optimistic about the possibility of the subject.

"Villa Moret, Inc., music publishers of San Francisco, are publishing a Mickey Mouse song, used in the pictures.

"Also in connection with our pictures we have launched a campaign for the formation of Mickey Mouse Clubs at theaters where the cartoons are shown. On the West Coast alone, the only territory so far we have worked, there are some sixty theaters successfully operating Mickey Mouse Clubs, which are a Saturday matinee proposition for the children. The idea is meeting with astonishing success . . ."

The comic strip had been Walt's idea. In 1929, he had asked Ub Iwerks to prepare a sample, and after several tries, Walt decided on one. Ub drew a month's supply of strips before leaving the studio. When King Features approached Walt for a Mickey Mouse strip, he was ready for them. The daily feature made its first appearance on January 13, 1930. It was followed over the years by Mickey Mouse and Silly Symphony Sunday pages, and strips featuring Donald Duck, Uncle Remus, and other characters.

At one time 800 theaters took part in the Mickey Mouse Club promotion.

"We formed them ourselves by selling the theater men on the idea of having a kiddies club," Roy explained. "You give them a little something on their birthday, and they all had to pay admission. They had a ritual of a club, and they all belonged. Then we got people to make pins for them and banners and so on. We used to charge the theater men $25 as a basic license fee, and then they bought all those accessories. The basic fee of $25 went to our salesman, and if he was on the ball he could make himself $100, $150 a week. That went along for a few years very, very successfully."

One day in 1932, a Kansas City advertising man named Herman (Kay) Kamen telephoned Walt with a proposal for promoting Mickey Mouse via merchandising. Walt was intrigued, and he invited Kamen to come to the studio. Kamen greeted Walt and Roy by saying, "I don't know how much business you're doing, but I guarantee you that much business and 50 percent of everything I do over that amount." The Disneys were impressed by his enthusiasm and gave him the go-ahead. "He was a terrific salesman, terrific merchandiser," Walt recalled. "He knew how to merchandise things. He helped many a concern out of a hole by showin' 'em how to use our products. One of them was Ingersoll watch. [The Mickey Mouse watch] pulled them out of a hole; they admit it. And Lionel Toys.

"During the Depression, it was just bad for the toy business. They made this little windup Mickey Mouse that ran around a track. It was a big item. It sold everywhere."

A s with Mintz and Powers, the honeymoon with the Disneys' third distributor, Columbia Pictures, was soon over. As Roy explained: "We made pictures there on a basis of $7,000, $9,000, and finally $11,000 advance when we delivered, against a contract that was sixty-forty-forty-sixty. In other words, 40 percent for distribution, 60 percent goes to pay for those advances plus prints and advertising, and when they were all paid, we got 40 percent and they got 60 percent. We saw very, very little overages."

The money situation wore on Walt's nerves, which were already frayed by the pressures of riding a runaway hit. He kept adding new animators and other artists, many of them escapees from the New York cartoon factories, and then he had to break them in to the Disney way of doing things. He sought perfection in the Mickey Mouse and Silly Symphony cartoons and fretted when he couldn't achieve it. Within two years, Mickey Mouse had become a national icon, and critics hailed Walt Disney as a genius. Yet for all the success, the company continued its slide into the red.

"In 1931, I had a hell of a breakdown," Walt told Pete Martin and Walt's daughter Diane. "I went all to pieces . . . As we got going along, I kept expecting more from the artists, and when they let me down, I got worried. Just pound, pound, pound. Costs were going up, and I was always way over what they figured the pictures would bring in . . .

"I just got very irritable. I got to the point that I couldn't talk on the telephone. I'd just begin to cry at the least little thing. It used to be hard to sleep. It was an emotional thing, so I had to go away. I just finished a picture that I was so sick of. Oh gosh, I was so sick of it! I went to a doctor, and he said, 'You've just got to get away, that's all there is to it. I can't do anything for you.' "

For their first real vacation since their honeymoon, Walt and Lilly visited the monuments in Washington, D.C., then traveled by train to Key West, where they cruised to Cuba. After a trip through the Panama Canal and up the coast to California, Walt returned to the studio.

Roy's concern about his brother is conveyed in a letter to their parents dated Dec. 30, 1931: ". . . Walt is feeling much better than he was before his vacation, but is not back to his old self. Confidentially, I am a little worried about Walt's health, feeling there

71

must be something basically wrong. There is consolation in the fact, though, that he is taking it very seriously himself and leaving nothing undone to find out what the trouble is and endeavoring to correct it, if possible. It seems that they have definitely determined right now that there is some sort of parasitic growth in his intestines of a vegetable nature. It is absolutely not T B, but more like a fungus parasite, which is sapping his strength and body nourishment. When this condition is cleared up he may, by building up his general strength and vigor, be okay again. The above is the substance of the doctors' reports after thorough examinations.

"Walt, like the rest of us, has been indifferent to his physical endurance or condition, seemingly taking good health for granted, never having had any trouble before. But his trouble now has woke him up, so to speak, and maybe in the long run will be very beneficial for him for that reason. Things are going much better at the studio so it is much less of a nerve-wracking job for him than before . . ."

By 1933, Roy had completely soured on the company's association with Columbia Pictures. Columbia had released fifty pictures but had yet to pay more than the advance. The amounts that were due to the Disneys were subtracted from the $50,000 Columbia had loaned to pay half of Pat Powers' ransom. Roy had learned from theater owners that Columbia's salesmen offered Disney cartoons as loss leaders in order to sell Columbia's other, inferior short subjects. Even so, Roy proposed to renew the contract at an advance of $15,000 per picture. Columbia refused the offer.

Joseph M. Schenck, president of United Artists, agreed to pay the $15,000 advance and promised the cartoons would receive special handling, since United Artists released no other short subjects.

"The contract with U.A. was on a straight distribution basis," Roy remarked. "We paid 30 percent for distribution. That's when we moved into the period when [United Artists] upped the grosses from Columbia, and we were suddenly in the pink, in the money. By the time we got with U.A., we were spending twenty, twenty-five, thirty thousand dollars [on the pictures], and they used to do about one hundred and forty or one hundred and fifty thousand dollars in the world with them.

"That was the first decent contract we had in the business, and they gave us good world distribution. [United Artists was] a company of very high standing in those days—Mary Pickford, Douglas Fairbanks Sr., Charlie Chaplin, Alex Korda, Sam Goldwyn."

Walt and Roy were honored to be connected with such giants. But, as with the Disneys' other distributors, the association would one day end.

SEVEN

❧

T he Hyperion studio was a fun place to work," said Dolores
Scott, who started there in 1930 and became secretary to Roy
Disney and then Walt. "Everyone was so young and excited about
what was being created. We all worked like dogs, but we enjoyed
every minute of it."

Others who started with Disney in the early to middle thirties
shared much the same view. They worked for Depression-style
wages, but there were few complaints. They savored the rare mix
of personalities, many of them richly talented, more than a few
genuine eccentrics. A few were hardened veterans of the New
York school of cartoon making. Many had recently graduated
from high school or college, bright young artists with no knowledge of how animation worked.

"The artists depended on Walt's words," said Dolores Scott in
1973. "Directors would hang over secretaries' shoulders; they
couldn't wait to get transcripts of Walt's remarks in story meetings.

Once a few of the animators were having trouble with a scene. They ran it in the sweat box, and afterward silence prevailed. One of the men asked Rollin 'Ham' Hamilton what he thought. Ham replied, 'I dunno, Walt isn't here.' "

Ward Kimball, who became one of the legendary Nine Old Men who made the Disney classic features, remembered Hyperion when he arrived in 1934: "The studio in those days was a very small place. They had just finished the new center building, the two-story one. The in-between department [where assistants made the drawings between the movements created by the animators] was down in the semibasement, right next to the inking department. And was it hot! No air conditioning. We called it the bull pen.

"Working at a new job made me very nervous. During those hot summer months they were excavating next door to add on another building. This big Caterpillar tractor was growling away when all of a sudden, WHAM—it sounded like a bomb hit the building. This thing came through the wall and stopped just about three feet from my back! Dust, plaster, wood splinters, and everything, flying all over my work. The driver had lost control and drove this big thing right through the wall. Everybody comes running down the stairs to see what happened. When the dust settles, I find that my nose is bleeding all over my face."

Ken O'Connor, later an art director, also came to Hyperion in 1934 and began as an in-betweener. "The studio had some odd little bungalows brought in from somewhere," he recalls. "To me it was mainly a hotbox. I was tried out as an in-betweener in what I called the black hole. It had no windows, no air conditioning, just a big black place to work in. In the summer I tried to avoid smearing my work with my own perspiration.

"I had very little contact with Roy. I was on one end of the assembly line, spending the money to get the quality that Walt wanted; Roy was on the other end, trying to get the money back any way he could. In a sense, we were almost enemies, but Roy never seemed that way. He was the bookkeeping man, the money man, the man trying to keep Walt under control. Walt was like a spinning flywheel, spinning revolutions that kept the thing going. When Walt wanted to spend everything on the next picture, Roy would say, 'Let's keep a little sinking fund—in case we sink.' I always felt he was a real steadying influence throughout the studio."

Roy was always affable, always approachable for workers at the studio. Walt was less predictable. Bob Broughton recalls his first day at Hyperion in 1937. He had been hired for the traffic department and was told everyone was addressed by his or her first name—"even if you bump into Walt." That happened on Broughton's first afternoon.

"I went out with a load of drawings to somebody's room," he remembers. "Here comes Walt walking down the hall. I had been told what to do, so I said, 'Hi, Walt.' He went by me like there was nobody in the hall. I thought those dirty buggers had set me up; I walked right into it. Five-ten minutes later, I'm walking back and here comes Walt. I'm not real bright, but I'm not stupid. This time I just walked by. He grabbed me by the arm and said, 'What's the matter? Aren't we speaking?' I learned later when he was onto something, he had that tunnel vision."

When Ward Kimball came to work at Hyperion, he recalled, about 160 people worked there, "and that included the night watchman and the janitors. The big boss was the guy that everybody called Walt. For idea incentives, he would pay $3 for a small gag, $5 for a good gag, and $100 for a complete story idea.

"When I worked in the in-between bullpen, you had to strip to the waist in the summer, it was so damn hot. We sat in a row, row after row, and it all looked like a slave ship, where you'd be perspiring and you'd do anything to break the monotony. 'Course everybody was young, and the gags were many and funny. Sheer desperation seemed to bring out a never-ending stream of humor."

One of the great gagsters was Ted Sears, a New York import with a delicious sense of humor that made him an accomplished story man. A new member of the story department was a Britisher who was devoted to health food. While his fellow workers drank Cokes and other soft drinks, he had tomato or grapefruit juice. Sears decided to remove the label from the grapefruit can and glue it onto a can of string beans. When the Britisher opened the can the next day, he was astonished. The next day he opened his grapefruit can and found pork and beans. He shared his amazement with his coworkers. "Gee, you ought to send that to Robert Ripley and his 'Believe It or Not' feature in the newspapers," Sears suggested. The Britisher did so. The next day his can turned out to be red cabbage. On top of the can was a note: "I don't give a damn—Robert Ripley."

Freddie Moore had arrived at Hyperion in 1930 with sketches he had drawn on laundry-shirt cardboards. He was only eighteen, but his talent for putting character into cartoon figures was unmistakable. Later he brought the Three Little Pigs to joyous life and transformed Mickey Mouse from his simple, primitive look to a fluid, nattily dressed personality. Moore was a free soul with unlimited imagination and a taste for spirits that ultimately destroyed him.

To Freddie Moore went the distinction of introducing the gentle art of pushpin throwing. Pushpins, which resembled tiny swords with a round handle, had always been standard equipment for animators since they were used to attach drawings onto storyboards.

"Freddie Moore was a natural athlete," recalled Ollie Johnston, who shared an animation room with Moore in the early thirties. "He used to throw pushpins—the long ones—into the door of our room at the old studio. Then he got so good he could throw one with each hand at the same time. Then he got so he could throw two at once with each hand. Pretty soon everybody up and down the hall was doing it. If Walt came down the hall, he would hear pop-pop-pop—pushpins hitting the doors. 'What the hell is that?' he would ask. He finally found out. Of course, he really didn't like the idea because it wasn't contributing to our work."

When the studio moved to new quarters in Burbank, pushpin throwing took on a new dimension. Now the artists competed on who could stick the most pins in the acoustic-tile ceiling.

EIGHT

After five years of marriage, neither Edna Disney nor Lillian Disney had become pregnant. It was a constant concern for both couples, but especially for Edna and Roy. Edna was approaching forty.

Edna and Roy were desperate, so desperate that they agreed to her doctor's recommendation that they have intercourse at his office, so he could immediately check to determine that the egg had been fertilized. It was a great embarrassment for two such modest people, but the experience brought success.

Edna suffered through three days of labor while doctors debated the advisability of a Cesarean section. Two Catholic doctors were opposed, but they were outvoted (Edna retained a degree of anti-Catholicism thereafter).

A boy was born to Edna and Roy on January 10, 1930, and they named him Roy Edward, after his father and mother.

For Lilly and Walt, things were simpler, and less embarrassing.

After returning from his forced vacation, Walt followed his doctor's advice to exercise more. He worked out at the Hollywood Athletic Club, played golf at the Griffith Park course before breakfast, and often came home early to ride horseback in the hills with Lilly. Her doctor had advised her to exercise as a helpful way to encourage pregnancy. Finally, on December 18, 1933, eight years after her wedding, Lilly gave birth to a daughter, Diane Marie.

An exuberant Walt dispatched a telegram to Albuquerque to Roy, who was en route to New York: "Am proud father. Baby girl. Lilly and baby doing fine."

Three years later, Lilly and Walt adopted another daughter they named Sharon Mae.

No sooner had the Disneys made the distribution contract with United Artists than Walt announced he wanted to make cartoons in color. Roy was aghast. He argued that color would add greatly to the cost of the cartoons, and United Artists wouldn't advance any more financing. Walt countered that color would enhance the popularity of the cartoons, and the additional play dates and extended runs would mean more revenue in the long run.

Years later, Walt commented, "I've said before [Roy] always lived with figures, and I've found out with the people who live with figures as a rule it's post mortem. It's never ahead, it's always what happened. Well, in my particular end it was always ahead. In other words, I was always working on things to come. I was always ahead, looking ahead.

"I can't blame him because he never had the same experience in the business I had. He came into business because of me and because of his respect for me."

Roy tried to argue that the company had already sold theaters a package of twelve films, half of which had been delivered. If the studio changed to color for the last half, the price would be the same. Result: a big loss.

Technicolor had offered Walt the chance to introduce its new process, which combined three negatives of the primary colors. Technicolor was not ready to propose the process for feature films, since it was still in the experimental stage; cartoon shorts would be a good proving ground. Walt told the Technicolor people Roy opposed color because he doubted they would ever get their money back. Walt hinted he might be able to sway Roy if Technicolor agreed to giving Disney a two-year exclusivity on the process. Technicolor consented.

Roy grudgingly accepted the proposal, insisting that color be applied to the Silly Symphonies only, not Mickey Mouse. That was all right with Walt. He had been concerned that the Silly Symphonies had never achieved the popularity and play dates of the Mickey Mouse cartoons. To help attract attention, the shorts were billed as "Mickey Mouse Presents a Silly Symphony." Color would give the Symphonies a needed boost, Walt believed.

Walt had started production on *Flowers and Trees*, which he described as "a spring type of thing with the birds in the trees and the flowers on the ground and the grace and beauty of the waving trees." He junked what had been done in black and white and started all over again with color. When *Flowers and Trees* had its first screening at Grauman's Chinese Theater in Hollywood, the reaction was almost as sensational as that for *Steamboat Willie*. Walt Disney was again hailed as a genius, and the Academy of Motion Picture Arts and Sciences on November 18, 1932, gave *Flowers and Trees* the first Oscar for a cartoon. Silly Symphonies in color became so popular that Walt was able to drop "Mickey Mouse Presents . . ." from the title.

"Our color pictures, while costing a lot more money, promise to be a very good investment," Roy conceded in a letter to his parents on April 14, 1933. "They have met with very wonderful success, and in England they are doing a much better business on color pictures than on the black and white. It is possible that we may go to all color for next year."

To Walt, Roy was less optimistic, still insisting that color be limited to the Silly Symphonies. Mickey Mouse remained in black and white until *The Band Concert* was released in 1935.

Three Little Pigs provided the triumph for Silly Symphonies in color. It brought much-needed lightness and hope to the gloom of Depression America, "Who's Afraid of the Big Bad Wolf?" becoming an anthem of defiance. The huge popularity of the song took the studio by surprise. No arrangement had been made to issue the song on sheet music or phonograph records. Roy quickly entered a contract with Irving Berlin's music publishing company.

Roy estimated that *Three Little Pigs* earned three times the money of the average cartoons. "It just got very, very popular," he remarked. "Theaters held it for a long time and played it over and over. There was a theater in New York that ran it so long, they got a picture of the three little pigs out in front and gradually put whiskers on them. The longer they stayed, the longer the whiskers got."

There was one discordant note to the success of *Three Little Pigs*. The American Jewish Congress complained that the characterization of the Wolf as a Jewish peddler was "vile" and "revolting."

Roy and Walt were disturbed by the reaction, and Roy wrote to the Congress's director: ". . . We have a great many Jewish business associates and friends and certainly would avoid purposely demeaning the Jews or any other race or nationality. One thing we have always kept foremost in our production efforts has been to give no offense to anyone and to please as many as possible.

"I regret that it is impossible to eliminate this scene from the picture . . . It seems to us that this characterization is no more than many well known-Jewish comedians portray, themselves, in vaudeville, stage, and screen characterizations." Years later, the scene would be changed.

B esides flourishing at the box office, *Three Little Pigs* was providing revenue from dolls, ceramics, books, and other products. Under the leadership of Kay Kamen, the merchandising of Disney characters had become a major source of income. Not only in America, but abroad.

As the Mickey Mouse craze spread across Europe and beyond, pirating of Disney characters became endemic. Roy hired lawyers and sales representatives to control the situation.

"We made new law in Canada, Australia, and Germany in fighting to retain our characters," he commented. "One time I went over to Germany and found at a trade fair that the jewelry part of it was just full of Mickey Mouse pins of all sorts—little cheap jewelry items with Mickey and Minnie Mouse on them. We sent a lawyer named [Bill] Levy over to Germany from London, and he picked on the biggest [manufacturer] and said, 'I'm going to sue you for infringement.'

"The guy said, 'Why sue me? There are a thousand others around here doing it.' And Levy said, 'Well, you're the biggest, and we can get something out of you. But here's what I'll do. You take out a license and then together we'll sue all the rest of them.'

"Which we did. They had so many defendants in that issue

that they held the court in the opera house, and with their lawyers and their clients it was chuck full. They said there must have been 1,500 in attendance.

"The judge appointed a referee, and by standing vote the defendants all voted and agreed that if the referee found our copyright valid they would all quit or take out a license. And that was written into the court record. The referee found our copyright valid, and we stopped all that in one fell swoop. By the time Hitler came in, we had Mickey Mouse stuff all over Germany going terrific. Licensed.

"Then Hitler banned it all with one fell swoop with one of his frantic speeches. He was quoted in the press as saying, 'Why are the blond youth of Germany wearing the emblem of this vile scum, Mickey Mouse? Down with Mickey Mouse! Wear the swastika.' And just like that, they all quit. Because he had the fear of God on them then."

B oth of us are taking things a lot easier than we used to," Roy wrote his parents in 1933. "We both played 'hooky' and went out to Riviera Country Club and played polo in the afternoon in a tournament. We did the same thing last Tuesday afternoon. We also play polo regularly on Wednesday mornings and Saturday afternoons with a number of the boys here at the Studio.

"Walt is in pretty good shape, physically, now—much better than he has been for a long time. As for myself, I am at my very best since the war."

Two former Missouri farm boys playing the elite sport of polo with some of Hollywood's biggest names seemed incongruous, but the Disney brothers entered into it with vigor. Walt was the instigator, as always. He had begun horseback riding as part of his health regimen after his breakdown. "Then someone put a polo mallet in my hand, and it all started," he said.

Both Walt and Roy had known little acquaintance with horses since their Marceline years. Walt enlisted six others from the studio, including animators, directors, and the company lawyer, Gunther Lessing, who claimed to have ridden with Pancho Villa. They met in a studio conference room where an expert lectured them in the elements of polo. The two teams staged their practices at DuBrock's riding academy in the San Fernando Valley, a few blocks from the site of the future studio. They also had a horse and net at the studio and practiced goals during the lunch hour.

The players began by playing matches among themselves, then took on other teams that were similarly unpracticed. Finally, they ventured to the Riviera Country Club in Brentwood, where the famous names of Hollywood watched the matches from their Italian-made roadsters parked along the sidelines. Roy and Walt found themselves competing with Spencer Tracy, Leslie Howard, Darryl Zanuck, Jack Holt, Frank Borzage, and Will Rogers.

"I played with Will Rogers, and I didn't like him," said Bill Cottrell, a member of the Disney team. "He'd ride up behind you just when you were about to make a shot, and he'd yell 'Leave it! Leave it!' You'd check your shot and he'd hit the ball. This was in pickup games when you weren't playing to an audience. He was selfish, he just wanted to have the ball all the time."

Cottrell, who had started at the studio in ink-and-paint at $16 a week in 1929, recalled: "Walt had more drive probably than anybody on our team, more ambition to play well. Roy, like most of us, was in the fair class of player. Not great. Walt was able eventually to buy his own horses, which makes probably 70 percent of your game."

In 1934, Roy was emboldened to buy the Tom Collins stable

of four ponies for $1,050. Roy had gone to New York, and the deal had been made for him by his best friend, Mitch Francis, Edna's brother, who now headed the purchasing department at the studio. Walt gave three of the horses practice runs, and he sent word to Roy that he would be "well mounted."

The Disneys' interest in polo continued until 1938, when the studio was expanding rapidly. Roy sold his ponies and urged Walt to quit the sport, especially after Walt had played in matches that resulted in two fatalities. Roy maintained that the studio's primary asset should not be playing such a dangerous sport. The end came when Walt took a spill and crushed four of his cervical vertebrae. A chiropractor manipulated Walt's back badly, leaving him with lifelong pain.

NINE

⁓

D uring the thirties, Roy dispatched a steady stream of chatty letters to his parents and Ruth in Portland, relating conditions at the studio as well as personal notes about members of the family in California. Herb and his family had left Portland in 1930, and he was delivering mail in Los Angeles. Ray had joined his brothers and was operating a general insurance company. The four brothers often met at Roy's house for Sunday afternoon picnics highlighted by fierce croquet matches that demonstrated the Disney sense of competition.

Flora Disney responded to Roy's letters, Elias seldom wrote. She often told of seeing the latest Mickey Mouse cartoon at a Portland theater, expressing her pride in her sons' achievements. Many of the letters concerned the health problems she and Elias suffered from, as well as their modest financial needs. Roy always sent checks by return mail. His attitude remained steadfast as a devoted son, but he also offered his mature judgment concerning his parents' health and money matters.

At first Roy dictated the letters to Walt's secretary, since he had none of his own. Later the force of business prompted Roy to hire a secretary for his own office.

In 1930 things were going well. Mickey Mouse was everywhere—in newspapers, on magazine covers, on radio (First Comic: "Did you hear Mickey and Minnie Mouse are getting divorced?" Second Comic: "No, why?" First comic: "She found out he was a rat."). It was a happy time for Roy and Edna. They doted on young Roy Edward, as did Edna's mother, who continued to live with the family until her death in 1942.

Roy to his parents, August 25, 1930: "I surely wish you could see our boy before he grows up. He is getting cuter every day; full of fun and a very good baby all around. He is getting to think an awful lot of his Grandma Francis, and I am quite anxious for him to see his Grandma Disney. Walt and Lilly are both crazy about him. He seems somewhat afraid of Walt, but goes crazy over Lilly. Walt just doesn't know how to play with him yet.

"We are all feeling fine, and working hard; getting in rather a better position every day, and getting a few of the 'wrinkles out of our stomachs.' Yes, we saw the write-up in the *Literary Digest*. We are getting to be publicity hounds, and never miss that kind of stuff. We have a great number of very good write-ups like that . . .

"Thanks for promoting our comic strip and keeping the newspaper on as a customer. Would you think that this little comic strip is bringing us in about $1,500 per month? Of course we have the expense of making it out of that, which takes about $800 . . . It is being syndicated all over the world, and we now have twenty-two foreign countries . . ."

In business affairs, Roy rarely exposed a sentimental side, but he could easily cry watching the son he had waited so long for. In his letters to Portland he customarily wrote about Roy Edward before reporting events at the studio. May 2, 1931: ". . . [the baby] is pretty good at taking falls and such sort of hurts and punishment. The thing that hurts him most is speaking to him crossly. If he realizes you are cross or angry with him, it breaks his heart. In that way he reminds me of Ray. His little chin will pucker up and start to quiver and then a cloud spreads all over his face and he goes into a real brokenhearted cry. I guess he takes after his mother and father that way, as they both have their feelings easily hurt . . .

"Our new buildings [at the studio] are practically finished. It is just a matter of landscaping, fencing, and putting in driveways, walks, etc. When it is all completed, we will have some good pictures taken and send some to you . . ."

To the outside world, Walt Disney Productions appeared to be prospering. To Roy, who viewed expense sheets daily, it was a different picture. May 8, 1931: ". . . Very frankly, our business has been growing so fast and expanding in two or three directions, that we are still about as close run for money as ever. This may sound odd, but yet when you realize that our expenses are increasing to a point where it costs us $1,250 a day for operation, you can realize that we have to have much more [money] to deal with than before. Also, we have tied into this new studio, which will be approximately $45,000 in buildings, with another fifteen to twenty thousand in equipment, and it will probably be a long time before we have it paid for . . .

"The situation regarding Pathe and the infringing Fables has changed. The court allowed them to put up a $50,000 bond and continue in distribution the six pictures I mentioned to you before, but they are not allowed to make any new pictures using anything like our character. So if you see any that look like

Mickey, let us know the name of them and we can find out when they were released . . ."

Flora Disney sometimes wrote Roy about her concern that Walt was endangering his health by working so hard. In his July 30, 1931, letter he was able to reassure her: ". . . Walt is feeling very good. In fact, is more like his old self than he has been in two or three years. His tonsil operation seemed to help him and he got over it just fine. Apparently he has even lost his hacking cough, which you recall he has had for a long time . . ."

Although he was not the eldest son, Roy assumed the often difficult role of family peacemaker. His letter of October 20, 1931: ". . . Right now [Robert Disney] has quite a peeve against Walt because he has never been invited up to the new house. But Walt takes the attitude that they never cared to come down to the old one, so why invite them to the new one?

"Edna and I have made two attempts lately to keep on cordial relationships with them, having visited Uncle Robert twice. We, too, never see them at our house. They are funny that way.

"Uncle Robert is still as rabid on politics as ever. I 'dared' not to agree with him the other night on some of his views, and a clash almost ensued. In fact, we had to go to our car escorted by only Aunt Charlotte and Robert Jr., big Robert peevishly walking away from us. Ain't life funny?

"Walt made the comment here not long ago, after a little dis-agreement with me: 'Us Disneys are the most peevish sort of peo-ple in the world, always taking offense at each other for something.'

"He mentioned at the same time that he had not written you folks in a long time, and he supposed you, too, were peeved at him. He said he was going to some day sit down and write you—but don't start counting on that letter! . . ."

In late 1931, while Walt and Lilly were on a lengthy vacation,

Roy wrote a comforting letter to his parents on Oct. 31: "I think they are having a good time. I talked with Walt by telephone from Washington, D.C. He said in Kansas City they would not let him spend a cent, and put him up at the Muehlbach Hotel, in a suite of rooms that had three baths. Walt and Lilly were kept busy all the time trying to keep three bathrooms busy. Lilly always did say Walt needed one entirely to himself; that when he 'retired' there, he stayed 'retired.' "

A postholiday letter, December 30, 1931: ". . . All the Disneys down here seem to have had a very good Christmas. All of them are well and seem to be happy, which is the most important thing. Ray spent Christmas Eve at Walt's house and our house. A number of friends dropped in, and it was during the course of that evening's affairs that Walt called you up and we all talked to all of you. Walt was about 'three sheets to the wind' about that time on some champagne he had blown himself to—not drunk, but just feeling good. Even Ray seemed to loosen up and thoroughly enjoy himself. Uncle Robert and Aunt Charlotte were to have been over, but were detained by company themselves, so we did not see them until Christmas Day."

Not until early 1932 did Roy feel the company was able to repay the loan Elias and Flora Disney had provided to help start the Disney Brothers studio. He wrote his appreciation on January 6: "Enclosed is our check for $2,500, plus $29.17 which represents interest for the two months up to January 14, 1932. We are sending this check air mail in order that it can be deposited and you can have the collection in your hands by the fourteenth. As it is now past banking hours, I would have to make a special trip to the bank tomorrow to get a bank draft and then the bank draft would also have to await collection.

"We are glad to do as you requested in this matter. I would like at this time to include another check in appreciation to you and Dad for the wonderful help that this was to us at the time you let us have it, and ever since then, in fact. You can rest assured that this appreciation is not idle talk and will be accounted for at some later date. Right now, to be frank, it would not be convenient to show the appreciation in terms of dollars and cents, as the bigger this place gets the more money it seems to take to run it. You know 'you can't have the roses without some thorns' and it seems we always have plenty of thorns mixed up with Mickey Mouse . . ."

Roy had been free of any symptoms of tuberculosis for ten years, yet he would always be conscious of the specter of the disease. A letter dated March 23, 1932: ". . . All of us are well, in fact have been feeling exceptionally so lately. Even Walt seems to be feeling much better . . . By the way, it will be interesting for you to know that I had a thorough chest examination recently by a very competent chest physician. The examination and the X rays showed me in fine shape. I took the examination merely to check up on myself and to attempt to get the New York Life Insurance Co. down on an excess premium they charged me [because of TB] of thirteen years. I think I will get it cut down to six or seven years . . ."

Roy appreciated a good joke and could laugh heartily, but he lacked the comedic sense of his famous brother. His attempts at humor were sometimes lumbering, as in his Father's Day letter to Elias, June 15, 1932: "I understand that Sunday, June 19, is a day dedicated to fathers, nationally known as Father's Day. Inasmuch as I am a father myself, it behooves me to encourage the observance of this day so as to set a good example for my son as he grows up. In addition to that, of course, there is the fact that you are my father . . . and since you are and also the fact that I cannot have any other one substitute, I just naturally feel that I should write you on Father's Day . . . Aside from all this nonsense, we are all feeling fine . . .

[Roy reports on the house and swimming pool Walt and Lilly were building.] "They are going to have a marvelous home. Yes, it will cost a lot to keep it up, but Walt is a great believer in enjoying life, and why not, after all? You can't take it with you, and if you put it in stocks, bonds, or a bank, you lose it anyway.

"That's where we have fooled the Depression. Anything that we had saved up was all put into our business. We have been doing our own gambling. This past three years will be a very good lesson to the people at large. For a while there, everybody and their brother were gambling in stocks. I believe however, after Congress adjourns the country will feel more at ease and probably show a little improvement . . .

"Between you and me and the gatepost, we are trying to so arrange our affairs that we will have the proverbial nest egg in the sense of meaning that the home's clear at last. Our entire studio has very little indebtedness against it and this will all be cleared off within months."

In a September 8, 1932, letter to his mother, Roy enjoyed teasing his secretary: ". . . [Miss Benedict] is writing this letter, and I am going to tell you what happened to her. She is a married woman now, so in place of having an innocent, young, sweet girl for a secretary, I have just a married woman! It makes it tough on me . . . but is probably a relief to Edna. I like to devil her about it, anyway . . .

"P.S. Thanks for the clippings. I met a woman from Portland the other day, and she told me she saw my picture in the paper there. My bid for fame!"

Ray Disney offered Roy his major challenge as family peacemaker. An eccentric who led a solitary life, Ray had an annoying knack of interpreting casual incidents as personal affronts.

Roy's letter of January 7, 1933: ". . . Ray was out to the house the other night for dinner. I overheard Roy [Edward] telling him the story of Black Sambo. Ray let me read Mother's birthday letter to him and the delayed one as well as the later letter. Ray was quite tickled to know that Mother had not forgotten him. I believe he was really disappointed, Mother, when he did not hear from you on his birthday. Ray is very sensitive. Sometimes I can't figure him out. We get along fine for the most part, but [I] occasionally find it very difficult to do so. He seems to imagine offenses . . ."

More and more, Roy seemed unwittingly to be assuming the role as leader of the Disney family. In a February 2, 1933, he seemed almost paternal to his own father: "This will go down in the records officially as a 'Birthday Letter' to Dad. Best wishes to you, Dad. Hope this finds you feeling fine, enjoying life, wanting to live a lot longer and that you actually get to do so.

"If life's varied experiences teach us anything, it should teach a man when he gets to be your age to know how to enjoy life, and to avoid worrying over the countless number of things that are really unimportant, but instead to make the most out of life as we find it. Judging by the doctor's report of your condition you should be good for a great number of years yet . . ."

The historic month of March 1933, brought the presidential inauguration of Franklin Roosevelt, who closed the nation's banks to avert fiscal disaster. A ruinous earthquake shook Long Beach and the rest of Los Angeles County. Flora and Elias Disney were greatly concerned about their Los Angeles families, and Roy wrote an apologetic letter on March 16: "When I received your letter this morning, Mother, written March 14, I felt rather ashamed to think that we had, none of us, thought of you enough to allay your uneasiness . . . Hollywood and this part of the city were not affected at all; in fact, Los Angeles was affected to such a trifling extent that we did not take it very seriously . . .

"We had a preview of a cartoon at the Ritz Theater Friday night, the night of the quake. The first shock was at about six o'clock. Then while we were in the theater waiting for our cartoon to be previewed, we experienced two or three pretty good secondary shocks. It did make you feel sort of nervous to have the darn theater shaking underneath you, and a number of people got up and went out . . .

"Well, our banks are all open again and everything seems to be better than ever before. Yes, I think Roosevelt is doing wonderfully and I am glad I voted for the wrong man. That is, I'm glad that the man I voted for did not get in. I still believe in Hoover, personally, as an individual. I do not believe he could have accomplished what Roosevelt has . . ."

Roy discovered that his letters to Portland provided a convenient way for him to put into words his long-range views of the Disney company. On April 14, 1933, he wrote an insightful statement of studio policy: ". . . Our difficulties are one of being undercapitalized. We still own our business, 100 percent, and have avoided taking in any outside interests to secure capital. We have had several 'squeeze plays' tried on us, but have been able to avoid them all, so far.

"We will probably never make as much money out of this proposition as some 'hard-boiled' type of motion picture producer would. Nevertheless, we have the satisfaction of running our business in a way that is fair to everyone connected with it.

"It is a very difficult problem, also, to produce something of a creative nature, like our product, without a certain amount of loss through waste and inefficiency in your organization. Considering the large amount of money we spend on our pictures, we should make good pictures, but I don't believe we get all that we should for the money expended.

"Walt, however, continually (without letup in the least) always strives for something that has not been done before. That sort of policy, of course, is always costly . . . you can't stop a person like Walt. He seems to have no end of energy and ambition . . ."

Roy rejoiced in the honors that continued pouring in for his celebrity brother, never betraying a shred of jealousy. In September 1933, the Writers Club, a social group of prominent writers and industry figures, gave a testimonial dinner for Walt. Roy sent a report to his parents on October 2: ". . . It turned out to be a very nice affair and very complimentary to Walt. There was quite a cross section of the community's leading individuals . . . Will Rogers was the speaker of the evening, with Rupert Hughes, the writer, as sort of master of ceremonies. It was all handled very nicely, and Walt conducted himself fine. I was very proud of him. Edna and I both went of course, all decked out in evening clothes. Edna had a new wrap she had just made, together with (she's bragging about them yet) a corsage of orchids, so a good time was had by all. You would have been proud of your youngest son had you been there."

TEN

❧

W ho wants to see a feature cartoon? Cartoons last eight
minutes. People would be bored if they were ten times
as long."

As often happened, Lilly's questioning only strengthened
Walt's resolve. He needed a new challenge, and producing the
first feature cartoon seemed the perfect solution.

Roy also expressed his doubt whether their company, barely
ten years old, could amass the resources to accomplish such an
ambitious project. Walt estimated the movie would cost a half-
million dollars.

Whatever Roy's objections had been, they melted under the
persuasion of his younger brother. In November of 1933, Roy was
in New York overseeing a lawsuit brought by Columbia. He had
lunch with Jock Whitney and his lawyer at the Rookery Club in
the Bank of Manhattan Building. The two men—one a scion of
immense eastern wealth, the other a former bank teller in Kansas

City—hit it off famously, especially when discussing their mutual interest in polo. Whitney was dabbling in film stocks, and he inquired about a Disney feature.

Roy wrote to Walt: ". . . I told them of the restrictions of our United Artists contract with respect to features, but we expected to have that condition removed very shortly under any new contract we made, and that we were interested in the feature idea, that Schenck and Zanuck [who had formed Twentieth Century Pictures] were interested in financing, but that we could not see our way to accepting their proposition because it called for such a big portion of the returns . . ."

Roy began further negotiations with Joe Schenck, brother of Nicholas Schenck, whose Loew's, Inc., owned MGM. Joe Schenck agreed to invest $400,000 in exchange for a one-third interest in Walt Disney Productions. Roy reluctantly agreed, figuring that amount would be enough to start the cartoon feature.

But Schenck encountered financial difficulties. Just before the contract was to be signed, he asked to be excused from the obligation. Roy was relieved. Bringing in Schenck as a one-third partner would have abrogated the Disneys' vow to remain independent. Roy had agreed to the arrangement in order to facilitate Walt's dreams of a feature.

"After we got shut of Joe Schenck, we got in better with the bank," Roy said later, "because we began to have a little substance, and they had more confidence in us. We told them our dreams and plans and they agreed to go along with us."

With the backing of A.P. Giannini and the Bank of America, the feature could commence. On a momentous summer evening in 1934, Walt summoned his artists to the sound stage that had been built three years before. He announced to them that the studio was going to undertake an animated feature, and it would be *Snow White and the Seven Dwarfs.*

For two hours Walt held his audience enthralled as he told the entire story, acting out each part with great verve. The images of his initial recital remained firmly in the artists' mind during the long months and years ahead. When *Snow White* ultimately reached the audience, it followed the same design that Walt had outlined on that summer night.

Much had to be done. Walt knew that the studio was not capable of realizing the work of art he envisioned. He initiated the Disney Art School and hired a teacher, Don Graham, to instruct the artists in drawing of humans and animals. He arranged classes with the Chouinard Art School and even drove some of the employees who lacked cars to night school. He launched a nationwide search for artists and interviewed hundreds of them. Roy uncomplainingly signed the checks.

I n 1935, Walt was having treatment for what the doctors said was a defective thyroid," Roy related. "He was taking a series of injections for it, but it seemed to me it only made him more nervous . . . I persuaded him to take the girls and get away from the studio for a while. It happened to be our tenth wedding anniversary." They began planning a grand tour of Europe.

Before the two couples departed, Roy with his customary thrift wrote out a code for the families to send cables to the traveling couples at a reduced rate. The cryptology:

> ITCER: Loving greetings.
> KOHOL: Diane well, rest of family O.K.
> KOJOC: Roy Edward and Mother well.
> ALBIV: Everything running smoothly. All well. Nothing here to hasten your return.

AUMAG: Hope you are all very well.

FYAPI: Be sure you have a good time and do not let matters worry you.

KESMY: With love and affection to all.

Edna kept a diary of the trip, with an occasional assist by Roy. In every capital he took care of business, Walt handled the press. Walt was besieged by reporters and photographers at each stop, and he graciously gave them hours of his time, much to Lilly's impatience. When they weren't sightseeing, the wives went shopping.

The tour began in New York, where the two couples boarded the *Normandie* on June 2, 1935. The Disneys had been threatened with a lawsuit, and they avoided process servers by entering via the galley gangway, through the galley to their cabins.

"What a relief when we sailed," Roy wrote to Edna's mother. "Such crowds, cops, confusion, tremendous, gigantic, colossal, etc., etc. Everyone aboard is 'somebody' or a reporter. My God, what a collection of snooty folk."

Edna wrote in her diary: "At dinner sat next to Baron Rothschild, who is very hard of hearing." She also noted that Walt drew a Mickey on the menu for the wife of the President of France. The *Normandie*, which set a new cross-Atlantic speed record on the voyage, landed at Plymouth on June 12, and "people almost mobbed Walt taking pictures and asking for autographs."

The Disneys attended the races at Ascot. Edna wrote in her diary: "The men in their cutaway coats, striped trousers and gray high hats were very funny to us. The women wore wilted-looking finery, and everyone had an umbrella and raincoat. Tradition makes Ascot a very ritzy affair, and in spite of the rain and miserable weather, they dressed for the occasion."

They visited Buckingham and St. James palaces, Eton, Oxford, and took the Sterling Collander train to Edinburgh, where they sat near the King's Box and watched the Duke of York (the future King George VI) review the troops at the Tattoo. They returned to London for Roy's forty-second birthday, which was celebrated with a play, *One Glorious Night*, and dinner at the Savoy Grill.

Between sightseeing trips, Roy spent time at the Disney office on Shaftsbury Avenue, one of the offices he had opened in Europe to attend to Disney merchandising. He wrote a five-page memo to the company lawyer, Gunther Lessing, describing new distribution deals for Holland and French Indochina, the mishandling of the comic strip by King Features, trouble with the Italian merchandising contract, and other matters.

In Paris Walt was to be presented with a medal by the League of Nations for the creation of Mickey Mouse. He and Roy had been warned that morning clothes would be required, but they had brought along sports clothes only. They hurried through fittings and arrived at the presentation in fancy duds, learning that the others had dressed informally to make the honored guests feel at ease.

The Paris visit included such sights as Notre-Dame, Montmartre, Versailles ("Louis XIV's old home"), the Grand Prix at Longchamps, and the Folies Bergères, which Edna called "a very poor, third-rate burlesque show with quite a bit of nude women (or nearly so) and lots of ham acting."

Roy wrote to his parents and Ruth from Paris: ". . . You have good reason to be proud of Walt. He has conducted himself in a marvelous manner. Aside from whether he deserves all the honors that have been conferred on him, he keeps his head and is still the same boy you knew. When we arrive in Rome it will be a repetition of the London and Paris receptions. In spite of the fact that all these things are wonderful and very valuable in our business, as well as a great tribute to Walt, they are all very trying and I am sure we will all be more than glad when we feel we are on our way home."

The foursome hired a seven-passenger Hispano-Suiza to tour Reims, Château Thierry, Belleau Woods, Verdun, and other sites of World War I that Walt had visited as a Red Cross driver. At Strasbourg, Walt was fascinated by the mechanical clock. He made sketches of it and tried to ascend the tower to figure out how it worked. He was denied permission, but twenty years later his observations provided inspiration for the mechanical clock at Disneyland.

The travelers stopped briefly in Munich, and Edna made no mention of the Nazi presence there. On to Lake Como, where Walt and Lilly celebrated their tenth wedding anniversary. In the morning all four went to the lake and the men did some swimming. Roy wrote in the diary: "Edna took a grand swim in the lake by wiggling her toes and dipping her hands in the water and then climbing up the ladder, exhausted but satisfied with her little bit of exercise . . . Lilly would not go near the water; she said it was too dirty."

The tour allowed only one evening in Venice, and it included dinner at the Hotel Danielli, visits to St. Mark's Square and the Bridge of Sighs, and a gondola ride. Edna sat down in one of the indented seats, which happened to be filled with splash water. Everyone laughed except Edna.

They rushed to the train station for the night train to Rome, discovering the Italian porter had taken them to the wrong side of the tracks. The frenzied porter led them across the tracks just as their train was pulling into the station. "What a risky thing to do," Roy commented years later. "Those crazy Italians, you know."

Roy continued: "We had a lot of fun on the train. In Europe, when you have second-class transportation, it is really first-class, but two to a room. Our tickets were marked second-class, so Lilly was kidding her husband quite seriously about what a big shot he was, with everybody meeting him and so and so, but he is riding in second class.

"After they were assigned and got in their berth and were trying to get straightened around in their room, Walt was investigating, and he found a commode down underneath. He said, 'Look, Mama, first class! A private toilet!' "

The reception for Walt's arrival in Rome was clamorous. He and Lilly were photographed at the train station and again at the Hotel Excelsior, where Walt attended a press reception. Dinner at Alfredo's, where Alfredo himself mixed the pasta with a gold spoon and fork given to him by Mary Pickford and Douglas Fairbanks. Visits to the Colosseum, Forum, St. Peter's, Naples, Pompeii, where Edna noted "a couple of the places the guide took the men only."

The highlight of the Rome visit was the audience with Il Duce.

It turned out that Mussolini had been a fan of the Disney cartoons. Learning that the Disneys were going to Naples, he bragged, "You can ride the trains unmolested now. A year ago the brigands and hold-up people would stop a train and go clear through it and rob everybody. They don't do it anymore."

"He had this real big office, real big," Roy remembered. "He was back in the corner. We had to walk across [that space]. The fellow who was taking us in had the squeaky Italian shoes that you may have heard. So it was squeak, squeak, squeak, squeak all the way down to Mussolini. He was sitting there, and he has a spotlight on you, and he sits in the relative shadow. You sat in a chair, right under a spotlight. But he was

most pleasant, most cordial." (Harry Cohn also met with Mussolini in the thirties and was so impressed by the office that he
had it duplicated at Columbia Studio as a method of injecting
fear in his visitors.)

The travelers boarded the *Rex* in Genoa and enjoyed a pleasant trip through the Mediterranean and across the Atlantic. The
brothers worked out in the gym, and Roy noted in the diary: "Walt
is going in for boxing—don't know what he has in mind, must
have someone he wants to lick."

Years later Roy commented on the trip's beneficial effect on
Walt: "When he came back, the first thing that happened was his
doctor's secretary called him to relay the doctor's message: 'You'd
better get down here and start taking your shots again.' Walt said,
'You tell Doc I never felt better in my life. He can shoot those
things in his own ass from now on.' "

In 1936, after almost five years with United Artists as distributor,
the Disneys made another change.

The UA contract had been a great improvement over the one
with Columbia. The cartoons were costing around $30,000, and
each picture was returning between $70,000 and $80,000. With
the studio producing twenty shorts a year, that meant a healthy
profit.

When the contract came up for renewal, Samuel Goldwyn,
one of the UA partners, insisted on retaining the television rights.
Television in the mid-thirties was little more than a flicker in the
laboratory. Yet the Disneys had the remarkable prescience to refuse to part with any such rights.

Charlie Chaplin, a founder-partner in United Artists, regretted
Goldwyn's intransigence and the loss of Disney. The Disney law-

yer, Gunther Lessing, talked with Chaplin and Paulette Goddard at the Trocadero night club and was told by Chaplin: "Anything I can ever do for Walt I will gladly perform. You will always have a home with us." He expressed great interest in the feature project and volunteered to see it before previews and "to give Walt anything I have learned from past experience."

Roy signed a contract with RKO, and it would prove to be the longest association of Walt Disney Productions with a distribution company.

A letter to Roy's parents on April 6, 1936: ". . . When we go with RKO, I don't know who will have the pictures in Portland. It will be the people they can sell them to. You know this picture business is quite a cutthroat game and sometimes you don't appear in theaters for the simple reason that the people won't pay you for your pictures what you think you should have. It is all a matter of fighting for a price. You never get one penny more than what you fight for.

"For instance, we practically stayed out of Chicago for a number of months, a couple of years ago, because the houses there wouldn't pay what we thought we should get. And so it goes all the way around the world; it is a fight continually to get decent prices. We are held down a great deal by cheap competition, and the big studios that have their own cartoons practically give away their cartoons with their feature pictures. We, all of the time, have to stand on our own feet without any tie-in with any other product."

Roy explained that although United Artists had done a good job on distribution, RKO agreed to a small fee and a guarantee of all of Disney studio costs. He added:

"Over all we have been doing exceptionally well and are not kicking, but there is so much possibility to do better, from year to year. At the last count there were 327 people working here, and that is a lot of people to pay salary checks to every week, including a lot of other expenses . . . So it is no different than it was years ago, only that we are dealing in larger figures . . ."

ELEVEN

❧

Walt sweated on *Snow White* from the time it was first started—the story, the animation, the music, the recording. There was a period of great tension, because for us a million and a half dollars was a terrific investment; we had been spending $30,000 on a cartoon short. It was guaranteed to us practically, by our distributor; we got paid when we delivered the picture. But if we had flopped with *Snow White*, we were gonna flop with our own money."

Roy Disney remembered the two crisis years as Walt struggled to achieve his vision of *Snow White* and Roy worked to placate the Bank of America, which was supplying the cash.

Despite the infusion of artistic talent from all over the country, Walt was disappointed in the results. For the first time, the artists were dealing with human figures: Snow White, the Prince, the Queen. The dwarfs were more cartoonlike, but they were human as well. The faces, the bodies, the movements of the human characters of an animated film would instinctively be compared to live-action actors by the audience. If the *Snow White* actors seemed awkward and unreal, the entire illusion would be destroyed.

"There were quite a few artists on *Snow White* who were not real good artists in those days," Roy recalled. "The good men were scarce. So Walt devised a way of breaking down the key work for the best artists and then have the secondary men do the fill-ins and the follow-ups of more simple art. That was another angle that a lot of the artists resented and didn't like.

"It was kind of making it a progression of work. Like almost, you might say . . . the assembly line. But that was the way he spread more good men over more work."

Walt was making dozens of decisions daily, and many of them required compromises of what he had envisioned. Yet he didn't hesitate to discard whole sequences in rough animation and start anew. Roy watched helplessly as the cost of *Snow White* mounted precipitously.

"Roy, of course, was quite different from Walt," observes John Hench, who started delivering mail at the studio in the late thirties, rose through many departments and remains a guiding force at Walt Disney Imagineering.

"Walt was prone to take risks. His security was the fact that he really thought the ideas that kept popping up—his own, especially—were good and valid. Roy had a much more conservative approach to things.

"It amused all of us when we used to take audience reaction [at the studio] to scenes or rough cuts of features. There was always one comment: 'Walt, stick to shorts.' We knew who that was: It was Roy. Walt was so annoyed. He'd say, 'I gotta find this guy and explain to him. He just doesn't have the right spirit here. He keeps saying "Stick to shorts" all the time.' He never did find out, because none of us ever told him."

Roy wrote to his parents in Portland with a mixture of concern and bravado: ". . . We are taking all the risk ourselves, so if it goes caflooey we may be up there living with you in your rooming house. Save me the front room on the other place next door to you, will you? But I have all the confidence in the world that Walt can build a good feature, and that it will go out and do a lot of money in gross. Three, four, or five years from now we can tell you much better. Anyways, that is life; you just have to keep on working and gambling. It is all a gamble."

The monolithic Bank of America had scant interest in gambles. The board of directors in San Francisco grew increasingly restless as Roy returned again and again to increase the Disney loan. Fortunately, the liaison between the bank and the Disneys was a sympathetic man named Joe Rosenberg. As much as any banker could, he understood the variables of the motion picture business. Still, he was the Bank of America's representative in Los Angeles, and he was required to do the board's bidding. He repeatedly telephoned Roy to inquire about the state of *Snow White* and to urge him to hurry his brother along.

It helped that Walter Wanger, an important producer and industry leader, told Rosenberg of his faith in the Disney operation. Walt also got a boost from W.G. Van Schmus, operator of the Radio City Music Hall, who agreed to book *Snow White.*

When Walt sought yet another loan for the feature, Roy realized that the bank would resist. He told Walt that the only way to increase the loan would be to show Rosenberg the work in progress. Walt protested that the film was too unfinished for any outsider to judge its value. "They insist," Roy said flatly.

Walt reluctantly assembled an amalgam of pencil sketches,

rough animation, a few scenes of finished animation, much of it still black-and-white.

"So Roy set up this date," Walt related. "It was a Saturday afternoon. Roy didn't show up. [Roy's version: Walt wouldn't let him in.] I ran it all alone, just the two of us in this big projection room. I don't know where Roy was, but he wasn't there . . .

"I'd sit there, and I'd put in my pitch and I'd say, 'You re-member this thing I did where I had this beautiful scene?' I said, 'This is going to be twice as beautiful.' I kept filling in all the way through it . . . Oh, it was a hodgepodge."

Rosenberg made no comment when the screening ended. Walt walked him to his car, and the banker chatted about other matters but not about what he had just viewed. He opened his car door and thanked Walt, then added: "That thing [*Snow White*] is going to make a hatful of money."

Walt commented: "From that time on I had more respect for bankers."

S *now White* had more of Walt's personality than any other pic-ture," says Ken O'Connor. "He hadn't diversified then. He knew what the hell everybody could do in the way of art and gags and music and had a director's overall point of view on the whole thing. He was a great leader."

Others who worked on *Snow White* agreed. Walt was always available to look at sketches, inspect storyboards, watch rough animation, audition voices. Animators cherished Walt's recitals of scenes; the tone of his voice, his gestures and facial expressions gave them the clues on how to interpret the action. He prowled their rooms after working hours, checking out the drawings, sometimes retrieving discards from the wastebasket.

"For an artist that delivered," Roy once said, "Walt didn't care how he combed his hair or how he lived his life or what color he was or anything. A good artist to Walt was just a good artist and invaluable."

As Walt continued at his meticulous pace, Roy's patience grew thin. By the summer of 1937, Walt was still tinkering with details, and the announced premiere date of December was in peril. Roy recalled the turning point: "There was a portion in the end, or near the end of the picture, where the Prince kisses the sleeping Snow White and brings her back to life. As the Prince approached the casket, in the shooting of it, a weave developed to where the Prince was shimmying.

"It irritated me a little bit, and I suggested to Walt that he ought to make it over. He said, 'Fine, I'd like to make it over. I've been figuring on it. It'll cost us about $250,000 to $300,000. Can you get the money? I'll be glad to make it over.' I said, 'Forget it. Let the Prince shimmy.' And he's been shimmying ever since."

BUILD-UP FOR 'SNOW WHITE' OPENING
DWARFS HOLLYWOOD PREDECESSORS

Beneath a star spangled sky while a multitude looked on and millions listened, the flower of Hollywood genius and glamour foregathered at the Carthay Circle theater Tuesday night to celebrate the most extraordinary world premiere in cinema history, the baptism of Walt Disney's "Snow White and the Seven Dwarfs."

In an enthusiastic report, *The Motion Picture Herald* trumpeted the premiere held on December 21, 1937. The account, written by William R. Weaver, continued: "For this was no mere premiere of a picture, but a premiere of an entertainment form, a crucial test of the vital new commodity introduced into a close drawn and cruelly competitive commerce."

The combined force of the RKO and Disney publicity departments made sure that the public became aware of the historic occasion. A thousand posters were pasted on billboards all over Los Angeles. The dwarfs traded banter with Charlie McCarthy on his network radio show. Cecil B. DeMille interviewed Walt on Lux Radio Theater. "Whistle While You Work," "Some Day My Prince Will Come," and other *Snow White* songs poured from radio loudspeakers. (Roy had given away the music rights for a small percentage of sales, as was the industry custom; the studios were interested only in the publicity value. Roy spent years trying to get the rights back.)

Bleachers were erected at the Carthay Circle to accommodate 4,000 fans. The premiere guests were greeted by a scene of midgets in dwarf suits using pickaxes on a full-scale diamond mine. The singers who recorded the movie's songs performed for the crowd, accompanied by a full orchestra. Usherettes wore Snow White costumes. Human-size versions of Mickey and Minnie Mouse, Donald Duck, and Pluto entertained the youngsters.

Don Wilson greeted the arrivals on coast-to-coast radio. Charlie Chaplin delivered high praise for Walt Disney, as did the distinguished George Arliss. Other stars included Bob Burns, Joe Penner, Amos 'n Andy, Norma Shearer, and Sally Eilers.

The applause was loud and prolonged at the end of the screening. The reviews were equally laudatory in Los Angeles and New York, where *Snow White* set a new record for the length of a run at Radio City Music Hall. After fourteen years of scrambling for every dollar, the sudden burst of prosperity thrilled Roy Disney. Yet he was less confident of the future than his brother. Events in Europe and the Far East disturbed Roy. But he was careful not to quench the enthusiasm of Walt, who was filled with ideas for expansion.

TWELVE

❦

Old habits die hard, and even as Walt Disney Productions basked in its first prosperity, Roy Disney clung to his thrifty ways. The lessons of the hardscrabble life he had known at Marceline and Kansas City remained with him to the end of his life.

While on a business trip to New York in 1937, he sent a memo to the studio: "Inform studio telephone operators to accept collect calls from New York and delay operator until the proper person is notified. I always place station-to-station calls, like a true Scotchman."

Roy's parents and sister Ruth often sought financial advice from him, and he gave it unsparingly. In 1933 when she was thirty, Ruth became infatuated with Ted Beecher. No matter that he had no job and no prospects. She aimed to marry him, and in a long, enthusiastic letter to Roy proposing "what we think 'wonderful' ideas . . . here is the big proposition—We want to build a little house!"

She wrote that she had saved $430, "which would be enough to get the thing started. And at the rate I am saving now, since I fell in love and turned Scotch, I can easily put away $50.00 a month or $600.00 a year. Ted hasn't anything, financially, but he has got time, and plenty of it, on his hands—and nothing to do." He had been a sheet-metal worker, she said, and could do much of the construction himself.

After detailing how she and Ted could buy the lot and build the house, Ruth asked if Roy could lend them $2,000. They would repay at any rate of interest he suggested and would give him a mortgage. She urged him not to mention the matter to their parents; she hadn't discussed it with them and was afraid they would not approve.

Roy answered by return mail, as Ruth requested. "I would be happy to secure you a home or do anything that would make you happy," he wrote. "I know that Walter would feel the same way about it . . . The idea, taken as a whole, is not a bad idea, or a foolish one. However, it offers considerable difficulties in working out."

He analyzed the various ramifications of financing the house, pointing out that if Ted swapped his labor for building materials, the newlyweds would have little to live on.

"You look at this as an opportunity to get a start and yet if you go into this, when you have your house completed you still have the problem of furniture, taxes, upkeep, etc.," Roy reasoned. "Money tied up in a house is hard to realize on, where cash in the bank is the most useful thing to have around."

He mentioned that Herb owned a lot in Portland and that he might consider lending it to her. "I will write you tomorrow, or wire you, after talking with Herb and Walt," he concluded.

"Please don't think I am trying to discourage you. I love you and want to help you in any way I can. All of us feel the same way."

Ruth and Ted Beecher married on June 19, 1934, without solving their housing problem. They had one child, Theodore Warren Beecher, born June 10, 1940. Ruth's husband remained a source of concern for the rest of the family. After two years of marriage, the Beechers' house still hadn't been completed.

An exasperated Roy wrote to his parents in 1936: ". . . I am glad that Ruth is taking steps to ease up on herself. That idea of working in the daytime and keeping house at night certainly is very tiresome and hard on anybody. I don't know what it is all about, but from a distance I am sure all fed up with that husband of hers and his activity or inactivity on that house.

"Good Lord, if he had any gumption he would get out now and get that house completed, if they had to borrow the money to do it . . . Oh, well, we have troubles enough of our own. So, as Ruth would probably say—I guess we better take care of those and not worry about hers."

In 1937, Flora Disney wrote to Roy about a proposal by the doctor of Elias, who had been undergoing a siege of bad health. The doctor had proposed a loan of $2,000 from the Disneys, to be paid off by Elias's future medical bills. Roy talked to Walt and Ray, and they came to the same conclusion. Roy wrote to his mother:

"Regarding the possibility of our loaning Dad's doctor $2,000, we haven't any business doing this, Mother. We have a tremendous load to carry the studio and we need the strength of all our resources . . . I wouldn't advise your borrowing money on your house to help him out. What you folks have, you should carefully nurse for your own good and use . . .

"We Disneys, I think, are chickenhearted. I gave in to a similar situation down here about six months ago and signed on a note for a man for $1,000 at the bank. I am now making payments to the bank to wipe out the note, so I have lost both my money and my friend . . ."

Roy wrote to the doctor explaining why the family was unable to help him in a financial bind. "That same [financial] trouble is no stranger to us, I assure you, and if you have difficulties in the conduct of your business, you can probably multiply them many times and have an idea of what we are contending with . . ."

Flora and Elias Disney had moved to Los Angeles in 1938, after Roy had flown to Portland to express the family's concern that they were working too hard on their properties. The family gathered at New Year's to celebrate the golden wedding anniversary of Flora and Elias. Only Ruth was missing. Among those attending were Aunt Charlotte and Uncle Robert, who had supplied the seed money to start the Disney Brothers Studio.

The New Year's Eve celebration was marked by much jollity, with retelling of old stories about life on the farm. If any resentment remained against Herb and Ray for disappearing in the night, it did not surface.

A group photograph reveals the remarkable resemblance between parents and sons. All had the broad forehead, the long straight nose, prominent ears. The sons inherited their mother's eyes—wide-spaced, penetrating, with a trace of amusement. Herb, the mailman, appears the handsomest, with oval face, sly grin, slick hair. Ray, the second oldest, looks the picture of an insurance salesman, eager eyes, Ronald Colman mustache. Roy's thin face and pointed chin accents the large ears; his hairline is edging backwards. Walt, exuberant as always, with the trademark mustache he grew in the 1920s so he would not look like a boy cartoon maker.

At the anniversary dinner, Walt conducted a jocular interview with his mother and father, suggesting that Elias would want to make whoopee on the occasion. "He don't know how to make whoopee," Flora replied. When Walt suggested that Elias could be ornery, Flora observed that Walt knew something about orneriness: "Do you remember the time you painted the whole side of the house when we were in town?" Walt claimed innocence, suggesting that Roy had been the culprit.

Roy took over as announcer of an imaginary broadcast from "Station D-I-S-N-E-Y." He introduced Herb's son-in-law, Reverend Glenn Puder, who led the singing of "Put on Your Old Gray Bonnet." Robert and Charlotte Disney and the Disney sons offered their congratulations, followed by grandchildren and the in-laws. When Walt suggested fifty more years, Flora cracked, "Oh, no, that's too many. I just made a date with the cameraman."

After a singing of "Old Black Joe," Roy called on his father for remarks. "This is my dear little girl that I got fifty years ago," Elias said, gazing fondly at Flora. She recalled their wedding "down in the Florida woods" and remarked of the anniversary party: "I think this beats all." She added: "There's just one thing to mar the happiness of this day, and that's because our daughter Ruth isn't here."

Roy asked his son, eight-year-old Roy Edward, to read some passages from *Pinocchio*. Roy and Walt discussed the book, and Walt announced that his second animated feature would be based on it.

On New Year's Eve, another broadcast came from Station D-I-S-N-E-Y, with Roy Edward sharing the announcer's duties with his father. There was much talk about the Pasadena Rose Parade they had witnessed that morning, especially the Snow White float. Roy needled his parents about the sunny weather for the Pasadena parade in contrast to "that Portland rain." He asked, "Are you content to stay down here now?"

"Why, yes," Flora replied. "We have to stay now because you're building us a house, and we've got to stay and live in it." Roy commented, "Let's hope we make more speed than Ted is making."

The new house was located a few blocks from the home of Roy and Edna in Toluca Lake. Under Roy's supervision, builders finished the parents' house in good time, and they occupied it in early 1938. It would be the scene of a devastating tragedy.

THIRTEEN

‹❧›

R oy Disney turned forty-five on June 24, 1938, and he had reason to be satisfied. The studio had prospered beyond his dreams; *Snow White and the Seven Dwarfs* became a sensational hit in every country it appeared. Money poured into the studio, and although Walt found ways to spend it, Roy managed to put some of it away.

All business aspects of the company received Roy's close scrutiny. When he noted a proposal to share costs of a banquet room for an RKO sales convention, Roy fired off a memo to his New York representative. After pointing out that Disney was supplying Mickey Mouse display materials, dolls, and novelties, Roy said RKO should supply decorations for the banquet room.

"Around our place we don't go in for getting salesmen drunk in order to encourage them to sell our pictures," Roy concluded, "so I am not hot about taking a suite at the Waldorf to set up a bar room to cater to RKO salesmen, or the salesmen of any other organization. We just don't work that way."

Roy Edward was a continual source of delight for his father. When his parents still lived in Portland, Roy sent them reports of the boy's activities in nearly every letter.

". . . Roy still attends kindergarten and gets a kick out of it. Edna has been taking him down to the Christian Science Sunday school lately. He likes it all right, although he is willing to put it off until next Sunday if he can get away with it. He came home last Sunday singing 'Onward Christian Soldiers.' He is a great little fellow . . ."

". . . Roy is spending the afternoon with me in my office. His school is out right now. He sits around and reads and behaves himself very nicely. He is a fine little boy. He said the other day that he thought Christmas was 'a fine idea.' I believe he is getting a bigger kick out of it this year than he has any year yet . . ."

". . . For Roy Edward, I can't think of anything he appreciates more than good storybooks. He loves that little Indian book you gave him when you were here. I am reading to him now *The Swiss Family Robinson* a little bit at a time in the evenings . . ."

Roy adored Diane and Sharon Disney when they came to visit. "Gosh, it makes me jealous," he wrote to Flora and Elias. "I wish we had a little girl at our place, but I haven't been able to talk Edna into it as yet. I thought we might be able to go down and adopt one, if we could find one we could fall in love with. But I think my wife is having too good a time right now and hates to take on the added responsibility."

Diane remembers many family parties at Roy and Edna's house: "Edna was true to her Midwest roots; she was a gracious hostess. In the photographs of Roy, he always seemed to have a sweet half-smile. That's the way I remember him." The home movies of the thirties, most of them taken around the swimming pool, illustrate the gaiety of the family gatherings. Roy is seen splashing the guests and diving in the pool with Roy Edward.

Despite his support of Franklin Roosevelt in his early presidential years, Roy remained a Republican. Along with other studio heads, he had been alarmed by Upton Sinclair's campaign for California governor in 1934. The muckraking novelist had won the Democratic nomination with his proposal of "End Poverty in California" (EPIC). Sinclair appeared the favorite until the *Los Angeles Times* and other conservative newspapers launched a smear campaign and Irving Thalberg made movie shorts slanted against the former socialist.

Roy chided his parents: "You sons of guns, I understand you were pulling for Sinclair. What do you mean by trying to wish us a socialistic governor? Of course, all the 'bridges' that we look forward to in life and dread crossing never turn out to be as bad as we anticipate . . . but I honestly feel that Sinclair was entirely too radical and too impractical to have ever made a good governor . . . Many of the things he advocated are going to come around in some form or other. However, I don't believe you can upset society overnight, and single out one state in which to do such a thing . . .

"I can hear Dad saying, 'Now, since the boys have joined the capitalist class and the employers' class, they sing a different tune.' Well, of course, it is true . . ."

Like all men in middle years, Roy was concerned about aging, especially in regard to his hairline. "Did I tell you about my hair treatments?" he wrote cheerily to his parents. "I am trying to keep from getting baldheaded, so I have been taking a lot of hair treatments. I have been after it now for four months, and I am beginning to show some results. So from now on, I am going backwards—I am getting younger." Unfortunately, his hairline continued to recede.

Perhaps because of his postwar experience with tuberculosis, Roy was almost hypochondriacal about his health. He took a variety of pills for ailments real and imaginary. After he quit polo, he exercised as much as he had time for. During the mid-thirties he took part in the studio bowling league every Monday evening.

Roy maintained friendly relations with the Hollywood press, but his name rarely appeared in print. Mainly that was because reporters were dazzled by Walt, who was masterful in an interview. While he was not at all shy, Roy was content to let his kid brother have the spotlight. But when it came to selling the Disney product abroad, Roy was accommodating.

In the spring of 1938, Roy and Edna traveled to Europe to oversee the premiere of *Snow White* in Paris and other cities. He also arranged for the dubbing of the film in Dutch, Italian, Spanish, Swedish, Polish, Czech, Hindustani, and Arabic. In London, Roy was interviewed by a reporter for the London *Observer* who commented: "Business managers are not, as a rule, very fascinating subjects from an interviewer's standpoint. Mr. Disney is an exception. A slight, soft-voiced, eager person, with a lighter version of his brother's keen face, and just his brother's sense of humour, he is financial brains, nurse, and guardian to the Disney organization.

"He has been with Walt as advisor and friend ever since the two young men went West to try their luck in Hollywood fifteen years ago. It is his job to keep a curb on Walt's artistic enthusiasms, to pull him off a picture, which Walt would love to make and remake, to say, 'That's enough' when Walt has spent so many thousand dollars."

The story pointed out that Roy didn't draw a line, nor did Walt, except for broad sketches to illustrate his ideas. "Walt is crazy about animals," Roy told the reporter. "When he was young he used to say that the only thing he really wanted to do was raise dogs and kids."

Roy went on to explain how the Disney organization operated and to report on future productions, *Pinocchio* next, then *Bambi*. He mentioned that Leopold Stokowski was preparing a score for *The Sorcerer's Apprentice*, which might be a full-length cartoon or a Silly Symphony. Observing that *Snow White* was "running like wildfire through America and here in London, in its ninth week, it has done the biggest business of the season," the reporter asked if he had expected such a success in England. Roy replied: "Nobody could be that conceited."

F lora and Elias Disney enjoyed their new life in Los Angeles, the last of their many moves across the nation. Flora especially was delighted to be near her grandchildren, Roy Edward, Diane, and Sharon, and Herb's daughter Dorothy, now grown-up and married to Reverend Puder. Elias listened to reports from Roy and Walt about happenings at the studio, and he repeatedly warned them to be prudent in their dealings, always saving for a rainy day.

"Those boys are always borrowing money; they're reckless," Elias complained to his wife. He never believed in borrowing money. He and Flora would save their money until they had enough to buy what they wanted. Elias believed it was bad policy to rent; every house he lived in he owned.

"My dad was very thrifty, very thrifty," Walt recalled. "He never spent a nickel on himself. He wouldn't take a streetcar; he'd walk. When he was in Kansas City, before they moved to Oregon, a nephew wrote and asked him to come out to California and build a home for him. It was in Glendale. Dad decided it was a chance to look over California and see if he wanted to live there. So he came out and stayed for over three months and he only spent one dollar!

"Of course he stayed in the nephew's house, and he went on all the free rides. Real estate developers advertised to come out and see their properties and get a free meal. So he saw all of California on one dollar. In Kansas City, he used to carry a little old pocket book, the kind that snaps shut. He carried a quarter in it. Every so often my mother would take the quarter out and put a new one in. The old one was turning green.

"The funny thing is, I didn't inherit any of that thrift, none of it."

Late in his life, Elias received the astonishing news: he was not an American citizen. He had been voting for fifty years—illegally. His father, Kepple Disney, had been naturalized after he moved the family from Canada to Kansas. His wife and minor children became citizens; Elias, who was over twenty-one, did not. He and Flora took immediate steps to be naturalized.

While Elias and Flora stood in line at the federal building in downtown Los Angeles, they spoke of their situation to other applicants. One of them cracked that a lot of aliens were getting their papers now that President Roosevelt had instituted Social Security and old age pensions.

Flora was furious. "I'll have you know that we are independent and don't need any help from any government!" she raged. She added proudly, "On top of that, if we weren't independent, my son is Walt Disney!"

Flora delighted in the house that Roy and Walt had built for their parents, and she decorated the place with her keepsakes from Portland. She had only one complaint about the house.

Her daughter Ruth related: "The lady who was working there, Alma Smith, a friend of Aunt Charlotte, told me Mother had said,

'We better get this furnace fixed or else some morning we'll wake up and find ourselves dead.' So Roy and Walt had sent someone over from the studio to fix it and they'd worked on it"

Her husband, Ted Beecher, explained: "The air intake from the outside had a lid on top of it, and that lid had fallen down and so the air was recirculated."

Ruth continued: "Instead of coming from the outside, it was drawing from inside the chamber of the gas furnace. It was on the same floor. It was pouring carbon monoxide through the registers . . . Mother had gone into the bathroom adjoining her bedroom, and there was a big concentration of it in there, and it just took her. Father, wondering why she was gone so long, finally got up and went in there. He started to pick her up, and he became so weak that he fell. He fell out in the hall, and his falling was what saved him because there was less gas down there."

Alma Smith had been in the kitchen making oatmeal, which she spilled and went outside to dump. Then she realized something was wrong and returned inside to find the Disneys. She hurriedly called Roy, then the next-door neighbor. The neighbor applied artificial respiration and was able to revive Elias but not Flora.

On the morning of November 28, 1938, Roy Disney was awakened with the horrible news. He rushed to his parents' house. Elias went by ambulance to a nearby hospital, where his condition was declared to be stable. Roy, Walt, and Herb found him to be alert and cognizant of what had happened.

Both Roy and Walt were brokenhearted. At seventy their mother had been in good health; never had she known a serious illness. The two brothers had planned the house as the perfect place for their parents' sunset years. Now that house had caused their mother's death.

Roy notified Walt of the funeral in a studio memo: "Arrangements are complete now for the burial services for Mother, to-morrow at 9:30 A.M. We are to meet with Mr. Weatherwax [a funeral director] about 9:20. Then we'll all go up to the mauso-leum.

"I've taken care of the flowers in conjunction with Mr. Weath-erwax, and I'm notifying Ray and Herb, and also Glen Puder def-initely knows of the arrangements and will officiate.

"So, we'll be seeing you at the Forest Lawn main office about 9:20 in the morning, with Dad."

Neither Roy nor Walt could ever talk about the horror of their mother's unnecessary death. Roy ordered an inspection of the furnace. The report: "The installation of the furnace showed ei-ther a complete lack of knowledge of the requirements of the furnace or a flagrant disregard of these conditions if they were known. The workmanship expressed in the installation is very poor and cheap . . ." The rest of the report analyzed various faults.

There is no record that Roy took any legal action against the manufacturer or the installer. More likely, he dropped the matter, not wishing to add to the heartache for himself and the rest of the family.

It was the darnedest thing after Mother died," Walt said many years later, "I never felt so sorry for anybody in my life as I did for Dad. He was really a lost person . . . a lonesome guy. I used to take my kids over to see him every Sunday. There was nothing, he was just lost. It was a very sad thing. But they were very happy before she died. She was very happy. She was very proud of Roy and me and what we'd done. She'd go to places and say 'Mrs. Disney.' They'd say, 'You any relation to the Disney boys?' She'd say, 'Oh, yes, they're my sons.' "

When Roy and Walt started building their new Burbank studio, they figured it would be helpful for their father, with his background as carpenter and contractor, to become involved. They gave Elias the number-one construction badge and outfitted him with a worker's uniform.

"I used to take him around on these big excavations, big things going in all these foundations," Walt recalled. "The animation building started to go up. I had him up there, and my dad was never happy walking around. I thought he would be excited about building this big thing. He was never happy.

"When the building was nearing completion, I was showing him all the rooms. He said, 'Walter, what can it be used for?' I said, 'It's a studio, a studio where I work.' And he said, 'No, Walter, what can it be used for?' I couldn't quite grasp what he was after, and suddenly it dawned on me. He meant if we failed how could we liquidate. How could we get our money back out of it . . .

" 'Oh, I see, Dad,' I said. 'This would make a perfect hospital.' The rest of the tour I didn't talk about a studio, I talked about a hospital. How they could put the operating rooms up above. The white corridors could be rooms. I went through the whole darn studio and explained the thing to him as a hospital. He was happy."

The studio as hospital was a legend that would not die. Walt escorted Eleanor Roosevelt on a studio visit during the war. As she was leaving, the First Lady remarked, "My, this would make a lovely hospital." Walt himself used the hospital argument whenever Roy became overly concerned about the company's state of affairs. Roy seemed to be reassured, temporarily.

The notion of conversion to a hospital seemed to make sense because of the building's rows of small rooms on long corridors. But John Hench says the theory was false: "I remember during wartime being part of a group of doctors who were looking for places they could convert to hospitals. They decided after investigation that [the studio] was not suitable for a hospital at all. But I think the possibility of a conversion assuaged some of the fear or the worry of Roy. And I think Walt invented it."

The legend of the studio as hospital continued its prevalence into the nineties.

FOURTEEN

∽

"W hile we are not making money hand over fist as the general public thinks," Roy had written his parents in 1933, "still we are making some money. However, it is all going back into our business. Just think, there are about 130 or 135 people around here, living on Mickey Mouse. He's a pretty good mouse, don't you think, to keep up so many families? Well, we are not particularly concerned whether we ever make millions or not. After all, what you get in this life is what you take out of it in the way of pleasure, fun, enjoyment, and accomplishment. I have made up my mind that I am not going to let this thing get me down just for the sake of some money, and I know that Walt feels the same way about it."

The Disneys' principles hadn't changed five years later. Since Roy and Walt were sole owners of the company, the returns from *Snow White* could have made them very rich men, even by Hollywood standards. Instead, they siphoned most of the money back into the company. Their own styles of living hardly changed at all.

In the later stages of the production of *Snow White*, Walt had begun preliminary planning for *Pinocchio* and *Bambi*. He had also become intrigued with interpreting classical music with animation. It had begun with his concern over the sagging career of Mickey Mouse.

During the late thirties, the founding star of Walt Disney Productions had been overshadowed by nouveau comics such as Donald Duck, Goofy, and Pluto. Walt gave Mickey a starring vehicle in a version of an old fairy tale, *The Sorcerer's Apprentice*, based on the music of Paul Dukas. At a chance meeting, Walt told the famous conductor Leopold Stokowski about the project. Stokowski volunteered to conduct the score, and his participation led to what became known as *The Concert Feature*.

Roy enjoyed telling of his own brief contribution to the planning of *The Concert Feature*: "You see, I was never in the creative side [nor did I] inject myself into the creative side. In fact, I remember a funny incident when Walt had Stokowski here and was making *Fantasia*. He and Stokowski and Deems Taylor were talking over the picture and the selection of numbers. Playin' the records and talkin' about it.

"I joined this session one day, and during the course of it, I dared to say something to the effect: 'My Gosh, can't you select some music that just the ordinary guy like me can like?' They all froze up and Walt ordered me out of the room. 'Go back down and keep the books,' he said."

Despite its pioneering aspect, the production of *Snow White* had few major problems. Partly that was because the concept of the film had emerged virtually full-grown from Walt's head. Compared to *Snow White*, *Pinocchio* was a nightmare.

Walt and his story men had struggled with the story. The book had been a biting social satire written in 1880 by an Italian journalist under the pen name of Carlo Collodi. It had none of the cuddly characters or the fairy-tale themes of *Snow White*. Pinocchio himself presented problems. He was a puppet turned boy, hence he was expressionless and moved awkwardly. After agonizing over *Pinocchio* for six months, Walt ceased production.

Roy fretted over the expense while Walt and his staff built a new structure for *Pinocchio*, adding more flamboyant characters, building up the role of the cricket who supplied the puppet-boy with a conscience, giving the cricket two surefire songs, "Give a Little Whistle" and "When You Wish Upon a Star."

Because of the production problems, *Pinocchio* ended up costing a half-million dollars more than *Snow White*.

"*Pinocchio* was a film that was very difficult in production," Roy observed, "and there again it was more [that] the artists weren't up to the animation. We didn't have enough of 'em. Walt was starting out trying to set up a pattern of making a cartoon feature every year. That was a phenomenal job he was never able to reach because of the talent available. I think anyway, lookin' back now, that's too many of a specialty kind of a product to go on the market, one every year."

Fantasia also disappointed Walt, Roy said: "He really didn't have the artists to do what he hoped to. He saw more possibilities than he got out of it . . . Walt made a lot of decisions against his will, when he had to put up with what he had available to work with."

While Roy was in Europe arranging the openings of *Snow White* in 1938, he received an urgent memo from Gunther Lessing. Walt wanted Roy to return as soon as possible. "The principal questions which are bothering him," wrote the com pany lawyer, "are the purchase of a piece of property which seems to be available near Warner Bros., the new distribution contract and the purchase of story properties."

The brothers had been discussing the need for a new studio for several months. It had become obvious that the Hyperion plant could no longer accommodate Walt's ambitions. Several of the departments had been shifted to a building near Hollywood and Vine, the *Bambi* unit had been set up on Seward Street. The rentals and transportation to and from the main studio placed added burdens on the company budget. Roy was receptive to Walt's arguments that a new studio was needed to take care of the studio's needs.

When Roy returned, he placed a $10,000 deposit on a property on Buena Vista Street in Burbank. The total price would be $101,897.10.

Even though he was in production with three feature films and still supervised the short cartoons, Walt plunged into the planning of the new studio with customary enthusiasm. After making cartoons in the cramped, makeshift Hyperion studio for a decade, he was determined to create the ideal animation workplace. He planned everything down to the smallest details of the animator's chair and worktable. No more the stuffy rooms where the artists dripped sweat in the summer months and smudged their drawings.

Walt chose his own office, a spacious suite in the northeast corner of the third floor. Roy's office would be an east wing in the center of the second floor, where he would be surrounded by lawyers, accountants, and others concerned with business matters.

"Each office in each wing was different, depending what was supposed to go on in there," remembers animator Frank Thomas. "If you were in the planning stage or the story stage, if your story sketches were layouts or backgrounds, you had a different type of window. You had a different type of light. You had a big sink where it would be easy to clean things . . .

"Walt called us back to night meetings, where he had little models of all the buildings. He'd say, 'How about if we put the theater here, the animation building there, the restaurant here, the sound stage there, the orchestra stage, the camera department, ink-and-paint, cutting, process lab, all those things. We would move all those models around, then someone would say, 'What do you do in rainy weather?'

"Then we'd figure, 'Well, how many rainy days do we get? Is that really a factor?' Walt put in underground tunnels that would connect you with ink-and-paint and camera so that in rainy weather you carried the drawings underneath. He really thought it through and involved us in it all the way."

In August of 1939, the *Pinocchio* unit began filming in the camera building, the first structure of the new studio to be completed. In the fall, the *Bambi* unit moved from temporary quarters in Hollywood to become the first occupant of the animation building. After Christmas the major exodus from Hyperion began.

At first, the animators were dazzled by their new surroundings. The Animation Building, which housed the artists and the business departments, rose like an art deco palace, gleaming white in the San Fernando Valley sun.

"It was fun after we all moved in," recalls animator Ollie Johnston. "We had all this freedom to begin with. We had a little snack bar next to the traffic department on the first floor. We had the Penthouse Club and a masseur. We could come up there and get a milk shake or something to drink any time you wanted, or get something to eat, or have traffic deliver it to your room. The restaurant was open longer hours. When you came to work, you could go there for breakfast for a dollar. And gee, it was just great.

"I liked it, but I liked the small place [Hyperion]. We all got together more for meetings. Like on *Snow White.* Walt had us all out on the soundstage discussing how the dwarfs would walk. Everybody got up and showed how he thought each one would walk. We talked about it, and it was really fun. We did a lot of that here.

"The meetings with Walt were really marvelous. He used to get me so enthused I couldn't wait to get back to my [drawing] board. He'd get you laughing and all excited about the personality of the guy you were going to work with. Of course the strike and the war hurt that. Walt, I don't think, ever felt as close to us."

The strike and World War II. Two unforeseen events over which Walt and Roy had no control and which would bring more troubles than the brothers and their company had ever dealt with.

FIFTEEN

❦

One month after the Disney company began moving into its grand new studio, Hitler invaded Poland. Roy's greatest fear was realized. The foreign market, which amounted to 45 percent of Disney income, collapsed under the onslaught of war.

Roy had witnessed signs of things to come in 1938 when he was in Europe to arrange the openings of *Snow White*. He visited Vienna a week after the invasion and saw Nazi flags flying everywhere and German military trucks parading around the Ringestrasse.

With the most important part of the foreign market virtually closed, the Disney company also faced an uncertain future in the United States. *Pinocchio* opened in February 1940 to a mixed reception. While technically superior to *Snow White*, it lacked the fairy-tale quality that had made *Snow White* so endearing. Theater business was good, but not good enough to offset the $2.6 million production cost.

Roy was concerned about the two other films that were near-ing completion. *Fantasia* represented Walt's biggest gamble yet. It was totally dissimilar from anything he or any other producer had attempted. Would American audiences pay to see a mix of artistic conceptions of classical music? Walt was convinced they would, and he demanded that *Fantasia* be presented like a con-cert in prestigious theaters equipped with the revolutionary Fan-tasound, which presented the music stereophonically.

Fantasia had its premiere November 13, 1940, in the same New York theater where Mickey Mouse first appeared almost ex-actly twelve years before. The film was well received in big cities, where it was presented as a road-show attraction, two screenings a day, reserved seats, higher admission prices. Other theaters ob-jected to paying $30,000 to install Fantasound, which could be used for a single movie only.

The Bank of America, represented by Joe Rosenberg in Los Angeles, had become increasingly concerned about Disney's bur-geoning debt. Rosenberg nudged Roy to cut costs and find ways to increase income. One of his worries was the flagging *Fantasia*.

On August 22, 1941, Roy wrote to George Schaefer, president of RKO Radio Pictures in New York, telling of a visit to Rosen-berg's office. Roy went there to outline plans for the company's future releases.

"Joe Rosenberg hit the ceiling with respect to my comments on the handling of *Fantasia*, and he says, 'George Schaefer doesn't agree with you, and George is in favor of putting it out immediately, in general release.'

"I explained to Joe that it wasn't a question of whether or not *Fantasia* should be released right now, but rather it was a ques-tion of considering all of our completed product and so spacing the release of the various pictures that it would work to the best advantage in their distribution.

"Right now we have *Reluctant Dragon* in release. We have *Dumbo* ready to be released the middle of October and *Bambi* practically finished, to be released right after Christmas. Even if we wanted to, I think it would be a bad policy to put *Fantasia* into general release right now because it would just conflict with and confuse the distribution of other pictures."

A showman as well as guardian of the Disney product, Roy reasoned with Schaefer: "It is true that the picture-going public think of pictures in terms of newness and firstness, and that because of the time involved they are apt to, in their mind, call *Fantasia* 'an old one.'

"On the other hand, we have to build up the idea that *Fantasia* is different from regular pictures and not to be considered in the same light. I think it is more comparable to a stage play that runs for a long time. I believe that *Fantasia* can run for a long, long time if we hold it on a proper level and don't make it common by showing it in the cheap houses, double-billed with *The Lone Ranger*, or some other ill-fitting companion picture." Roy's reasoning was borne out by the company's policy of rereleasing the animated classics every seven years, making each revival an "event."

Fantasia proved its capacity for long runs by appearing at a New York theater for more than a year. But in the end Roy lost the fight to the bank and RKO. Because Walt couldn't bear to cut *Fantasia*, RKO assumed the chore. *Fantasia* was butchered from two hours to eighty-one minutes and, as Roy had feared, released on a double bill with a western. With a cost of $2,280,000 it had been Disney's biggest loss.

Dumbo provided the only light amid the gloom.

"*Dumbo* was a very happy little experience we had around here trying to get something on the market," Roy recalled. "That picture was made for $800,000, I remember well. And it made a lot of money for its negative cost . . . *Dumbo* was only sixty-four minutes long, and it always suffered in the marketplace because it needed a little more length, really, to be sold as a feature picture. Had it been feature-length and kept up the same interest and entertainment, it would have been a really top grosser."

RKO urged Walt to make *Dumbo* longer. He refused. As Roy remarked, "After we finished 'em and put 'em on the market, Walt left 'em like a dirty shirt. He just turned his back on 'em and went ahead."

Dumbo eventually earned $850,000, but it was not enough to erase the red ink created by the other features. The idyllic *Bambi*, released while America was enmeshed in a full-scale war, brought more disappointment.

I n 1940, Ub Iwerks returned to the studio where he had been one-third partner and chief animator.

Ub had left Disney ten years earlier, lured with promises of riches by Pat Powers, the fast-operating nemesis of Walt and Roy. Ub had produced thirty-six Flip the Frog cartoons for release by MGM, but the series never caught fire. "There was nothing sympathetic about Flip," veteran Disney producer Ben Sharpsteen observed. "Ub never learned how to put character into his characters; Walt did. Walt had made too much of a smart aleck out of Oswald. He made Mickey Mouse more human."

During the 1930s, Ub worked on other cartoon series, while also designing and building his own cameras and special effects techniques. Ub had neither the talent nor the patience to be an entrepreneur, and he put out a feeler to Sharpsteen. Ub was too proud to ask Walt for a job; Walt had not forgotten that Ub had deserted him.

Walt finally agreed to place Ub in checking, the final phase between animation and photography. It was a comedown for Ub, but he accepted it gracefully. Later Walt told Sharpsteen, "We don't need Ub in checking. He's an outstanding man in optics; I don't think anybody knows more about optics than Ub. I'm trying to develop a new printer. I'm going to put him on that."

For the next thirty years, Ub Iwerks proved an invaluable asset to the studio. He developed techniques that won him two Academy Awards, provided special effects for all the major films, perfected the transfer of 16mm film to 35mm for the True-Life Adventures, and helped create It's a Small World, Pirates of the Caribbean, and other Disneyland attractions.

One writer claimed Walt and Ub didn't speak to each other after Ub's return. "Poppycock, pure poppycock," Roy responded angrily. "They were the closest of friends. We have been close friends with the Iwerks. Their kids [David and Donald] work at the studio. Ub is a fine man."

As the debt to Bank of America continued to rise and the expensive features performed poorly, Roy realized the company needed another source of financing. His solution: a stock offering.

From the beginning, Roy and Walt had resisted inviting any outside investors. They had worked as a partnership until they incorporated Walt Disney Productions in 1929. Walt and Lilly owned 60 percent of the stock, Roy 40 percent. In 1938, the company was reorganized to include three subsidiary companies. Of the 150,000 shares, 45,000 apiece went to Walt and Lilly, 30,000 apiece to Roy and Edna.

Walt had long opposed a public stock offering, fearing that his total autonomy over creative matters might be challenged by investors. At Roy's insistence, Walt agreed to issuance of preferred and common stock in April 1940. The prospectus listed Walt as president and executive production manager and Roy as executive vice president and business manager. The company's assets at the end of 1939: $7,000,758.

Roy himself had misgivings about issuing stock. "When you go public," he said later, "it changes your life. Where you were free to do things, you are bound by a lot of conventions—bound to other owners."

The sale, on the over-the-counter market, infused a much-needed $3,500,000 into the company, but Roy realized that drastic measures were required for survival. In a memo dated April 30, 1940, Roy told all department heads that "present world conditions have brought a new and urgent need for rigid economy. Other motion picture studios have already effected drastic reductions of all kinds, including severe salary cuts, and the Walt Disney Studio finds it cannot escape adopting economic measures."

He called for a cost reduction of 25 percent, explaining, "To recover a dollar wasted or unnecessarily spent, we must earn an additional ten dollars at the box office."

Roy issued these regulations, effective immediately:

1. No additions to the payroll without his approval in writing.
2. No purchase of materials, equipment, supplies, etc., without his approval in writing.
3. No new jobs to be established "without a complete review of the needs, objectives, and costs," and with his approval in writing.

In a memo to Walt on March 14, 1941, Roy reviewed the company's overall position. He pointed out that his initial estimate of income from *Fantasia* was "proving itself each day more and more to be completely wet." The downward trend meant "a further serious crimp in our already severely strained financial condition."

Roy said he was convinced that studio production operations were healthier than in recent years and suitable for the company's world market, which had shrunk to the United States, Canada, and Latin America.

"Our problem is one of indebtedness and the need of cash for production of new product," he continued. "I know the bank is nervous now about our indebtedness and is going ahead to a higher figure reluctantly and because they are on a spot and can't do otherwise. Just how far they will go in that frame of mind, I don't know, but we are getting on very thin ice." He suggested a further reduction of 20 percent in expenditures.

When Disney's debt to the bank reached $3 million, a gravely concerned Joe Rosenberg was summoned to a board meeting in San Francisco. He took Roy and Walt along. Roy recalled the scene: "A chair was at the head of the table for A.P. Giannini. After we waited for him for fifteen or twenty minutes, A.P. came in and didn't sit down at the chair but walked around the whole table. As he passed Walt and me a couple of times he nudged us in the back and said, 'Don't look so downhearted; it isn't that bad.'

"So then he turned on the board and said, 'You've been loaning Disney a lot of money. Have you been following any of their pictures?' 'Oh, yes. Oh, yes,' said several of the members. 'Well, which ones have you seen?' And he put each of 'em on the spot as to which pictures they had actually seen. He didn't let the general remark go. He found a lot of 'em hadn't seen any of 'em.

"Finally he said, 'Well, look, I've watched Disney's pictures quite closely, 'cause I knew we were lending them money way over their financial risk . . . There's nothing about those pictures that's gonna be changed by the war. They're good this year, they're good next year, and they're good the year afterwards.

" 'Now there's a war on. And Disney's markets are all in trouble. His money is frozen or he can't work in a country. You have to relax and give them time to market their product. This war isn't going to last forever.'

"And with that he left the board meeting. Needless to say, the committee saw fit to extend our loan. Well, that was the kind of friendship we had out of the Bank of America."

Despite A.P. Gianinni's blessing, Roy realized the bank would not extend its goodwill and its money forever. The studio needed to extend its economies to demonstrate its good faith. In a memo to Walt on March 14, 1941, he painted a dark picture of the company's condition and urged planning for a further 20 percent reduction in expenses. He proposed stopping work on all product beyond the present year, closing the process lab, curtailing the training school, going "down the line of our personnel and releasing everyone who can possibly be released without affecting the immediate work in process," and asking all employees to take a graduated pay cut.

Drastic measures, Roy agreed, "but this method is to be preferred to the other alternative possibilities that are staring us in the face, such as selling our product out through a franchise or otherwise on poor terms and conditions arising out of emergency action, or even by being forced to go through receivership or bankruptcy. To me, it seems that serious."

For once, Walt agreed with his brother's reasoning. Years later he recalled that "hectic period": "My brother went through as much hell as I did. I became all confused. I didn't know where I was. I had a big staff. I hated to lay off anybody. I tried to hold on to 'em. I tried to think for different ways. The war was not here yet. But they were still drafting; some of my boys had to go. It was a terrible period.

"I just became so darned confused that I just didn't know what the heck I was doing. I should have had a big layoff. I should have practically closed the doors until I straightened the mess. But no, I tried to keep 'em. The boys should have had increases because of their time. I couldn't give 'em an increase; I was fighting like the devil even to pay 'em.

"I learned my lesson there. You don't do a person good sometimes by keeping them. I learned a lot on that. I think the best thing is to face up to it. I always hated to fire anybody. I'd always think, 'Well, gee, he's got five kids.' I began to let that enter into it, and it's wrong. The best thing is to face up to it. Because sometimes I've seen some of those kids go out and be very successful outside. In other words, it could have been a favor."

For eighteen years, the Disney company had increased its number of employees, seldom firing anyone. Now the layoffs began.

The pink slips were a blow to those who believed they had found a lifetime job at Disney. Some of them grumbled that the Disney brothers were profiting from the situation, skimming the profits to make themselves richer. There were complaints about low wages, little chance of advancement, work drudgery.

Those who remained on the payroll felt an unease, wondering whether they would survive, whether the studio would survive. This air of uncertainty made many of the employees prime targets for union organizers. Confusing the situation was the presence of two warring unions seeking to organize Disney: the unaffiliated Federation of Screen Cartoonists and the Screen

Cartoonists Guild, affiliated with the A.F.L. Painters and Paper-hangers Union. The Screen Cartoonists Guild was led by Herbert Sorrell, a firebrand organizer connected with radical causes.

A picket line appeared outside the studio gate on May 29, 1941. Herb Sorrell had called a strike.

What had gone wrong with Walt's dream of a "worker's paradise?"

"The first seeds of the strike were sown by the Penthouse Club," says Ken Peterson, who had started in 1936 as an in-betweener, joined the strike and survived it to become a Disney executive.

"I was at Hyperion for four years, and we were all one happy family. It was a wonderful time, people coming from all over, all funny guys, offbeat. We'd lunch 'on the [drawing] board' and go out and play touch football in Griffith Park on the noon hour. There wasn't anybody you couldn't ask for help, a top animator or whoever. There were different salaries, but nobody worried about that. We all figured we were learning something, and it was true.

"When we moved to the new studio, Walt's paternalism was expressed in the Penthouse Club. The dividing line for membership was money; you had to earn two hundred a week, something like that. I didn't qualify, and a lot of others didn't either.

"When the union came in, I don't think any of us knew anything about unions. But we were all feeling sort of left out . . . The strike was about economics, but it was also a rebellion about the kind of management Walt had."

Roy's daughter-in-law, Patty Disney, believes that the strike angered Walt and saddened Roy. At first bewildered, Walt became incensed by the strikers. He defied them, driving through the picket line and responding angrily to their taunts. One day he almost got into a fistfight with one of the strident hecklers.

While Walt continued to be visible, Roy remained in his office, arranging for negotiations, struggling to keep the studio functioning with the reduced staff. He made no public statements, and he was alarmed by the fierceness of Walt's attacks. Walt took a trade paper ad in which he declared: "I am positively convinced that Communistic agitation, leadership and activities have brought about this strike . . ."

It became apparent that the company lawyer, Gunther Lessing, had Walt's ear during the tumultuous period. "Walt believed everything Gunnie told him, and some of it was wrong," animator Ward Kimball commented. "Gunnie would read a Hearst editorial and report it as fact to Walt—and Walt believed him."

Roy became convinced that Walt's presence at the center of the strike firestorm was neither good for Walt nor the studio. He yearned for some way to remove Walt from the scene. The U.S. government came to the rescue.

Nelson Rockefeller, Coordinator of Inter-American Affairs, shared the government's worry that the many Germans and Italians living in South America would sway the countries to favor the Axis powers instead of the Allies. Jock Whitney, with whom Roy had once discussed polo, headed the motion picture division of the agency and suggested that Walt Disney would be an ideal ambassador for the American cause. Walt at first was reluctant, but he was enticed by the government's offer of partly financing films to be made about South America. And the trip would provide escape from the damnable strike. He accepted.

"Don't worry, Walt, I can take care of this," Gunther Lessing said reassuringly. "I know the boys [the union leaders] over there. I play golf with them, and we'll make a deal under the table."

The deal Lessing made created as many problems as it solved. Roy was disappointed, but he wanted the strike to be concluded by the time Walt and his crew returned from South America. Both

Roy and Walt remained convinced that Communists were behind the strike, and there was evidence that Communists and "fellow travelers" were involved. The experience made the brothers more conservative and outspokenly anti-Communist. It also changed Walt's attitude toward his workers.

"I think the strike changed everybody," animator Marc Davis observed. "I think that Walt became resigned that he had to operate in a more hard-nosed way, like a lot of other people who have something forced on them that they don't like. I don't say that he was less benevolent. But I think that a lot of the frills that he thought were so wonderful when we first came out to the new building . . . went by the boards. I'm sure that he had to feel that [the strike] was a thing against him personally, and I guess in some areas it certainly was."

Elias Disney died at the age of eighty-two in September 1941, while Walt toured South America. He had been in failing health for some time, and his daughter Ruth thought that the gas that killed Flora may have affected his mind. "At times he slipped back into thinking that Mother was there," she said.

Elias was buried alongside Flora at Forest Lawn in Glendale. Often when Walt had taken them on a drive, they asked to visit Forest Lawn. "They enjoyed it," Walt once said. "I left them at the gate, and they would walk around all afternoon. Then I'd pick them up toward evening." He said they both drew inspiration from the cemetery, with its wide hilly lawns dotted with reproductions of classic sculpture.

Years later, Evelyn Waugh visited the studio and urged Walt to read the manuscript he had written, titled *The Loved One*. After reading it, Walt asked Waugh, "You're not going to publish this, are you?" Waugh replied that he certainly was, that he considered it an interesting view of American customs and mores.

"I think it's in extremely bad taste," Walt said sternly.

"What's bad taste?" Waugh replied. "I think it's funny."

"My mother and father are buried there," Walt said. "There are many people who consider it to be a sacred place."

SIXTEEN

◆

In October 1941, while Walt was still on his good-neighbor tour, Roy sent him a four-page memo from New York, outlining the studio situation. On the day Walt left, Roy had flown to Washington in an attempt to break the strike stalemate. A labor department official agreed with Roy's suggestion of a studio layoff to cool down the situation. The union bluntly refused, and Roy believed their action angered the labor department and "put the monkey on their back." Roy then shut down the studio for two weeks or until the layoff was decided, thus avoiding accusations of a lockout.

"I must say here," Roy wrote to Walt, "that personally I came to the realization after seeing the attitude of official Washington in the matter, that we are bucking a national trend and that the unions were definitely in the saddle.

"So I altered my personal approach to the entire matter. We are definitely in a period of social revolution and changes, and if we're going to continue to conduct our business, we're going to have to find out how to work with the present social problems and the Washington administration attitude."

The Bank of America had vetoed any work on a new feature. So Roy and the production staff worked out a program for production:

1. Regular short subjects.
2. The South American short subjects [which were compiled into two features, *Saludos Amigos* and *The Three Caballeros*].
3. Completion of *Bambi*.
4. The completion of the Mickey feature [*Mickey and the Beanstalk*, released as part of *Fun and Fancy Free*] or *The Wind in the Willows* on a slow schedule.
5. A very modest story development program.

Roy had flown to Washington four times to negotiate with labor department arbitrators, making the thirty-hour flights in DC-3s. "The union also sent their delegation, and after a two-day session in Washington, [the government official] 'arbitrated it' by giving the union what they demanded," he told Walt. Having no recourse, Roy ordered the union demands carried out. They included a set ratio of strikers to nonstrikers in each department, strike pay and retroactive salary increases. The settlement did not include twenty-eight contract workers, who had been paid their salaries during the strike but did no work.

Roy made another trip to Washington for the contract agreement. "While it is lousy," Roy wrote, "we have managed to save management rights for the greater part."

Roy promised to return to Burbank and meet with Walt in early December "at which time, in conformity with *our promise to the bank*, we will set up an executive committee, which will function as a governing body of the studio, where all matters of general policy will be discussed and agreed on before action is taken.

"The bank's attitude is very good. They don't lack confidence in us. However, they do have some qualms about your 'enthusiasm and possible plans for future production.' They want to be sure we follow the outline that's been set up by them until such time as we have reduced our indebtedness to them to a 'safe figure.' "

The letter ended with a note of optimism: "From all reports I get and my own observations, I feel there is a new life, understanding and appreciation, on the part of the present studio personnel. I really think a lot of good will come out of all our past trouble and that we are now on a firm basis on which to go ahead."

A month after Walt returned from South America, the Japanese bombed Pearl Harbor.

"The forties brought the war and our frozen markets," Roy reflected in later years. "It was a bad decade for us; we really got in a tight bind around here. We were a young organization, and our fellows were subject to the draft. We lost many, many of them.

"To counteract losing our boys, Walt jumped in and started making films for the services. On the strength of that, we were able to keep some of the boys and keep a nucleus of an organization going."

On the afternoon of December 7, 1941, five hundred soldiers of an army antiaircraft unit moved into the Disney studio unannounced. The soldiers stripped the sound stage and installed equipment to repair antiaircraft guns. Three million rounds of ammunition were stored in the parking sheds. Sentries were placed at all entrances to the studio. The Disney brothers and all their employees were fingerprinted and given identification badges.

With the theatrical product in low gear, the Disney studio virtually became a war plant. Earlier in 1941, Walt had produced a training film for aircraft workers, *Four Methods of Flush Riveting*. It became a vital tool for Lockheed Aircraft and so impressed the Canadian government that it ordered films about promoting war savings bonds and how to operate an antitank gun.

After Pearl Harbor, orders for training films poured in from all the U.S. armed services. Subjects included everything from aircraft spotting to water purification. For other branches of the government, the studio produced films about malaria prevention, paying war taxes, mass hysteria, and Nazism. The most memorable of the latter was *Der Fuehrer's Face*, in which Donald Duck dreamed of being in Nazi Germany. The title song featured a succession of "Heils!" followed by loud raspberries. The Motion Picture Academy named the film best cartoon short of 1943.

The studio dubbed *Der Fuehrer's Face* into Russian, using war personnel who were in the United States. Dozens of prints were given to Russia at no cost (the country didn't recognize copyrights and had been a notorious bootlegger of Disney cartoons).

"That was just a little war gesture on our part," said Roy. "The army dropped prints of the film over the German army, just to irritate them."

Funding of the instructional and propaganda shorts was haphazard, bordering on chaotic. Since all of the assignments were on a rush basis, Walt sometimes gave a rough estimate of the cost over the telephone. Usually the estimate was too low, but the government held him to it. Payments slowly trudged through the bureaucracy, sometimes didn't arrive at all. The studio didn't charge for the expense of designing 1,400 insignias for fighting units.

Roy watched helplessly as the company's already depleted finances dwindled further. Both he and Walt had been involved in the First World War, and they were intensely patriotic. They shouldered the loss without complaint.

"Walt accepted the tasks with enthusiasm," Ben Sharpsteen recalled. "He was excited about what he called 'visual education.'"

Since most of the films had to be delivered on a tight schedule—some within a few weeks—Walt was not able to apply as much showmanship as he desired. But the use of the Disney characters and the studio's advanced animation techniques made the films superior to those of other suppliers.

Bill Anderson, who later became a Disney producer, arrived at the studio in February 1943 and was assigned to keep track of the war work. He recalls: "There was great pressure within the services of trying to get everything out. The navy wanted their thing. The army wanted their thing. The air force had projects. The marines had projects. So there was competition, and each branch of the service was fighting to get theirs.

"There was still security when I came, because certain projects were secretive. You had to be cleared to go into certain wings of the studio . . . Walt was getting calls almost daily: 'Can you handle this project?' 'Can you do this for us?' And Walt would say, 'Hell, yes, we can do it for you. We'll find a way to do it.'"

The training films were sometimes subject to the whims of changing times. Wilfred Jackson recalled being assigned a film for the Royal Air Force on how patterns of light were used to direct bombers to their night targets. As usual, the order was on a rush basis. After working day and night, Jackson's unit completed the film. Then one day he was told to destroy it.

"Two R.A.F. men and some American officers stood by as everything went into the incinerator," Jackson related. "I wept for a day and slept for a week. I knew I'd failed miserably. What I didn't know was that Ike was planning to go into Normandy, and the pattern bombings weren't necessary anymore."

While Walt occupied himself with war work, Roy dealt with RKO on the releases of *Fantasia* and *Dumbo*, tried to placate Joe Rosenberg and the Bank of America, presided over board and stockholders meetings, worked with the union and National Labor Relations Board on the new contract, and tended to other corporate matters, no matter how small.

Roy dispatched a memo to two New York executives saying he was upset that they purchased a thousand *Dumbo* books for more than the wholesale rate and had mailed them to the studio at a higher rate than necessary. "I think this is a case of gross negligence and results in an absolute waste of $300 or better," he wrote. "I want to impress on both of you the need for using some common sense in our everyday transactions."

He criticized another New York executive for ordering a message sent to the studio by straight wire at a cost of $6.64 when it could have arrived two hours later for $1.80. When two department heads quarreled, Roy sent a telegram on December 29, 1942—by overnight wire—declaring, "I don't see why you two can't work together. You are both working for the same company . . . None of us should have any pride of authorship of ideas but give and take and work with each other amicably. Happy New Year."

. . .

Before the war, Walt had been engaged in the early stages of two classics, *Alice in Wonderland* and *Peter Pan*. Those projects had been indefinitely postponed. Walt suggested combining a short feature starring Mickey Mouse and *The Wind in the Willows*. Roy advised Walt that they couldn't afford to spend more than $400,000 to $450,000 on the picture.

"The very nature of this picture—combining two stories in one—is a different type of presentation, and nobody can say what sort of an experience we will have with it," Roy reasoned in a memo. "To me it seems certain, however, that it will not be as salable as a feature comprising one story of a conventional type." The project was abandoned, and the two segments were later packaged into other feature presentations.

Roy kept a close eye on his brother, knowing Walt's propensity for taking on new projects that would overload his capacity for dealing with all his responsibilities. During the war, George Sidney was preparing an MGM musical starring Gene Kelly, Frank Sinatra, and Kathryn Grayson, *Anchors Aweigh*. The film would include a dance number featuring Kelly with a cartoon figure. Since Kelly was playing a sailor, his ideal partner would be Donald Duck.

Walt was immediately receptive. He saw the drawings for the dance and heard the music and told Sidney he would like Donald to join the movie. The next day, Sidney received a telephone call from Roy. "You son of a bitch, trying to get my brother over there!" Roy exclaimed. "He's got four pictures to finish, and if he doesn't deliver them, we're in real trouble." Donald missed his chance for musical fame. The role was given to Jerry of the MGM cartoon team, Tom and Jerry.

Victory through Air Power became an anomaly in the Disney oeuvre, the sole blatantly propaganda film for the mass market. After hopping over the Andes and to the capitals of South America, Walt returned with a profound interest in flight. He was over-whelmed by the 1942 book by Major Alexander P. de Seversky, who argued that strategic bombing could win the war. Walt brought Seversky to the studio for consultations and placed a production crew on a rush basis to turn out a film.

"The film had wide distribution," Roy explained, "because the air force sent it far and wide to other countries and to military establishments. As a motion picture for the theater it was a big flop. We lost most of our money [$436,000] on that picture, but we did it as a patriotic gesture."

After the war had ended, Walt Disney Productions faced more hard times. No major films had been put into release, nor had any begun production. Receipts from Europe had been frozen by the war-impoverished countries. Joe Rosenberg called Roy repeatedly to underscore the bank's concern about its loan, now swollen to $4.5 million. "I kept working on Walt and with Walt," Roy said later, "[but] there was only so much he could do without wrecking the organization."

Exhausted, Roy told Rosenberg to "stop beating on me so much" and come out to the studio and try to reason with Walt. Roy continued the story: "The morning he came out it was rain-ing, and it was a real California rain. We're sitting in Walt's office, and it's raining outside. Joe starts lecturing Walt about our con-dition. The dangers involved in it. The extent the bank could go, and so forth. That it was really their stockholders' money they were loaning, and they had restrictions. No matter what their hearts felt, it came down to a situation where they had to act.

"So he builds it up, and he says, 'Roy and I see the situation this way: You should cut down your outgo here drastically.' (It seems to me we had some $30,000 in weekly expenses.) Walt would interrupt every once in a while, and Joe would say, 'Let me finish, let me finish.' It got to be like that vaudeville gag. Walt would say, 'Now? Now?' Joe would say, 'Not now. Let me finish.' It went on this way until it got quite comical.

"Finally Walt said, 'Now?' and Joe said, 'Yes. Go ahead. What have you got to say?' So Walt says, 'I'm disappointed in you, Joe. I thought you were a different kind of banker. But you turned out to be a regular goddamn banker. You'll loan a guy an umbrella on a sunshiny day, but when it rains, you want it back. Okay. You can have it back. We'll take our business to another bank.' Which was quite a joke because you don't take a four-and-a-half-million-dollar bad loan to a bank.

"Joe's mouth dropped open, and he finally laid his head back and laughed out loud and said, 'Walt, you take the cake.'

"So that was the long story, and Walt used to claim that he just called him a 'goddamn banker.' The way Joe and I remember, it is different, slightly."

SEVENTEEN

❧

After the war Walt Disney seemed to experience a lack of confidence for the first time in his entire career. Those working closest to him noticed it. Always he had possessed a crystal-clear vision of where the future would take him and the studio. Never had he been without with an abundance of ideas.

He had brought to his war work all the skills he possessed, but, except for the knowledge that he was performing his patriotic duty, it was unrewarding. His professional life had been devoted to pleasing the public. The instructional and propaganda films had been fashioned to the demands of generals, admirals, and bureaucrats.

In the sweet glow of *Snow White and the Seven Dwarfs*, Walt had resolved to release one animated feature per year. But with the box office failures of *Pinocchio*, *Fantasia*, and *Bambi*, he had to change his thinking. Perhaps it would have to be one feature every two or three years. At any rate, the company was so broke after the war that not even one feature was in production. There was only enough money to piece together a handful of musical shorts and release them as *Make Mine Music* and *Fun and Fancy Free*. Or combine segments of animation with live-action films such as *Song of the South* and *So Dear to My Heart*. These were stopgap measures, designed to bring desperately needed revenue into the company.

In December 1945, Roy met with Joe Rosenberg to outline the company's financial needs. When Roy mentioned the figures of $4.5 million for expenses in 1946 and $5.8 million for 1947, the banker was shocked. He recovered after Roy explained how the money would be used. Rosenberg became "quite cooperative," Roy remarked in a confidential memo to Walt, and he even suggested a term loan of $1 million to take care of capital investments in soundstages and equipment.

"So I think it behooves us to strengthen our foundation so that we can do the job as we see it now, without financial handicaps or possible pitfalls," the memo continued. "This is a much better way to go, I believe, than to consider making any deals with third parties or other studios whereby they would put up the money and take half the profits. Deals of this sort would only partially solve our problem and could be more expensive."

Three months later, Roy sent another confidential memo to Walt, reporting on the state of the studio.

"Our company is stronger today than at any time in our past," Roy began cheerfully, then adding: "The size of our program is such that it will tax our financial strength to handle it. Our bank borrowings for probably four years will be the heaviest in our history, and might reach $6 or $7 million dollars in March, 1948, on present production planning. That is why, for safety, get in more ballast—additional capital to reduce our borrowings to a lower and safer level."

Roy foresaw expanding markets for Disney films, and he offered suggestions for improvement: "The injection of new selling angles, personalities, appealing songs, etc., into our films will provide more potent ammunition for exploitation and thus win for us greater box office acceptance where we are now weakest."

The ideal program, he proposed, would be three features a year—one a package of short films, one combining live-action and animation, one full-length cartoon feature—plus eighteen shorts. Roy gave a complete rundown of revenue prospects for pictures that had been planned.

Roy ended with a plea: "Above, Walt, I have tried to give you a brief picture of the reasons why, in my opinion, we must have a meeting of minds on our program for the years ahead; and why, once that agreement is reached, we must take the necessary steps to hew to that program. Otherwise we will be drifting with an increasingly heavy burden on our shoulders."

The advantages of setting such a course:

"1. It means you can go forward in your desire to make fine pictures with fewer uncertainties and restrictions.

"2. It means you can plan a more specific property-buying program. This is vital, because it is where everything starts.

"3. It means we can make long-range distribution, selling and exploitation plans.

"4. It means we can build a sound program for securing new capital and thus strengthen our financial structure.

"5. It means we can meet our financial obligations to the bank and our stockholders.

"6. It means we can have a busy, successful, inspired studio which, in turn, means the solution of a thousand and one trivial, yet aggravating problems."

This would prove to be the formula that would restore the Disney Company's fortunes and provide the guidelines for years to come.

The Disney methodology stressed preparation. Walt always had three or four, sometimes more animated features in various stages of development. First he worked with the story men, exploring how a fairy tale or fable could be converted into a Disney entertainment. If the subject matter seemed appealing, it would be outlined by sketches on storyboards. If Walt saw promise in the result, the storyboards would include individual scenes. Again Walt would weigh the possibilities.

Projects that passed the various tests might not be completed for five or six years, often longer. Many would never be made.

Preparation of animated features remained at a standstill during the war. Now Walt needed to put one into production in order to fuel the studio's recovery. He considered *Alice in Wonderland*, *Peter Pan*, and *Cinderella*.

Sensing Walt's indecision, Roy voiced his opinion. He opposed *Alice in Wonderland* and *Peter Pan* because he feared they would require "terrific negative" costs.

"*Alice in Wonderland* never appealed to me as a property that would make a motion picture," he recalled. "*Peter Pan* I was against for some of the same reasons. But Walt wouldn't shelve them.

"I remember one night he came down to my office, and we sat there from quitting time to eight or so. I finally said, 'Look, you're letting this place drive you nuts, that's one place I'm not going with you.' I walked out on him.

"I didn't sleep that night, and he didn't either. The next morning I'm at my desk, wondering what the hell to do. We were in a hell of a fix, tight payroll on our hands and everything. You don't worry about yourself, you worry about your commitments, your involvements.

"I felt awfully low. I heard his cough and his footsteps coming down the hall. He came in and he was filled up, he could hardly talk. He says, 'Isn't it amazing what a horse's ass a fella can be sometimes?' And he walked out. That's how we settled our differences."

Walt placed *Cinderella* into production.

Roy concluded: "Walt always had his way around [the studio]. He was the guy, he was just irresistible, and he was so damned right about it. That's why I say, if I contributed anything, I contributed honest management for him. It wasn't that he wasn't smart enough if he applied himself. He was always disinterested in figures, legal work, and all that stuff. It just took time away from what he wanted to be thinking about. So he'd have been easy prey for somebody to twist him and take him."

I could always tell when Dad was having a fight with Walt," Roy Edward Disney says. "When he came home in the evening, I could hear his car slam into the driveway. I learned to stay in another room when he came in the house."

Except for the fraternal battles, Roy seldom brought his work home. He preferred not to inflict his studio problems on Edna and young Roy. He lived simply, not indulging in the social life of Hollywood. While Walt and Lilly moved to an elite neighborhood in Holmby Hills, Roy and Edna remained in the San Fernando Valley. When the studio prospered after *Snow White*, they had moved into a large house surrounded by landscaped gardens on Forman Avenue in Toluca Lake. Roy decided to economize during the studio's postwar money pinch. He sold one of his cars and moved to a smaller house on Clybourne Street in the same neighborhood.

After quitting polo in the late 1930s, Roy acquired no new hobbies. Living close to the Lakeside Golf Club, he seemed a likely candidate for golf. He dismissed the suggestion: "That's a stupid game."

"I think we were the only residents of Toluca Lake who didn't belong to Lakeside," says Roy Edward. "When I started playing golf in college, Dad decided we should join the club. I begged him to play with me, but he never would." Edna also urged him to take up the game. "I don't want you to be a golf widow," he replied.

For a couple with such resolute personalities, Roy and Edna remained surprisingly close. Family and acquaintances never heard them exchange harsh words. It was different in the privacy of their own home. Housekeepers told tales of shouting matches over domestic matters.

Whenever possible, Edna accompanied Roy on his business trips. He relied on her to help entertain at receptions and dinners, and she proved a valuable asset. Her down-home manner put strangers at ease immediately, and she asked them about their families and especially their children. Formality went out the window.

"Mom and Dad always held hands," their son recalls. "They had a ritual whenever they came home from a flight. Dad would mix Mom a Scotch, then pour one for himself, quite a bit darker. Then they'd sit and hold hands, and Dad would say, 'Well, Mother, we cheated death again.' "

Did Roy have a temper?

"Oh, yes," Roy Edward says. "It was sudden, usually. It was not the kind that he struck out physically with. His chin would move forward a little bit, and his eyes would narrow. That's all you needed to know. I think he only swatted or spanked me once. Which was all he needed to do, because you just did not want that to happen again.

"I'm sure he was that way in business. Not in terms of anger, but if you saw the chin get set, you would know there was no further negotiation. He knew what he wanted and where he wanted to get. He knew that this was the line; don't cross it. Everyone who did business with him always talked about knowing where you stood, a deal was a deal, and a handshake deal was as good as anything. He meant what he said, and he said what he meant."

His business associates agree. Says Mickey Clark, Disney attorney: "Roy was very strong-willed. Like Walt, he would listen to everything those around him said. Then he would make up his own mind on what he wanted to do."

"In business negotiations, he was always saying, 'Don't make it too complicated,'" remembers Mike Bagnall, who became a financial executive. "It was not because he couldn't understand; he knew that if a deal was too complicated it wouldn't work. Sometimes during a meeting he would get up and leave because he didn't want to be bothered with the details. That forced you to try to make something simple.

"He always said, 'Explain it to me in a sentence or don't talk to me about it.' I tried to simplify matters so he got down to the bottom line real fast."

"He was very direct," says Neal McClure, a studio lawyer. "I remember a favorite saying of his when things got too complicated: 'Let's not get tied up in our shoelaces.' He was always trying to cut through the verbiage and get to what was really important."

In correspondence and personal matters, Roy relied on Madeleine Wheeler, the Scottish-born secretary who remained with him for thirty-four years. She was ever loyal, reminding him of birthdays and anniversaries of family and friends so he could send flowers and a note. Whenever he went on a trip, he always brought her gifts such as silk scarves or perfume.

"You know, Madeleine, I can never pay you what you're worth," he once told her. To compensate, he gave her shares of Disney stock from his own portfolio. Many years later, Madeleine attended a stockholders meeting with her niece, Janet Spurgeon. The niece happened to notice the number of shares on Madeleine's proxy statement. It was between five and six thousand shares, worth more than $1 million.

Roy had friendly words for all of the women employees. Jo Sears worked the teletype machine in the wire room. One day she received a message from the New York office reporting excellent returns at the box office. She ripped off the sheet of paper and ran down the hallway to Roy's office to present him with the good news. Roy, who was conferring with Gunther Lessing, was pleased with the message and thanked her for the prompt delivery. As she was leaving, Roy looked up and remarked, "You know, Jo, Gunther and I just came to a decision. We have decided that you have the prettiest feet and legs of any gal on the lot."

Although he remained in good health, Roy was ever watchful. He installed exercise equipment in his basement and used it before bedtime because, he told his son, it helped him sleep. His medicine chest overflowed with prescription bottles of curatives or preventatives. He sometimes took extreme measures to prevent illness, as exemplified in this memo to Walt on May 21, 1946.

> I am going into St. Joseph's Hospital on Thursday evening, and on Friday morning at eight o'clock Dr. Laughlin is going to take out my appendix. I won't be laid up over one week and will be available after two or three days for anything that comes up. My appendix is not bothering me,

and the doctor's study of it does not disclose any absolute necessity for taking it out, although they do express some doubt as to the shape it is in, judging from the X rays. So I am having it removed in the hope that it will help my general condition and especially this arthritis that has been bothering me for the last couple of years.

(In the 1920s, Roy had had his wisdom teeth removed, not because they troubled him, but because they might.)

If Roy had a hobby, it would be touring in his car. When he could afford it, he bought big, comfortable sedans, which he enjoyed driving around town, and especially, on longer trips. He welcomed the completion of the Los Angeles freeways, which allowed him to drive at a comfortable speed without concern about traffic. He particularly liked the Ventura Freeway, which ran past the studio and a few blocks from his house. He used it every morning and night, even though it only carried him a mile to the next off-ramp.

His greatest treat was taking a break from the studio worries and touring through America with Edna and other members of the family. He planned the trips with great care, spreading maps on the dining table and plotting distances and destinations.

In the fall of 1948, Roy, Edna, and her niece, Lettye Vogel, embarked on a cross-country journey that would take them through thirty states and two Canadian provinces. It was a trip that Roy had always dreamed of, visiting the national parks and monuments and making a pilgrimage to his father's birthplace. Of course Roy would also do some business for the company along the way. Lettye kept a diary, and it reveals the care of Roy's planning.

The travelers departed from Toluca Lake on Monday, September 27, pausing for lunch with Roy Edward at Pomona, where he was attending Pomona College. The first night was spent at the Hotel Last Frontier in Las Vegas, still a small desert town with a handful of casinos. On to Salt Lake City, Bear Lake ("part of the old Oregon trail"), Jackson Hole country, the Grand Tetons, Yellowstone, Cody ("we saw Buffalo Bill's monuments and spent the night in the hotel he built, the Irma; it was named for his daughter").

More sights: Big Horn mountains, Mount Rushmore, Rapid City, Sioux Falls, the lakes and farms of Minnesota, the autumn leaves of Wisconsin. In Chicago, Roy met with RKO people while the women shopped at Marshall Field's. More business in Detroit, then crossing the Blue River Bridge to Canada. At Goderich, Roy could find little evidence of his father's youth except the school he attended and part of the home where he was born. At Montreal, the travelers enjoyed turkey and champagne on Canada's Thanksgiving Day.

At Plattsburg, New York, they crossed Lake Champlain by ferry, then bought maple syrup and hams in Vermont, shopped for antiques in New Hampshire. A night in Saratoga Springs, then straight to New York City. Instead of staying in the city, they found hotels in Scarborough, Tarrytown, and Ossining, driving or taking the train into New York each day. Roy spent much of his time at the RKO office, but he joined his companions for dinner and shows (Beatrice Lillie and Jack Haley in *Inside U.S.A.*, Robert Morley in *Edward My Son*, Tallulah Bankhead in *Private Lives*).

They left New York to visit the battlefield at Gettysburg and George Washington's headquarters at Valley Forge. Back to New York for another round of shopping, dinners, and theater.

The homeward journey began November 13. To Washington, D.C., Alexandria, Williamsburg, Jamestown, Duke University, Atlanta (where the new governor, George Wallace, was being inaugurated), Pensacola, Biloxi, New Orleans, Natchez, the battlegrounds at Vicksburg, Dallas, Carlsbad Caverns.

"Now we are getting anxious to get home," Lettye wrote in Stafford, Arizona. For once they gave up sightseeing and headed west, stopping for ice cream in Wickenburg before crossing the desert. They arrived home just past midnight on their second Thanksgiving Day, having traveled 10,600 miles.

EIGHTEEN

〰

The postwar period remained filled with headaches for the Disneys' business.

Their situation would not have been so dire except for the continuing postwar depression in the parts of the world where the company once earned almost half of its income. *Pinocchio*, *Bambi*, and *Fantasia* were now playing in Europe and Asia with good results, despite the widespread poverty. But most of the countries did not allow their currency to leave the country. As a result, Disney was piling up blocked funds.

Roy and his staff surveyed the world situation country by country, and he sent a memo to Walt. Among the findings:

ARGENTINA—The Minister of Finance was coming to Washington, and there was hope that 50 percent of the blocked money would be released. "Most people are pessimistic about any improvement so long as the Peron government is in control." One suggestion: making a film with an Argentine producer.

BRAZIL—"The same comments go for Brazil, Chile, Colombia, and Peru, except that there is no worthwhile production facility in any place in Latin America except the Argentine and Mexico City."

AUSTRALIA—"Australia is one country where I believe our blocked money will turn out to be good."

NEW ZEALAND—The country was not blocking its currency because "they are having an argument with Great Britain, in a way similar to South Africa. In other words, New Zealand is not so Empire-minded as Australia."

NORWAY, SWEDEN, DENMARK—"These Scandinavian countries will probably pull out of their difficulties after a few years because they are sane and more balanced and reliable. I would say that ultimately we can get our money out of them . . . We don't actually know, but we believe the blocked money can be spent for production in the Scandinavian countries."

EGYPT—"While Egyptian currency has been blocked, they have been permitting transfers from time to time . . . Egypt may be a wonderful country from the standpoint of getting [film] material, such as the River Nile."

Great Britain, which had always been Disney's best customer, held the greatest amount of blocked currency. RKO, which also had funds frozen in Britain, suggested that Walt use both funds to make a movie.

Walt welcomed the opportunity to make a live-action film. As he explained in later years: "When I came to Hollywood, I was fed up with cartoons. I was discouraged and everything. My ambition at that time was to be a director . . . I tried to get into the live-action end of the business, but I just couldn't get anywhere. Before I knew it, I was back with my cartoons.

"All along, as I was making cartoons, there were a lot of times when an idea would come up; I kept feeling that I was competing

169

with live action and was trying to do it with my cartoons. But that was my medium. That was the thing I had. So what happened? Finally I decided to diversify."

For his first venture in England, he chose *Treasure Island.* In the summer of 1949 he took Lilly, Diane, and Sharon to London on their first trip abroad as a family. The experience of filming *Treasure Island* with the English cast and crew proved immensely stimulating for Walt. After years of spending two or three years or more to produce an animated feature, he delighted in creating an entire movie in three months. Walt returned to England for three more summers of filmmaking with frozen funds. He realized he could apply his talents to something beyond the world of the cartoon. The future was limitless.

I n his search for ways to restore the company's financial health, Walt considered the making of commercial films. But after attempting a few for major corporations, he shut down the commercial unit. He was ill-equipped for dealing with company executives and fashioning product to fit a message.

Walt also considered educational films. After all, he had been making them during the war, teaching bombardiers how to sight their targets and sailors how to identify enemy planes. And, as Roy pointed out, "From the very beginning of Walt's career he was very interested in the use of the cartoon medium for educational purposes.

"[In the 1920s] there was a man in Kansas City, a dentist, that every now and then would get a grant from a Kansas City merchant to make something on dentistry. Looking forward to preventive dentistry, you know. And so Walt made two or three reels for him.

"Then for a time [after the war] we had a national committee of five leading educators work with us for three or four years trying to find a way to make educational pictures. We had some very wealthy, well-known names in America that kept urging Walt on a program of educational pictures. So we made a serious study.

"But after a while we found out that the educational world is as confused and different in their various opinions as any other group in the world and that you can't find a happy medium on what you want to put on film.

"So Walt, in a huff one day, said, 'Oh, to hell with it! From now on let's make the word "educational" a dirty word around here. Let's just stick to entertainment.' So followin' that he said, 'We'll give 'em sugar-coated educational stuff.' "

The True-Life Adventures resulted from that thinking. The first featurette, *Seal Island*, won widespread praise, and it was followed by six more half-hours on such subjects as bears, beavers, elk, and water birds.

"Just beautiful, splendid little subjects," Roy once remarked. "We in the marketing kept pleading with Walt: 'Look, it's a thirty-minute subject. We can make so little on them. If you could only stretch those, make 'em seventy minutes, we could market 'em as a feature and make real money.'

"He used to come back with this: 'Well, we can't make a thing bigger than it's worthwhile to make. And if it hasn't got the substance in it you can't make it longer than the material merits.'

"Finally, though, there was a boy [N. Paul Kenworthy Jr.] come out of UCLA, and he liked the camera. And he practically lived down in the desert, like a desert rat, many months in his little hut contrived with cameras all set up, photographing tarantulas and lizards and desert flowers blooming, and floods, the sudden flash floods they have in the desert. And we got the most wonderful batch of material, out of which came the theme of *The Living Desert* that made a wonderful, wonderful picture."

I n a memo to the Bank of America dated 1953, Roy outlined the postwar diversification of Walt Disney Productions. He noted that in the past the company had been a one-activity business: the making and marketing of cartoon product. But cartoons had become expensive. With most theaters offering double bills, the market for cartoon shorts had dwindled. The Disney shorts were just breaking even or losing a little money.

The cost of cartoon features had inflated alarmingly. Hence diversifying had been vital for the company's survival.

Roy cited the live-action films made with frozen funds in England; *Treasure Island* and *Robin Hood* had been moneymakers, and the same could be expected for *Rob Roy* and *The Sword and the Rose*. The popular True-Life Adventures could not be expected to earn much profit because of their length. But they were useful in contributing to a Disney package: a feature, a True-Life Adventure, and a cartoon short. (The company had long been plagued by theater owners who played a Disney feature with a B movie, paying the same rental for both.) A documentary series called People and Places was being produced, as well as live-action featurettes. Walt was now planning live-action films to be made in the United States, the first being *20,000 Leagues under the Sea.*

"We are not going into these things because we are feeling our oats or getting ambitious," Roy stressed. "We are doing it for common-sense business reasons, realizing the hazards of our basic cartoon business."

Roy noted the turmoil in the movie business, caused in part by the U.S. government's consent decree, which resulted in major companies' divesting themselves of their theater chains. No longer were producers assured of profits because of ready bookings for their product; each movie had to stand on its own merits. Hence the opportunity for a company like Disney, "making fine product intelligently, and intelligently marketing it."

In his review of other activities, Roy reported that merchandising had increased, 16mm nontheatrical distribution appeared promising, as did the music company. Finally, television.

"We have made up our minds to go on television and have set ourselves a beginning date of September of 1954," he declared. "Our approach is the same as our approach to the making and marketing of a motion picture. We are going to make good entertainment and go after public support and following, and then couple that with the advertiser's interest and make him pay the freight, with a healthy profit to us.

"But overall, the whole activity will be designed to aid in the exploitation and marketing of all our motion picture product."

The *Living Desert* would provide the impetus for one of Roy's biggest gambles: the establishment of a distribution company.

From Charles Mintz to Pat Powers to Columbia to United Artists, the Disney brothers believed they had suffered loss of income by underhanded or incompetent distribution of their pictures. RKO had been an improvement. The distributor had performed adequately with *Snow White* and other features. Roy had established a friendly relationship with the RKO salesmen, though he was disturbed by the instability of the company, traditionally the sick man of Hollywood. Regimes had come and gone during the 1930s and 1940s, but Roy had confidence in the sales force.

The RKO salesmen had disturbing blind spots, however. They were baffled by the True-Life Adventures. They had no notion of how to sell half-hour featurettes about seals and beavers and elks. And they drew a complete blank when Roy proposed releasing a feature-length documentary about creatures of the desert.

In 1948, RKO was acquired by one of Hollywood's authentic eccentrics, Howard Hughes. In between setting flight records and establishing an airplane industry, Hughes had dabbled in films since the late 1920s. His purchase of RKO and its theater chain for $9 million startled the Hollywood community. His curious ways and neglect of the studio brought wholesale defections.

Roy's first meeting with Hughes provided some indication of what it would be like to deal with the man. Roy was asked to come to the Beverly Hills Hotel, where Hughes maintained his offices in a bungalow on the grounds. A Hughes official met Roy in the hotel lobby and said, "Mr. Hughes is in the men's room. He will meet you there."

Howard Hughes was standing at the urinal. Roy joined him in the next stall, and they began conducting their conference.

Though he was concerned about having the fate of the Disney product in the control of this man, Roy was amused by his peculiar habits. Edna was not.

Hughes customarily began his work day at midnight, and his associates could expect telephone calls from the boss in the early hours of the morning. At two o'clock one morning, the telephone rang in the Disneys' bedroom. Edna answered, fearful that some family catastrophe had occurred.

"This is Howard Hughes. Can I speak to Roy?"

"No, you may not. My husband works hard all day, and he

deserves his rest. If you want to speak to him, call him during regular business hours. Good night, Mr. Hughes."

Hughes never again called Roy late at night.

Roy could have tolerated the erratic behavior of Howard Hughes, but he was disturbed by what was happening to RKO. The company once ranked among the best distributors in the film industry; lacking a roster of big stars, RKO had to seek bookings aggressively. Under Hughes, the sales force had deteriorated. The studio's product had become sparse and mediocre, and salesmen began leaving for healthier companies.

When RKO balked at handling *The Living Desert*, Roy decided to release it himself. He had already gathered his own sales organization, which had worked hand in hand with the RKO salesmen, approving trailers and ad campaigns and assuring that all was done in the Disney manner.

In a July 31, 1953, memo to Walt in London, Roy explained: "We have squared away with [RKO] the idea of our distributing *The Living Desert* show, so that they understand and don't feel hurt, or feel that we have any mental reservations about leaving them . . .

"The first screenings on *The Living Desert* met with a truly wonderful reception. We can make deals, and quickly, with our pick of good small theaters in all the principal cities. However we are going to open in New York first and be careful to give it a fine buildup and to watch it, and out of it develop our method of handling our whole press book and presentation. So we are very strong on this one."

Roy told a gathering of his sales force, "I think we can do better if we fend for ourselves." He outlined a campaign to sell *The Living Desert*, together with a cartoon featurette, *Ben and Me*, at handpicked theaters across the country. The first booking, at the Sutton theater in Manhattan, brought laudatory reviews and strong business among adults as well as children. The result was repeated at specialized theaters, many of them close to college campuses. *The Living Desert* produced a healthy profit for Disney: $4 million vs. $300,000 production cost. And no distribution fee to RKO.

Roy had originally appointed Bill Levy head of the distribution company. "He was a peculiar guy, very tough on secretaries," Irving Ludwig recalls. "We would check into a hotel, and he would make his presence known immediately. He berated waiters left and right, he enjoyed it. He was a nice guy, but he didn't have the right tactics. So there came a day when Roy said, 'We've had it; Bill, thank you very much.' " Roy had seldom been known to fire anyone, even drinkers, as long as they did their jobs.

He replaced Levy with Leo Samuels and made Ludwig vice president in charge of domestic distribution. After appointing the pair, Roy walked them to the elevator on the twentieth floor of the RKO building in New York. He took Samuels and Ludwig by their arms and said, "Look, guys, take care of the little people. The big guys can take care of themselves."

After the success with *The Living Desert*, Roy invited Samuels, Ludwig, and Ned Clarke, head of foreign distribution, to the studio. Roy talked about Walt's promising new attractions, including *20,000 Leagues under the Sea* and *Lady and the Tramp*.

"What do you think of forming our own company?" Roy asked. The response was enthusiastic.

Roy reached for the telephone and placed a call. "Walt, we've decided to form our own distribution company," he said. "What do you think?" Walt agreed.

The four mulled over what to call the new organization. Finally Roy said, "What's wrong with Buena Vista?" All agreed on the name of the street the studio fronted on.

Buena Vista began modestly, opening small offices in New

York, Boston, Philadelphia, Chicago, Dallas, San Francisco, and Los Angeles. Roy knew the names of the salesmen in each office, and many of the secretaries. He asked about their families and made sure they were happy in their work. In return, the salesmen accorded him a fierce loyalty.

NINETEEN

❦

"Junior's got his hand in the cookie jar again."

That was Roy's favorite expression when he learned, not from Walt but from a studio employee, that his kid brother was plotting another big project for which Roy would be required to round up financing. What Roy didn't know when he first learned of Walt's plan for an amusement park was that it would be the company's biggest and chanciest gamble.

Walt traced the seeds of Disneyland to the Sunday mornings when he picked up Diane and Sharon at Sunday School and took them to an amusement park where they rode the merry-go-round and other attractions. He was repelled by the dirt and litter and unfriendliness of such places. He knew he could do better.

The idea became an obsession. As Walt toured the United States and Europe, he studied amusement parks and tourist attractions and talked with their operators. His vision of a place to amuse and dazzle children and their parents began to take shape.

When Walt first proposed his plan, Roy responded with customary caution. The studio was slowly recovering from its wartime paralysis, Roy said, but its financial health fluctuated from picture to picture. *Cinderella* brought a handsome profit, *Alice in Wonderland* did not. The company remained deeply in debt to the Bank of America, which had grown more impatient following the death of the Disneys' chief booster, A.P. Giannini.

"I couldn't get anybody to go with me because we were going through this financial depression," Walt recalled. "Whenever I'd go down and talk to my brother about it, why he'd always suddenly get busy with some figures. I didn't dare bring it up."

Walt, of course, was not dissuaded. He first planned to build the park on two-and-a-half acres of studio property on the back lot. He asked his production manager Bill Anderson if he needed that area for anything. Anderson replied that it was only used to store old sets. "Well, don't build anything on it; I'm gonna put my park there." A couple months later, Walt told Anderson, "You can forget about that place. I'm gonna go across the street." He said he would need five acres of a sixteen-acre plot the company owned on Riverside Drive, south of the studio. Shortly afterward he reported he planned to use the entire property.

John Hench, who lived on Riverside Drive in the 1950s, recalled seeing Walt alone on the weed-filled lot. He seemed deep in thought as he surveyed the acreage, occasionally pacing off dimensions.

On March 27, 1952, the Burbank *Daily Review* headlined:

WALT DISNEY MAKE-BELIEVE LAND PROJECT
PLANNED HERE.

"Disneyland," a spectacular world of make-believe made reality by the genius of famed cartoon producer Walt Disney, is being planned as a $1,500,000 development on Disney property at Riverside and Buena Vista.

A statement by Disney described the project as "something of a fair, an exhibition, a playground, a community center, a museum of living facts, and a showplace of beauty and magic." His proposal won the tentative approval of the Burbank Board of Parks and Recreation after hearing Walt's assurance that Disneyland was not intended as a commercial venture.

The Burbank plan was not to be. Walt discovered that negotiating with local politicians was not the same as dealing with his employees. The Burbank people balked at some of his requests. Also, he learned that the state of California had plans to construct the Ventura Freeway adjacent to the Riverside property.

Lacking any encouragement from Roy, Walt decided to finance the planning stages of Disneyland himself. He established Walt Disney, Incorporated, installing himself as president. He asked Bill Cottrell to manage the infant company and serve as vice president.

Roy had been responsible for Cottrell's coming to the studio in 1929. Roy did the company's banking at a branch on Hollywood Boulevard, where Cottrell's sister worked as a teller. One day she told Roy that her brother, who had worked as a newspaper cartoonist, needed a job, perhaps in cartooning. Roy mentioned that Walter Lantz had an opening for an animator at Universal, but the position turned out to have been filled. Roy told the sister: "Tell him to see my brother Walt." Cottrell started in ink-and-paint and worked his way through departments and became a writer. He was to prove an important figure in making peace between the two sometimes contentious brothers.

"I don't know why Walt chose me," Cottrell said during a series of interviews a few weeks before his death in 1996. "I could only assume that he had known me for a period of years and he knew that I was completely honest. Also, I think I knew his philosophy and his policy, and I agreed with most of it."

Roy was deeply concerned that stockholders would be disturbed over possible conflict of interest between Walt Disney Productions and Walt Disney, Incorporated. He suggested that Walt change the name of his company, and it became WED Enterprises, the initials of Walt's name.

Disneyland's birthplace was a rickety bungalow without heat or air conditioning, the last remnant of the old studio; the building had been moved from Hyperion to Burbank. Cottrell installed WED headquarters in the bungalow in early 1953, hiring a tiny staff despite not knowing what he and the employees were supposed to do. The studio had ventured warily into television with a couple of specials, and Walt decided that WED could earn some income by producing a television series. He bought the rights to the Zorro stories and appointed Cottrell as producer, since conflict-of-interest concerns prohibited Walt from producing. Cottrell assigned writers to prepare fourteen Zorro scripts, and Walt personally made presentations to west coast executives at the three television networks. All expressed interest but insisted on seeing a pilot film.

"Let's put Zorro on hold and get started on the park," Walt said. It was the first time Cottrell had heard about Disneyland.

Walt hired Harper Goff, an illustrator, to create depictions of Walt's concept for Disneyland. Richard Irvine, an art director who had worked on *Victory through Air Power* and *The Three Caballeros* then moved to 20th Century-Fox, had been added to the staff to design sets for *Zorro*. He was now assigned to make models and drawings for Disneyland. He also served as liaison with the architectural firm of William Pereira and Charles Luckman. Another distinguished architect, Welton Becket, told Walt that no one could design Disneyland but Walt Disney. The Pereira-Luckman connection was dropped.

Roy's concern for his brother was illustrated in a luncheon conversation between Roy and Bill Cottrell.

"Roy told me that after the success of *Snow White* he tried to get the rights to the Oz books," Cottrell related. "He found out that the heirs of L. Frank Baum, the author, did not own any of Baum's writings. [The studio acquired all the Oz rights except *The Wizard of Oz* from the publisher.] Roy said, 'That concerned me, and I began to worry about Walt's family. What would happen to them if something happened to Walt? He had no ownership in the company outside of his stock.' He suggested that Walt form a personal holding company and lease his name to the corporation on a royalty basis. He said to do it with attorneys so there would be no question of it being approved." Roy's suggestion was implemented, and over the years it provided considerable income for Walt and his family.

Cottrell continued: "After viewing the conceptual plans for Disneyland and hearing Walt's dreams, Roy finally became a convert. He realized that nothing could stop Walt from pursuing his desire for a park. But he objected to Walt's plan to locate the place somewhere in Burbank." Edna Disney recalled Roy's comment to Walt: "Oh, we can't do that; we should do it in a bigger way."

Bigger meant more money. Roy doubted that the Bank of America would ever consider investing in something as risky as an amusement park. Other banks would likely decline, or demand excessive terms. Walt provided the solution: television.

The Disneys had considered television as a medium for their pictures ever since the mid-thirties, when they ended their relationship with United Artists because the distributor insisted on retaining the television rights. In 1950 and 1951, Walt had produced special programs for NBC, and he was impressed by the huge audiences they drew. All three networks had urged him to produce a weekly series, but he had declined. Disneyland provided the impetus. He figured a network could help him finance the park. And the series would publicize both Disneyland and the theatrical product.

Roy said he would go to New York and try to sell one of the networks on helping to finance the park in return for a television series. But he needed something to show them. On September 23, 1953, two days before Roy was scheduled to leave for New York, Walt telephoned Herb Ryman. An accomplished artist, he had worked at the Disney studio, had made the South American trip, then left for 20th Century-Fox.

Walt urged Ryman to come to the studio immediately. Walt explained that he needed a rendering of the park he planned to build, which would be called Disneyland. With a deadline of less than two days, Ryman agreed to do it. Walt worked with him all weekend, and Roy carried the drawing onto the plane Monday morning.

Roy began shopping his brother's dream in the towers of Manhattan. He struck out with CBS, which was content with its programming. Next he approached RCA, the parent company of NBC, starting at the top with David Sarnoff, founder and chairman of the board. Roy was encouraged by Sarnoff's enthusiastic response, then Sarnoff turned the negotiation over to Joseph McConnell, the president of RCA. Roy strove for a commitment, but McConnell kept stalling. After a frustrating session in McConnell's office in the RCA building, Roy returned to his suite at the Waldorf Astoria and called Leonard Goldenson.

Two years before, Goldenson had come to the Disney studio, along with Robert Kintner, the president of ABC, and Donn Tatum, West Coast vice president of the struggling network. Goldenson had risen through the theater business to become head of Paramount Pictures' chain of theaters. When the federal government forced the Hollywood studios to divest themselves of theaters, Goldenson became president of United Paramount Theaters. In 1951 he bought the fourteen-station American Broadcasting Company, and tried without much success to compete with NBC and CBS.

In 1951, Goldenson and his ABC chiefs tried to interest Walt Disney in producing programs for the network. Walt converted the meeting into a word picture of his dream for Disneyland. Donn Tatum recalled that he was thrilled by Walt's spiel. As for Goldenson and Kintner: "They seemed not to understand what he was talking about. They were thinking in terms of Coney Island, I'm sure, and missed the point completely."

By 1953, Goldenson had grown impatient with the lack of growth at ABC, which had been the butt of comedians' jokes; cracked Milton Berle: "In case they drop the big bomb, go to ABC; they've never had a hit." Goldenson had heard through banking circles that the Disneys had been turned down for loans. He also learned that CBS and NBC had both declined the Disneys' offer.

The ABC boss hurried to meet Roy, and the two men agreed to form an alliance. Disney would provide ABC with a one-hour weekly program, and ABC-Paramount would help finance Disneyland. Goldenson's opinion of Roy: "He was a very good businessman, and not easy to get along with. He bargained for the last cent."

Flora Call, 19, and
Elias Disney, 28,
at the time of their
marriage in Florida on
New Year's Day, 1888.

Above:
Students of Park High School in Marceline, circa 1910. Roy is the earnest fellow second from the left, front row.

Right:
After graduating from high school in Kansas City, Roy walked more than 200 miles to western Kansas. He worked on his uncle's farm to regain his strength before going to work in a bank.

Flora Call, 19, and
Elias Disney, 28,
at the time of their
marriage in Florida on
New Year's Day, 1888.

Above:
Students of Park High School in Marceline, circa 1910. Roy is the earnest fellow second from the left, front row.

Right:
After graduating from high school in Kansas City, Roy walked more than 200 miles to western Kansas. He worked on his uncle's farm to regain his strength before going to work in a bank.

"at Salute".

Left:
A sharp salute from recruit Roy Oliver Disney outside the family home in Chicago, 1917. He was in training at the Great Lakes Naval Training Station.

Below:
Roy poses in a Chicago photo studio with his kid brother. Walt, dressed older than his 16 years, was working for the post office.

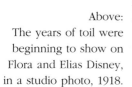

Above:
The years of toil were
beginning to show on
Flora and Elias Disney,
in a studio photo, 1918.

Right:
Newly arrived
in California in 1923,
the Disney brothers pick
oranges from a tree
for a photo to impress
their family in Missouri.

Left:
Young entrepreneurs in front of the storefront Disney Brothers Studio on Kingswell Avenue, 1925. Their seed money came mostly from relatives.

Below:
On location for the Alice Comedies. Walt (seated) directs star Virginia Davis while Roy cranks the camera and the girl's father looks on, 1925.

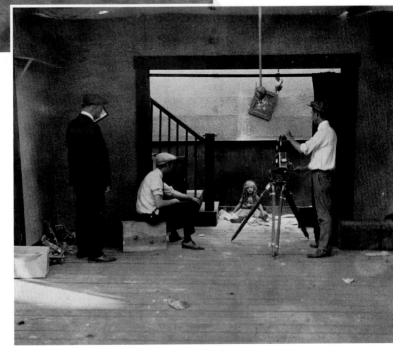

Left:
After an eight-year engagement, Roy Disney and Edna Francis marry on April 11, 1925, at the home of Uncle Robert, smoking a cigar in the background.

Below:
Walt and Roy savor the studio's first Academy Award®, for *Flowers and Trees* in 1932. Walt also received a special award for the creation of Mickey Mouse.

Above:
A variety of hats
on a sunny afternoon
at Walt's new
house in Los Feliz:
Walt, unidentified,
Kay Kamen,
the wizard of
merchandising,
and Roy.

Right:
Roy and Walt
during their
polo period,
at the Uplifter
polo grounds,
1934.

Above:
Roy Edward Disney,
named for his father
and mother, was
born January 10, 1930.
He often accompanied
his parents on trips.

Right:
Night of triumph:
Edna and Roy arrive
for the premiere of
*Snow White and the
Seven Dwarfs* at the
Carthay Circle Theater
on December 21, 1937.

Roy (right), accompanied by his Italian representatives, arrives in Rome on his grim tour of the European markets in 1938. It was his last visit until after the war.

Flora and Elias Disney's Golden Wedding Anniversary (1938).
Seated: Herb, the mailman; Flora, Elias, and Walt.
Standing: Raymond, the insurance salesman; and Roy.

Left:
Elias Disney, now a
widower, enjoys a
visit with his grandson,
Roy Edward, 1935.

Below:
Roy, Edna, Lilly, and
Walt savor a tropical
drink on the beach
at Waikiki, 1939.

A musical evening in the Disney box at Hollywood Bowl: Roy, Lilly, Edna, Walt, 1950.

Walt Disney Productions moves from Over the Counter to the New York Stock Exchange on November 12, 1957. Left to right: Roy, Edward C. Gray, exchange vice president, broker John O. Regan. Roy bought the first 100 shares for his grandson, Roy Patrick.

The wedding of Roy Edward and Patricia Dailey, September 17, 1955.
With Edna, Monsignor Harry C. Meade, who performed the ceremony,
and Patty's mother, Abigail Dailey.

Roy receives the royal treatment at a restaurant in Tokyo, 1960.

A study in profiles: the Disney nose.

One of the last pictures of the Disneys together.
At Mineral King, the proposed resort in the California Sierras, 1965.

A portrait of Roy and Edna taken by Dave Iwerks.
Friends remarked how much they resembled Harry and Bess Truman,
both in appearance and their relationship.

Roy inspects the horses for the carousel at Walt Disney World, 1970.
With Walt gone, Roy assumed responsibility for final decisions in building the new park.

Left:
After agonizing over the succession of power at the company, Roy selected Card Walker.

Below:
Roy surveys the vast wasteland on which the Magic Kingdom would rise, 1969.

Left:
With Cinderella Castle in the background and Mickey Mouse at his side, Roy O. Disney dedicates Walt Disney World, October 23, 1971.

Left:
The building plaque at the
Roy O. Disney Building in Burbank.

Below:
Ceramic portrait of Roy O. Disney
as a young cameraman on the
Alice Comedies. It appears in the
foyer of the Team Disney Building
in Burbank, facing a portrait
of Walt and the shadow of
Mickey Mouse.

THE ROY O. DISNEY
BUILDING

Dedicated to the life and works of Roy O. Disney.
President, Chairman of the Board, Chief Executive Officer.
With his brother Walt, he founded
Walt Disney Productions in 1923... and for
half a century thereafter, his creative financial leadership
helped make Walt's dreams come true.
The spirit and strength of this man,
his devotion to his brother, his family, and
to talent, honesty and integrity
will always stand as a model for those
who follow after.
Dedicated this 22nd day of September, 1978.

"I asked how much Disneyland would cost," Goldenson recalls, "and Roy said Walt figured from two to five million to get it started. I thought it would probably cost ten million. It ended up costing seventeen million."

Roy in early 1954 established a new ownership agreement for Disneyland, Incorporated, which Walt had founded in 1951. Walt Disney Productions and ABC-Paramount would own 34.48 percent apiece after each contributed $500,000. Western Printing and Lithographing, which published Disney books, added $200,000 for 13.79 percent, and Walt provided $250,000 for 17.25 percent.

Most importantly, Roy had exacted from Goldenson the condition that ABC-Paramount would guarantee loans for Disneyland up to $4.5 million. That meant immediate entrée to the banks and security houses whose financial support the Disneys would need.

The Disney-ABC deal stunned Hollywood. The movie bosses still considered television the enemy. Stars were forbidden to appear on TV. Even though millions of Americans had TV sets in their living rooms, you never saw one featured in a movie.

Goldenson, whose Paramount theaters were important buyers of films, remembers being invited to lunch with the top executives of MGM. "You're being a traitor to the motion picture industry," he was told. "You'll take all our directors, producers, and talent over to television, and we won't have anybody to carry on ourselves."

"That's silly," Goldenson replied. "Let me ask you: If I were able to put a trailer of your next picture into every home in the United States, how much would you give me? A million dollars? Well, I rest my case."

Goldenson reflects: "I had to find a way to crack the market and get Hollywood into production. Otherwise we'd be dead pigeons."

It is a fiction that Roy was only the numbers man and Walt was the artist. They were both bird dogs analytically. 'Why?' 'Why?' 'What?' 'How Much?' Walt was just tenaciously interested in that stuff, along with Roy. Both of them were smart as hell."

Harrison "Buzz" Price gives his assessment of the two brothers with whom he was intimately associated from 1953 until their deaths. One of the heads of Stanford Research Institute (SRI), he was summoned to the Disney studio in April 1953. Walt told him about the park he planned to build. Now that he had Roy's consent to "do it in a bigger way," he was looking for a location. Price offered to conduct a two-phase survey: first, a ten-week study to determine a geographical location; second, a four-month analysis of amusement parks and public attractions as part of a feasibility study. Roy authorized both for a fee of $32,000.

Ten weeks later, Roy and Walt traveled to downtown Los Angeles and the SRI offices in the Pacific Finance Building. Buzz Price and C.V. Wood, the president of SRI, presented ten possible sites.

"We did a general look first," Price says. "We even looked at Chavez Ravine, which wasn't a [Dodgers] baseball park yet. The general thought was: we had to get away from the center of the city, go out. But which way?

"There were huge temperature differences in Pomona, ten degrees hotter in the summer, and that freeway system wasn't developed yet. We didn't want to go in the beach direction, say, Santa Monica, because you'd have only half the market, half the apple. We wanted to be inland.

"I did a center of gravity of the population of five counties of Southern California. It was on Long Beach Boulevard about where the Long Beach Freeway is. The birthrates indicated it was moving southeast. So we made a survey of a five-mile area along the Santa Ana Freeway from the Orange County line to the city of Santa Ana. Then we zoomed in on that for specific sites . . .

"Roy and Walt bought our first site, in Anaheim. Except that we had it at Harbor Boulevard and the [Santa Ana] freeway, butting up. They moved it a quarter-section down. It was a smart move, because they got away from some hold-out type of properties on the freeway. It improved access, it improved entry."

Keeping their identity secret, the Disneys employed a real estate agent who bought 270 acres at $4,500 an acre. They wanted more land but ran out of money.

Buzz Price would continue making dozens of surveys for the Disney brothers, first for SRI, then for his own company, Economic Research Associates. The subjects included everything from Walt Disney World to CalArts. With his long and intimate association with the two brothers, Price was able to assess their differences:

"I think Roy had a little more funny bone," he observes. "Walt was almost too busy for humor at that time [the building of Disneyland] on a day-to-day basis. But that's an overstatement. He could relax and laugh, but he was always driven. Roy could laugh real quick. I've always been a joker and a smart-ass, and it was old-home week with Roy. He liked to laugh."

Walt had set a near-impossible schedule for himself. He promised to present the first television show in October 1954 and to open Disneyland in July 1955. He implemented his policy of using television to sell his product. The premiere show would be *The Disneyland Story*, which would relate the planning and building of Disneyland and provide a glimpse of future TV programs. Among them would be *Operation Undersea*, which told of the making of *20,000 Leagues under the Sea.* Both *The Disneyland Story* and *Operation Undersea* unabashedly pushed the Disney product, but the public didn't mind, and the Television Academy even awarded an Emmy to *Operation Undersea* as best individual show of 1954. *Disneyland* gave ABC audience ratings it had never enjoyed before. In the first two years, *Disneyland* placed sixth and fourth in overall audience ratings; no other ABC series appeared among the top twenty shows. On the strength of the *Disneyland* performance, Goldenson convinced Warner Bros. to supply programs, and the struggling network began its rise to parity with its two more established rivals.

"We only covered about 35 percent of the country at the beginning of the industry," Goldenson explains. "CBS and NBC already had about 85 percent coverage. They were taking all their stars from radio and taking them over to television. We had no stars, except for *Ozzie and Harriet.* I knew if I could get Disney, maybe that would help me crack the market and get other major companies to come along."

The Disney-ABC marriage proved fruitful for both parties and produced two more series, *The Mickey Mouse Club* and *Zorro.* Like many show business unions, it would one day end in rancor.

A mong the Stanford Research Institute representatives, Roy was most impressed by the president, C.V. Wood, who had dominated the presentations. Wood called himself "C.V." because he didn't like his name; reportedly his train conductor father named him Commodore Vanderbilt. At an early age Wood became chief industrial engineer of the airplane plant, Convair. He considered himself an expert at master planning, taking a complex project and making it work.

Roy hired Wood as executive vice president of Disneyland, in charge of building the park. One of Wood's first acts was to enlist Admiral Joseph Fowler as construction supervisor. A graduate of the Navy Academy and M.I.T., he had served thirty-two years in the navy, specializing in naval architecture. As an admiral in World War II, he had supervised ship construction. After retiring from the navy, he advised Congress on standardizing procedures for government purchasing. Fowler met Wood when he hired SRI for a survey on guided missiles for all three services.

Fowler established an immediate rapport with Roy and Walt; both admired his can-do attitude, perfected while meeting stringent schedules in wartime shipbuilding. Accustomed to keeping his superior officers informed, Fowler asked Walt if he should submit a weekly report of activities at the park. "Joe, when something doesn't suit me, I'll let you know," Walt replied. "You just keep right on going the way that you are."

Clearing of the Anaheim property began with the removal of the first orange tree in August 1954, eleven months before the promised opening. Soon the 270 acres in the city of Anaheim were swarming with bulldozers, earthmovers, ditchdiggers, cherry pickers, lumber-laden trucks, towering cranes, building equipment of all kinds. Rivers were dug, mountains raised, railroad track laid. Walt made frequent visits to bump over the rough terrain in a Jeep and survey his domain, correcting the sight lines, changing the paint color, attending to a thousand details. Throughout the frantic months, Fowler never expressed doubt that the park would open on time.

Roy occupied himself with Walt's ever-increasing need for money. Because of ABC's line of credit, the Bank of America had helped with financing despite the bankers' lack of confidence in the project. Estimates of the cost skyrocketed from $4.5 million in July to $7 million in September. By November it had reached $11 million.

"Roy did everything he could to raise the money," says Luther Marr, a Disney attorney. "He hocked the pictures, using them as collateral for the Bank of America loan. He hocked the leases at Disneyland; the whole thing had been borrowed on. He used ABC's credit line. He used everything there was to use.

"ABC was furious; they thought it was going to cost a million seven. Gunther Lessing and I had a meeting with the executive vice president of ABC-Paramount; he was the head of the whole theater chain. We had lunch at the Beverly Hilton, and this man said, 'Walt Disney is a wild man! We can't control him. It's like a tiger by the tail. We thought it would cost a million seven, and it's just going and going. There's no limit to what it will be, and we're on the line for it. Do something about it!' "

Of course neither ABC, nor Roy, nor a force of nature could deter Walt from fulfilling his vision of the park, no matter what the cost. One day in the midst of construction, he and Herb Ryman drove from the studio to the park. The long drive permitted Herb to unburden himself of something he had been agonizing over. Walt had assigned him the task of designing a restaurant to be situated on the hub at the end of Main Street. "I've been working three weeks on it, and I'm not getting anywhere," Ryman complained.

Walt remained unconcerned. "Herb, don't worry. You know the worst thing that can happen to you?" he asked.

"What's that?"

"You could go broke."

"Yeah, I guess so."

"I look at it this way: I've been broke five times in my life. One more time won't hurt."

In December, Joe Fowler faced a major crisis.

"By that time I had made up my mind we simply could not get the mill work done to the degree of perfection we needed or with regard to volume," recalled Fowler. "I went to Roy and told him the steel for the Opera House had been delivered. I needed $40,000 to put my steel up and get a roof on so I could put the mill inside."

Roy replied, "Jesus, Joe, I can't do it. We've borrowed on the life insurance and everything. Can't get any more."

Fowler returned the next day and asked Roy if he could somehow manage to finance the construction. "Yes, Joe, I've got your money," Roy replied, not explaining where it came from. "Go ahead." Fowler considered that the turning point.

However, another crisis arose after New Year's 1955. Plans for Tomorrowland had scarcely grown since Herb Ryman's original sketch. With little planned and the schedule to finish Disneyland ever tightening, C.V. Wood advised boarding up Tomorrowland. Walt reluctantly agreed. He quickly reversed himself. To open an unfinished Disneyland would be an embarrassment to him and a disappointment to the customers. He told his team to make Tomorrowland as attractive as possible. He would fix it later.

Roy continued courting investors, sometimes giving them a tour of construction to demonstrate that Disneyland was really happening. In April Roy and Joe Fowler escorted a Bank of America executive down the unpaved Main Street, inspecting the store buildings as they were being constructed and painted.

"Roy," the banker said, "you know if ever I have seen anything that appeared to me to be a little bit of a variance, this is it. I think you're looking at fifteen million rather than eleven."

Roy was greatly relieved, knowing that the bank would submit to more loans. The Bank of America now shared the burden. When the loan had risen to $11 million, it had brought in the Bankers Trust Company of New York as a co-investor.

The financing had been assured, but there was no certainty that Disneyland would open on July 17 as promised. Joe Fowler remained confident, always replying to Walt's concern with "We're gonna make it." C.V. Wood was less optimistic. In June, he commented, "Joe, we might as well postpone until September. We're not going to make it." Fowler's reply: "Woody, we have to make it."

Fowler explained years later: "Of course, I'd been indoctrinated during the war. I was working right under limits. I had twenty-five private shipyards, and by doggie, we had to make dates! There wasn't any two ways about it.

"That probably was the greatest thing in the world, that we opened in July. If we had waited until September, when the crowds sloughed off, we might never have gotten it off the ground."

During the construction period, Walt was omnipresent, often sleeping overnight in his apartment above the firehouse. He rose early and prowled the park in the chilly predawn, always visualizing.

"If he didn't like the scale of a fence or something, we'd rip it out and redo it," Dick Irvine recalled. "That was particularly true of Frontierland. He was upset because he didn't get the scale right for Frontierland. It was always too heavy.

"It's hard to get the scale in timber and make it strong. You can do it in iron or steel and make it fine and thin and light. But not in wood. The eucalyptus poles were always too big; he wanted the smaller ones. The funny thing to me was his view of landscaping. He didn't want small trees, he wanted big ones. He said, 'Trees have no scale.' "

Walt constantly sought perfection, yet he was no profligate.

"He was the first to criticize spending money that you didn't get your returns on," Joe Potter observed. One thing that exasperated Walt was cement. He had been accustomed to movie sets, which were erected as facades and would be dismantled after the movie's completion. He couldn't understand why so much cement had to be poured to support the railroad station. He hated the waterfall in Adventureland because it had required so much cement. Fowler and the engineers explained to Walt that if he wanted the exhibits to endure, they needed solid foundations.

During his cross-country trips to research Disneyland, Walt had interviewed several carnival operators. Not that he wanted to duplicate their tawdry shows; he thought he could learn from them about crowd management and other matters. He invited some of them to visit while he was building Disneyland.

All of them were case-hardened veterans of the "Hey, Rube!" tradition of carnivals, ever ready to pull stakes at dawn in case angered citizens or the local authorities should descend. Walt became fond of a few of the raffish types, and he listened to their advice. "You should never pay more than $25,000 for a ride," one of them told him. "Anybody who does that should have his head examined." Walt listened and then proceeded on his own. Early in the game, he had decided to buy rides from no one. All of them would be original, and they would cost much more than $25,000.

One of the top executives at Disneyland was a drinker, and he had a smashup in a company car. The incident appeared in the newspapers, causing embarrassment to the company.

Fowler made an appointment to see both Roy and Walt. "I think this man has learned his lesson," Fowler said. "If it's agreeable to you, Walt and Roy, I'd like to keep him on. I'll take his resignation, and if he gets out of line again, well, that's it."

Roy replied, "Well, you know, Joe, we've had lots of experience with people who couldn't hold their liquor. Go ahead, go ahead, if you want to. That's fine." The man never got in trouble again.

Labor problems repeatedly bedeviled the building of Disneyland. The planners and designers of the park were mostly art directors who had worked in the movie studios. They were skilled in creating sets for films, and hence they were ideal for realizing Walt's vision of a storybook atmosphere. They were also accustomed to producers' stringent deadlines, so the rush schedule of Disneyland did not dismay them.

The art directors found that some of the work could be produced faster and better at the Disney studio, particularly painting. Studio painters worked on many of the artifacts and furniture pieces, applying many coats for a fresh appearance and for durability. When the objects arrived in Anaheim, the Orange County painters stripped the paint and applied their own. Not only was precious time lost; the painting was inferior to the studio work.

As the opening day approached, union strikes caused major problems. The plumbers went on strike in Orange County just as the fixtures had been delivered and were ready to be installed. Learning of the fix the Disneys were in, the Teamsters Union volunteered to install the plumbing. The word reached the plumbers, and they agreed to return to work. Fowler volunteered to pay them at the rate they would achieve in the strike settlement.

Another strike: the asphalt plants of Orange County. With the opening only days away, Fowler was forced to truck the asphalt from San Diego at considerable expense.

• • •

Roy gazed out the window of his Toluca Lake home shortly after dawn on a July Sunday, and what he saw pleased him. The sun was rising in a cloudless sky. Of course rain was highly improbable in midsummer Southern California. But so many things had gone wrong in the building of Disneyland, Roy was prepared for anything.

He and Edna left early, heading south in their Cadillac sedan. Both were in a state of high anticipation. As Roy crossed the line into Orange County, he noted that the volume of traffic had increased. A good sign. He approached Anaheim, and the cars and pickup trucks and mobile homes crammed bumper to bumper. Roy was further encouraged. Finally he turned south on Harbor Boulevard. Instead of approaching the main entrance, he continued driving until he reached Katella Boulevard at the southern boundary of the park. He headed right and continued to West Boulevard, where he again turned right. He had covered the periphery of the parking lot, inspecting the number of cars inside. He was pleased by what he saw.

Roy parked the Cadillac in his reserved space. He and Edna stayed in the car, and she produced homemade cake and a thermos of coffee she had packed at home. Roy sipped the coffee and watched with delight the faces of the children as they pulled their parents in the direction of the entrance.

A young park worker ran up to Roy's car.

"Mr. Disney, I'm glad I found you," he said breathlessly. "A lot of these people have been stuck in traffic for hours, and the kids need to go to the bathroom. Now they're peeing all over the lot."

"God bless 'em," Roy replied with a broad smile. "Let 'em pee."

TWENTY

⤮

W alt Disney was fortunately unaware of the chaos that accompanied opening day. He was too busy rehearsing and
performing a ninety-minute special on ABC television. Roy was
also not informed of the snafus that were happening all over the
park. He enjoyed watching the happy faces of the children and
observing the size of the crowd. And what a crowd. Eleven hundred invitations had been extended to the press, Disney employees, the construction crew, politicians, and celebrities. The
invitations had been hastily printed and were easily duplicated.
The official tally on July 17 came to more than 28,000 people, but
there had probably been more. Many had climbed over the fences
and berms in remote areas of the park.

The problems around the park reflected the hell-bent schedule to open Disneyland on Walt's promised day, July 17. Women's
heels sank in the newly laid asphalt. There were very long lines
at every toilet. Eating places soon ran out of food and drink.

Thirsty visitors sought vainly for drinking fountains, a casualty of the plumbers' strike. Families stood for hours, waiting to enter the few rides that were operating.

"I got a call that we had a problem in Tomorrowland, and we did—a gas leak," said Joe Fowler. "You could smell gas coming up through the courtyard. The question was: What the hell do we do? Will we close her up and get everybody out of the park? I got ahold of the fire chief, and we decided we'd rope off the area. I don't think half a dozen people knew we had the problem."

Another problem developed in Fantasyland: sabotage. Someone had cut the electrical cables, and the rides shut down, stranding people in the cars and gondolas.

Many of the accounts of the opening in the Monday newspapers were critical. The Disneys also got bum reviews from the country's carnival owners who were invited to the event. They gathered for dinner afterward, and with two exceptions all predicted Disneyland would fold within six months. Their reasons were threefold: No alcoholic beverages were sold in the park; a beer or liquor sponsor was needed. People wouldn't stand for a fee to enter the park. Walt's insistence on a clean atmosphere would break him because of the expense; besides, people liked the clutter and hurly-burly.

Walt's responses, according to Herb Ryman: First, "I like a drink. If people want one, they can get it elsewhere, not in my park." Second, "We gotta charge people to get in. If we don't, we'll get all kinds of drunks and molesters; they'll be grabbing girls in the dark. You'll get a better class of people if you charge them to enter." Last, "One of the things I hated about carnivals and piers was all the crap that was everywhere. You're stepping on chewing gum and ice cream cones. I think people want clean amusement parks."

Walt and Roy became painfully aware of the problems on

Monday when they read the press accounts. Roy was not discouraged. The public seemed to disregard the bad reviews; a million people passed through the gates of Disneyland during the first eight weeks, and they were spending 30 percent more money than had been predicted. Although the *Disneyland* television show itself produced little or no profit, the residual benefits were satisfying. Davy Crockett had been the big hit of the first *Disneyland* season, and millions of merchandising items were sold, especially the coonskin hats for kids. *Davy Crockett, King of the Wild Frontier* was also released as a feature in theaters, bringing additional income.

The Mickey Mouse Club, an innovative late-afternoon television show for children, would premiere on ABC on October 3, 1955, and was certain to sell more merchandise, primarily the mouse-ear caps. Excessive plugging on *Disneyland* had helped propel *20,000 Leagues under the Sea* and *Lady and the Tramp* to excellent theater business.

Nor was Walt dismayed by the adverse press reaction.

"He had sensed the great reaction the public had given the park," remembered Joe Fowler. "He was more interested in new things, in changes, in modifications than he was in the operation. That was a great characteristic of his: He was always facing the future."

Walt directed his staff to improve the crowd control, so the visitors would not bunch up in certain areas or be bored by long waits. In the frantic weeks before opening, Walt had filled empty places, especially in Tomorrowland, by inviting corporations to install exhibits.

"We had to install some things that savored of the commercial aspects," said Fowler. "For example, Crane Plumbing was in there with a static exhibit, as well as one or two others. We learned one lesson: Never put anything in Disneyland that isn't animated, that doesn't have a story, that hasn't some audience participation."

Walt blamed C.V. Wood for the opening day foul-ups. Said Dick Irvine: "Walt always said that Woody was a great salesman, but he was a lousy administrator, and terribly ambitious."

A few weeks after the opening, the two men had a fierce argument in New York over why the Maxwell Coffee House remained unfinished. When Walt returned, he told Dick Irvine: "I want all the information you have on why that shop wasn't opened." Irvine discovered that the delay was caused by lack of decisions by the Maxwell House officials and Disneyland food people.

Armed with the evidence against Wood, Walt told Roy: "Fire him."

"Walt didn't like Woody," observes Buzz Price. "He was too fast-moving for Walt. C.V. *was* capable of making a fast deal. He wasn't corrupt, he was just fast-moving. Walt didn't trust him. The opening was a mess . . . Walt blamed the mess on C.V. By that time he had decided he didn't like him and didn't want him there."

Even though Roy had been initially beguiled by Wood and recommended hiring him as executive vice president of Disneyland, Roy had soured on him. In a review of Disneyland contracts, Disney lawyer Luther Marr discovered that Wood had granted the rights to all Disneyland merchandising to a souvenir company that no one had heard of.

"Roy Disney was furious that C.V. Wood had signed away all the merchandising rights to this company for some piddly amount," Marr recalls. "That was a big thing; they were going to make a lot of money off that and help pay for the park. We investigated for years to find out who this company was. It had some dummy names in the east, and we couldn't find the people. Years later, after C.V. Wood was fired, it turned out that he and a buddy had quietly set this company up, and they were going to get all the merchandising money."

The Disneyland firing did not deter C.V. Wood. He went on to a series of achievements that included building Six Flags in Texas, London Bridge in Havasu, and the Warner Bros. theme park in Brisbane, Australia.

At last Disneyland had opened and was producing revenue. Roy Disney could breathe more easily. He had hocked everything—real estate, the movies, life insurance—to pay the $15 million in bills that had been presented. Now he could relax and watch money flow back into the treasury.

Then came a shattering blow. Two months after opening, Bruce McNeill, the general contractor for Disneyland, appeared in Roy's office and reported that more money was needed. Because of the rush to finish the park, bills had been stuck in drawers. The additional expense amounted to almost $2 million.

"Roy was furious; he thought we'd been had," says attorney Luther Marr. "McNeill explained that Walt went around and changed things at the last minute, saying, 'These pots are too small—bigger ones!' That would be a hundred-thousand-dollar item.

"Walt would do that, without any reference to the cost. 'This needs to be done, that needs to be done. Buy this, buy that.' He didn't add it up; Walt didn't care about the cost at all. It was a matter of what it looked like, the result. So Roy had to dig up some more money. I don't know where he got it, because he had used up all the credit he could come by."

. . .

Roy's check writing would never be over. Walt was constantly "plussing" Disneyland, making improvements and additions, all of them with a price tag. When attendance fell during the first winter, Walt decided he wanted a circus. He had been fascinated with circuses since his boyhood in Kansas City. Now he could run a circus all his own.

As with opening day, the Disneyland Circus adhered to Murphy's Law. Walt had gathered some good circus acts and impressive animals and had enlisted his vastly popular Mouseketeers of *The Mickey Mouse Club* to be acrobats and other performers. The Mouseketeers were no problem; their mothers were, constantly complaining about how their children were treated and seeking better roles for them.

Remembering his Kansas City days, Walt insisted on a parade down Main Street. He waved to the crowd on the leading wagon, followed by a steam calliope, which had been laboriously restored to working order. Next came some old circus carts that had been renovated. One of them had a partition in the center, with a tiger on one side and a black panther on the other. The tiger managed to wedge his paw around the partition, and the panther chewed it off.

"My boys tackled the panther with two-by-fours to get him off," Joe Fowler recalled. "By the time we finished, we destroyed fifteen thousand dollars worth of cats." Roy got the bill.

On opening night, Walt basked in the sights and smells of the circus as he waited with Joe Fowler in the stands for the grand parade to begin. Owen Pope, who had built the stagecoach and wagons for Frontierland, entered with the pumpkin coach drawn by six handsome Shetland ponies. Fowler looked in horror as the coach wheel caught in one of the diagonal posts that held up the tent. Fortunately, no harm was done.

Next, Fowler was approached by an assistant with the urgent message: "Joe, the llamas have escaped!" Fowler led a posse that chased the llamas down the railroad tracks, finally capturing them at the main station. When he returned to his seat, Walt said, "Joe, you missed the best part; one of the leading ladies split her tights."

Placing circus personnel amid the wholesomeness of Disneyland presented problems. Boozing, gambling, and cussing constituted their way of life, and they didn't care if the squeaky-clean Mouseketeers were nearby.

The Disneyland Circus played mostly to half-filled tents, and it was never repeated. Walt tried puppet shows and other traditional attractions, but none worked. He learned that people came to see Disneyland.

On a Saturday in January 1956, Walt and Dick Irvine made the trip from Burbank to Disneyland in a driving rainstorm. The Santa Ana Freeway hadn't been completed, and Walt's car sloshed through flooded streets until he arrived at the park. Joe Fowler was there to greet him.

"You know, Joe," Walt reflected, "I come down here to get a rest out of the great humdrum of making pictures at the studio. This is my real amusement area, my relaxation."

The park was virtually deserted. Only a few tourists from far-away places huddled under umbrellas and dashed from one ride to another. The storm was developing into one of the heaviest in recent Orange County history; seven inches of rain would fall.

Walt wanted to see what was happening in the park, and he and Fowler and Irvine donned foul weather gear and set forth. The docks of the Rivers of America were submerged, and Fowler feared that the *Mark Twain* would float over the banks. Workmen struggled to dig ditches and unclog drains so the water would flow out of Disneyland.

The radio reported flooded streets throughout Anaheim, and Walt decided to stay the night. He and Irvine and Fowler slept in the administration building. The storm continued on Sunday, and that night the three were able to reach the Disneyland Hotel.

Walt spent the two days expounding on what he envisioned for the park. He wanted to build a skyway, with cables carrying gondolas for a bird's-eye view of the colorful activities below. He talked of erecting some kind of transportation system that would take visitors around the periphery of the park; this was the start of the Monorail. Later he conceived a submarine ride in Tomorrowland and a sled ride down the inside of the Matterhorn.

"That weekend cost Roy three million dollars," Fowler commented.

L ike most marriages of entertainment giants, the one between Disney and ABC soon soured. After a euphoric two years, with *Disneyland* constituting ABC's sole approach to respectability, rifts between the two companies began to appear. In an effort to recapture Wednesday night, NBC scheduled an expensive western, *Wagon Train*, opposite *Disneyland*. After three winning seasons, *Disneyland* dropped out of the top twenty in ratings.

Westerns were glutting all three networks, and ABC programmers panicked. They argued that Walt should inject westerns and action into his show. Walt detested being told what kind of entertainment to provide, but he realized the value of *Disneyland* in promoting the park and the theatrical movies. He made several programs based on western history and legend.

In 1957, ABC scheduled *Zorro*, which Walt had been planning since the inception of WED. After two successful seasons, ABC summarily cancelled the show. The reasoning: The network could make more money financing their own shows rather than buying them from producers.

Despite the immense popularity of *The Mickey Mouse Club* with young viewers, ABC claimed not enough sponsors could be found for a show aimed at children. The series was cut to a half-hour in the third season and then canceled the following year. Walt wanted to offer *Zorro* and *The Mickey Mouse Club* to other networks. ABC said no, that Disney productions for television belonged to ABC alone. Walt had proposed other series to the network, only to be turned down with the instruction that they could not be sold elsewhere.

The Disneys considered such tactics unreasonable and intolerable, especially coming from their partner in Disneyland. Roy decided the contract had to be broken.

There was another reason for terminating the contract. As part of the original agreement, ABC was granted food concessions in various areas of the park. ABC-Paramount may have been proficient in selling popcorn in its theaters, but as caterers of snacks and meals, they were far below Disneyland standards. Walt's plans for upgrading the food aspects of the park were stymied because ABC was so entrenched.

Roy assigned his lawyers to the matter, and they decided that the company could reasonably sue to end the contract on the basis of antitrust. Trouble was, antitrust suits could drag on for years before reaching the Supreme Court. Roy was hopeful of finding a way to buy out ABC's interest without resorting to a lengthy and costly court suit.

Leonard Goldenson tried to avoid a confrontation with Roy. Finally, the Disneys' New York lawyer, "Shorty" Irvine, warned

Goldenson that no meeting would mean immediate action against ABC. A meeting was set for June 30, 1959, in New York.

On June 19, Roy sent a memo to Walt: "We are approaching this—first—from the angle of gaining our freedom from their restraint or threats against our selling TV product to others after they have failed to make a deal with us. In this case *Zorro* and *Mickey Mouse*. We are planning a motion for a declaratory action. In other words, an interpretation of contract, so that publicly we are not out to break our contract.

"On the first action, if we file it, we will sue on that one point only, so that the first press reaction should be solely that we are trying to break the stranglehold of ABC and the 'dog in the manger' attitude on their part that prevents us from marketing *Zorro* and *Mickey Mouse*. We are avoiding the antitrust claim because we are also a party to the illegal contract (if it is such) and by the declaratory action we don't deny the legality of the contract that we signed.

"They may cross-file and probably will, with a counter-complaint, which would open up the case completely to all phases. If they do, that will be good, but the first impact on the public is the important one, and the cross-complaint will be second news and from their defense position instead of our attack position.

"Our three causes of action were we to file directly would be as follows: 1. The antitrust action, or their denying our right to sell to others the product they don't want or don't deal with us on. 2. Their claim for recoupment. 3. Some miscellaneous amounts we claim they owe us for union increases and some additional sales of *Mickey Mouse*.

"I would suggest you take the position to know nothing about the money arguments of recoupment or union increases and stick to the premise that you are not going to be restricted by them in marketing product that they don't deal for. If Leonard were to come out at our luncheon and ask what if they gave us in writing our freedom with respect to the sale of *Zorro* and *Mickey Mouse* or any other product, and if they would renounce their claim for recoupment, we on our part would in good faith carry out the deal with them for the rest of our contract period and renounce our claim for miscellaneous union increases, etc. . . .

"In all common sense and business reasoning I can't believe they would let this go to a big court fight. They have too many reasons to avoid that open action before the public. They have too many things they would rather keep quiet and not be brought out in court, plus the fact that all the attorneys feel the contract will fall—at least in part—on the antitrust count. Surely their attorneys, too, must realize that. However, they are unpredictable, so I guess we can expect anything. But we are well prepared to fight it out."

Roy's daughter-in-law, Patty Disney, recalls: "I remember how nervous he was when he went back to New York to see Goldenson. He studied so hard. I'd never seen him that nervous. He was playing with the big guys."

The meeting with Goldenson produced no agreement, and Roy ordered his lawyers to file suit. Later Goldenson indicated a willingness to sell his interest in Disneyland and release Disney from the television contract. Roy returned to New York for the negotiations. He got no help from Walt.

"We had ABC in the park for a 34 percent interest," Roy told Richard Hubler in 1968. "It wasn't working, which usually turns out that way when you have a fella like Walt. So I brought it along to the point where I bought them out. They had put in $500,000, and I kept hounding Walt [about the settlement]. I think my first offer was $3 million. That's a lot of money for the $500,000 they put in.

"I wound up paying them $7.5 million. And I didn't have a soul around to really get close to me and study it and say, 'Let's do it.' I had it in my lap.

"Just an hour before I closed the thing on that basis, I called Walt again on the phone and said, 'Walt, look, I'm going to offer them $7.5 million unless you strenuously object.' He said, 'I don't know, I don't know. You're a better judge of that than I am. Do you think it's necessary?' That was all I could get out of him. And I know he thought that was ridiculous: fifteen times what they had put up there."

Roy was determined to gain total ownership of Disneyland. After settling with ABC, he bought out the 13.79 percent share of Western Printing and Lithographing, as well as Walt's 17.25 percent. Then there was the matter of the shops and concessions. Before the opening of Disneyland, Walt was concerned that areas of the park would look empty. He sold rights for friends, company associates, and others to operate their own enterprises inside the park. One by one, Roy paid off the concessionaires and returned control of the areas to the company. He was able to make the buyouts because of a $15-million-dollar loan from Prudential Insurance and a revolving credit line from the Bank of America for $5 million.

When Disneyland was finally a wholly owned subsidiary of Walt Disney Productions, Walt acknowledged Roy's astuteness.

"That's the thing my brother's been fighting for," he said. "He's done a perfect job there. The way I back him up is if I make a good product and the money comes in, then he can do those things. And I think he's really fought there. He fought a long battle to get that thing financed and then freed. Actually, Roy is basically a banker. He's pretty shrewd on the money . . . I leave all those things to him. I don't question him on those things at all."

The ABC people were elated over exacting fifteen times their original investment in four years. History questions their judgment. As Disneyland developed into a mammoth success, ABC could have reaped far more if it had continued as an investor.

Roy scoffed: "They're just a dollar-minded bunch. They run the business for money first."

TWENTY-ONE

❧

In 1930, an enterprising young French journalist named Paul Winkler appeared at the Disney studio on Hyperion Avenue after a journey by boat and rail from Europe. He had been fascinated by how Mickey Mouse had enthralled Parisian movie audiences, and he wanted to introduce Mickey to newspapers. Roy gave him permission to pursue the idea. The agreement was made with no contract, nothing written. Just a handshake.

Winkler introduced Disney to Europe with a daily Mickey Mouse comic strip in *Le Petit Parisien*, a cartoon album that sold a half-million copies, and a magazine *Le Journal de Mickey*. His enterprise ceased with the German occupation of France. Having interviewed Hitler as a newsman and written derogatory articles and books, he fled the country, and traveled through Spain to Portugal where he was able to take the *Pan American Clipper* to New York.

After the war, Winkler returned to France and introduced Mickey and Donald Duck to a new generation of children. Not until 1960 did he and Roy enter into a written contract.

Paul Winkler was the first of a cadre of Europeans who spread the Disney characters and product throughout Britain and the continent and who were fiercely loyal to Roy. Their number grew after the war as the Disney fortunes improved.

Following V-E Day, Roy realized the need to reestablish the company's presence in Europe. RKO had begun the process of releasing the post–*Snow White* Disney features and the cartoons to those theaters that had not been destroyed by the war. The reception was warm, although the box office take was limited because of postwar poverty. Profits that accrued to RKO and Disney were frozen by the cash-poor nations.

Merchandising served the double purpose of providing revenue while helping to publicize the Disney characters and films. That revenue could be exported, based on the legal argument that Disney was the "author" of the products.

In 1947 Roy met in Brussels with a Frenchman named Armand Bigle. He had been a war correspondent for Hearst's International News Service. After the war, International News Service made him manager for Belgium, Holland, and Switzerland. Part of his duties was selling newspapers the King Features comics, including Mickey Mouse. When *Bambi* was being released in Europe, Bigle introduced a comic strip based on the movie characters. Walt and Roy were impressed, and Roy came to Brussels to offer Bigle a job.

Bigle reintroduced the Mickey Mouse magazine, and soon it was selling 50,000 copies. In 1949, Roy promoted Bigle to run merchandising in most of Europe except for Scandinavia. "How much are you going to pay me?" Bigle inquired.

"Nothing," Roy replied. "But we will pay your expenses and give you fifty percent of everything you generate."

"Fifty percent!" Bigle said incredulously.

"That's right. I figure fifty percent of something is better than ninety percent of nothing."

The first postwar Disney merchandising office was established in Armand Bigle's three-room Paris apartment. The place was divided: half for the living quarters of Bigle, his wife Betty, and their first child, half for Disney business.

Bigle struggled during the first year, because Disney had been absent from Europe for ten years. He expanded the Mickey Mouse magazine to other countries and introduced other Disney magazines and books. "Merchandising was not as easy," he recalls. "At first manufacturers wanted to know how much we would pay to have them put Disney characters on their products. In the end they were convinced to pay us ten percent because the characters helped their sales."

By the end of his three-year contract, Bigle was producing so much revenue, Roy reduced his share of the profits to ten percent.

As the European economy revived and Disney movies became popular, Roy established subsidiaries in major capitals. Once or twice a year he and Edna spent six weeks touring Europe. Roy's visits to the offices became routine. Always he wanted to meet the newest employees, and he spent time inquiring about them and their families.

Horst Koblischek, who became head of merchandising in Germany, remembers meeting Roy in Stuttgart in 1959. Roy had gone there to visit Disney's German publisher. He told Koblischek: "I would like to come and see your family."

The German was concerned. He and his wife and two young children lived in a modest three-room apartment with a small kitchen. "But I've just moved in," he protested.

"I'm not interested in your apartment," Roy said. "I'm interested in your family." The Disneys came to visit the Koblischeks, and Edna sat on the couch and held the children, one and three, on her lap. A close, enduring relationship between Roy and his German representative was established.

Gunnar Mansson, who rose from Stockholm manager to Disney head in all of Scandinavia, was a constant concern for Roy. A handsome Swede and expert skier, Mansson clung to his bachelorhood. He recalls, "Every time Roy saw me, he said, 'Are you married yet?' He was always disappointed when I said no. 'We don't like that,' he said. 'We run a family business, and we like our managers to have families.' He added with a smile, 'Then we can keep them under our thumb.' " Mansson finally married late in his career and retired to Australia.

Antonio Bertini became sales manager for Disney's Italian subsidiary in 1961. "Don't grow too fast," Roy advised him. "Be satisfied with 5 percent increase a year. That's better than having 20 percent one day and nothing tomorrow." Bertini comments: "Roy was always looking to the future. Not two or three years, but ten years ahead."

Roy also counseled in a fatherly way, "Look, Tony, in your job there'll be a lot of opportunity to do dirty business. Please, don't do anything under the table." Bertini replied: "I have no problem with that. In Italy, we discuss, we fight. But I promise: nothing under the table."

To the Europeans, Roy seemed to be a different kind of American. Many of the American entrepreneurs who came to Europe following the war appeared intent on making deals that would take advantage of the financially strapped countries. Roy insisted on contracts that were fair to both sides. As in Wall Street, his folksy manner was sometimes mistaken for weakness. He could be ruthless with anyone who failed to honor a contract. If an employee was found guilty of dishonesty, he would be fired summarily, often with a blistering sendoff.

Business in Europe had traditionally been conducted by a code of formality. That wasn't Roy's way, and some people had trouble with his style. One of the London managers was disturbed that everyone in the office called Walt Disney by his first name. "Even the office boy calls him Walt," the manager sniffed. London was not Walt's favorite office; he considered the employees "cold fish." Roy was more tolerant of English formality.

Marc Davis, one of the Nine Old Men, tells a story about the Paris office: "Edna would go along with Roy for meetings at the various foreign offices. She got upset with the Frenchmen, because they would talk French between themselves before they would speak in English. This really got to Edna, so when she came home she took a course in French. After she and Roy returned to Paris for meetings, there were a lot fewer Frenchmen working in the office."

Roy's associates rarely saw him angry. Don Escen, a company lawyer in charge of oversight of thirteen foreign subsidiaries, recalls one such occasion. Roy and Edna were leaving Paris en route to Copenhagen, where the European managers were assembling for a conference. Someone in the Paris office had sent the Disneys' car to Le Bourget airport instead of Orly.

"I can still see Edna sitting in the terminal with her fur coat on her lap and all of their luggage around her," says Escen, who was in the airport at the same time. "Roy had been around to all the airlines, trying to find a flight to Copenhagen. He was just frothing at the mouth. In fact, Edna was apologizing for him."

By the time they reached Copenhagen, Roy's anger had abated. He and Edna were greeted by Gunnar Mansson, who took them to the Hotel Angleterre, where the conference was to take place. A dinner for the European managers, their wives, and the Disney clients in Scandinavia had been planned for that evening.

"I would like to see the seating arrangements," said Roy. Mansson conducted Roy and Edna to the banquet room. As was her custom, Edna supplied gifts for all the wives, this time Hermès scarves she had selected in Paris.

Roy studied the place cards on the tables and asked who the people were. When Mansson identified their affiliations, Roy started changing the placement of the cards, putting those he wished to talk to close to him. "Roy, you can't do that," Edna protested. "This dinner has been planned. You can't come in here like a bull in a china shop and change everything around."

"Well, it's my party, isn't it?" Roy replied. "I can do anything I want."

When Roy planned to entertain groups at European hotels, he would stay in a suite. Otherwise he reserved less ostentatious quarters. Bob King, a Disney publicist, recalls that a studio executive occupied one of the most luxurious suites in the George V in Paris. When Roy and Edna arrived, they stayed in a room near the elevator.

In spite of the gastronomic enticements of Europe, Roy remained a meat-and-potatoes man. In every capital, he located a restaurant that served plain food, and he had most of his dinners there. His favorite in London was the Guinea, a small restaurant and pub on Berkley Square. "They have the best steaks in London," Roy proclaimed.

When Roy was in town, European managers sought to find entertainment that would please the boss. During a visit to London, Roy was invited to attend a football game between two of the major teams, the Arsenals and the Tottenham Hotspurs. Roy agreed, and he was joined by a half-dozen of the London staff members.

Roy was perplexed by the British sport, so unlike American football, but he enjoyed the spectacle of thousands of fans cheering for their teams. After the match, he and his companions joined the throng pouring out of the stadium.

"My God, we've lost the boss!" exclaimed Andy Thewlis, one of the London staffers. Roy was nowhere to be seen amid the shoving, hurrying crowd. A search party was organized, the men fanning out to the streets of Tottenham. Still no Roy.

Finally Thewlis searched the main street and found Roy. He was standing in front of a movie house, talking to the manager. "Why don't you play Disney pictures?" Roy inquired.

Periodically Roy brought the managers from Europe and from other countries to Burbank to show them upcoming films and infuse them with the Disney spirit. They met with Walt in his office, and he would deliver one of his spellbinding, forward-looking monologues. Roy and Edna entertained the visitors at their home with her fried chicken and corn on the cob and artichokes, two vegetables that were a mystery to the Europeans.

During one visit to California, Armand Bigle and Horst Koblischek were told by Madeleine Wheeler not to make any appointments for the following day. "Be at Roy's house at nine o'clock," the secretary said. "He will take you to our Golden Oak Ranch." When they arrived, Roy gazed at the pair in their dark suits, white shirts, somber ties, and polished shoes. "You guys look too European," Roy complained. "We'll have to fix that." He drove to a western apparel shop on Lankershim Boulevard called Nudies, which numbered among its clients Roy Rogers and Elvis Presley. When Bigle and Koblischek emerged a half-hour later, they were outfitted in cowboy boots, Levis, plaid shirts, bandanas, and Texas-style hats. "We came out of the store looking like Hopalong Cassidy," Koblischek recalls.

Roy announced they were going to the ranch for a family day with a picnic, games, and horseback rides. Koblischek protested that he had never been on a horse in his life. Bigle remarked that he had served in the cavalry in the French army. At the ranch, Koblischek was counseled on how to avoid falling off the western saddle by holding onto the horn. The experienced Bigle was given a horse that had performed stunts in movies. Its name: Tornado. Afterward, Bigle noticed that his inner legs were as devoid of hair as if they had been shaved. Both men limped through the next days like saddle-worn cowpokes. Roy was delighted.

TWENTY-TWO

✀

Roy's hair-growing potions didn't work. By his sixties, Roy
Disney had a high, shiny dome, with a fringe of greying hair
along the sides. With his horn-rim glasses and smiling manner,
he seemed more like a Midwest Rotarian than an important Hollywood executive. His appearance and demeanor sometimes led
New York power figures to expect him to be a pushover. He
wasn't, as Leonard Goldenson and others discovered.

"Roy was very folksy," says Luther Marr. "He often came
across to the New York boys to make them think, 'Well, this is a
country boy, and we're going to take advantage of him.' [The
negotiations] would get to some stage when all of a sudden they
realized they weren't taking advantage of the country boy; he
knew what was going on."

As Walt Disney Productions expanded in the 1950s, the studio
was divided between Walt's Boys and Roy's Boys, and often it

was an adversarial relationship. Walt presided over the creative side, and he ruled with a firm hand. Discontent was common, since he goaded his artists to achieve what they thought was impossible for them. He expected perfection and was frustrated when they didn't achieve it. He almost never complimented an artist for his work. Most old-timers can recall only one or two instances when Walt praised what they had done, and usually they heard of his approval from a second party. Walt's Boys were motivated not by being stroked, but by the sheer power of his genius.

Roy's Boys on the financial and legal side felt affection for their boss. Just as Edna accompanied Roy on most of his business trips, he encouraged his executives to travel with their wives. Like Edna, the wives could be valuable in entertaining clients; not incidentally, it would help solidify marriages which might be endangered when husbands ventured alone to far-off cities.

Jobs well done always won praise from Roy. He was especially attentive to young members of his staff.

"Both Roy and Walt were very tolerant of young people," recalls Marty Sklar, who was writing annual report messages for both while still in his twenties. "It always surprised me that they weren't interested in how old or how young anybody was; they were just interested in what he did. Roy especially was very encouraging; you'd never get that side out of Walt."

Harry Archinal came to Disney in his mid-twenties after serving in the Korean War. "Roy was a father image for me, because my father died young," says Archinal. "Roy always reminded me of him. They were very philosophical guys; they tended to fall back on the basics on anything.

"Roy had a way of putting you at ease. He always stopped whatever he was doing and talked to you. Having been in the service, I 'sirred' him to death: 'Yes, sir. No, sir.' One day he said to me, 'Harry, I'm going to kick you in the ass if you "sir" me once more. My name's Roy.' "

Archinal worked in the foreign department under Ned Clarke, a tough Irishman of the old film-selling school. Clarke deprecated the young man's ideas, often bitingly. When Archinal suggested bringing South American salesmen to the studio for a convention, Clarke scorned the proposal. Roy approved it.

Amid the success of the convention, Roy confided to Archinal: "I'm pleased with your idea, Harry. You're the guy for the future. Don't let anybody piss on you. If they do, come to me." Archinal understood to whom Roy was referring.

On Archinal's first trip to Europe, he attended a sales meeting in Paris conducted by Roy. One of the veteran salesmen was noted for his drinking. During an elegant lunch in a suite at the Plaza Athenée, he drank too much wine, and he fell asleep in the meeting. "Put him over on the couch," Roy suggested to Archinal and another young salesman, and he conducted the meeting while the old-timer snored in the corner.

"Roy brought a calming presence to everything," Archinal observes. "You knew you weren't going to get your ass chewed out, as with some bosses. There was absolutely zero fear in whatever the group was, as long as Roy was there."

He was loyal to his longtime employees, keeping them on long after their value to the company had diminished. Gunther Lessing, who had been with the studio since the 1920s, jealously maintained his leadership of the law department. This disturbed some of the junior members who felt that his secrecy and erratic decisions were harming the company.

When Neal McClure came to the studio to work in the law department, he lunched with Roy, Lessing, and Dick Morrow, a school chum who had offered McClure the job. Lessing dominated the conversation, though some of his comments made little sense. Afterward Roy took McClure aside and remarked, "Neal, don't think too harshly of Gunther. You might be that old yourself some day."

Even though he was co-founder and business chief of a rapidly expanding entertainment empire, Roy remained remarkably modest. When he was holding meetings in New York, arrangements had to be made for dinner. Roy insisted that restaurant reservations be made in someone else's name. He disliked flaunting the name Disney.

Jack Lindquist remembers being at the Disneyland Hotel one Sunday in the 1960s when he felt a tap on the shoulder. It was Roy Disney. "Jack, can you help me?" he asked. "I came down here with Edna, and I don't have my silver pass. Can you get me on the monorail?"

Says Lindquist: "So I used my Disney I.D. to get a Disney into Disneyland. I'm sure that if Roy had gone up to the person on the monorail and identified himself, he could have gotten on. But he wasn't that kind of person."

Robert Foster, a staff attorney, recalls being in Roy's office in the 1950s when Madeleine Wheeler entered with an envelope containing Roy's weekly salary, $1,000 in cash. Roy commented: "A thousand dollars a week! I'm the cheapest, lowest paid chief executive officer in the whole industry!"

Luther Marr tells the story that became legend at the studio. True or not, it fits Roy. Rarely did he enter the realm of Walt's Boys, but one day he stopped by the workroom of an animator who was agonizing over a piece of movement. "Why don't you do it this way?" Roy commented, suggesting a different approach.

The exasperated animator snapped, "Who do you think you are, God?"

"No," Roy replied, "I'm his brother."

. . .

For the first twenty-five years of their marriage, Roy and Edna never owned two cars. With their customary thrift, they saw no need. During the 1930s, they always bought Buicks, since an old pal from Roy's veterans' hospital days owned a Buick dealership in Pasadena. As the Disney company grew in the 1950s and Roy's duties increased, he realized the need for two cars. He was disappointed. Ever since the studio began, Edna had driven him to work and picked him up in the evening. Roy regretted the loss of companionship.

Never an early riser, Roy seldom arrived at his office before nine o'clock. He studied the box office returns from across the country, analyzing the performances not only of Disney pictures but those of the other studios as well. Copies of all of the company's cables and outgoing checks were sent to his office, and he reviewed those that Madeleine deemed important. She also presented him with the morning's correspondence, which he customarily answered on the same day. He reviewed the advertising art work that had been prepared for forthcoming productions and conferred with his executives from Buena Vista on how the films should be released.

Roy devised a special pattern for releasing *Alice in Wonderland,* a picture he had disliked from the beginning. After viewing the finished production, he realized that it had none of the endearing qualities of *Snow White* and other Disney animated features. He told the Buena Vista bookers to contract for as many theaters as possible for the opening of *Alice.* He instructed the advertising and publicity departments to prepare extensive campaigns for the film. The strategy worked. With *Alice* playing in double the normal number of theaters, the first two weeks produced greater ticket sales than for any Disney film. Then theater business plummeted as that essential element of every movie's success—word of mouth—turned negative, as Roy had predicted.

Roy rarely discussed business over lunch in the Coral Room of the studio commissary. He often entertained bankers, financiers, and other visitors, but the conversation remained social. The same when he lunched with members of the law and financial departments.

Except during conferences, the door to Roy's office remained open, and staff members were welcome to stop by to ask questions. Often he would question them. "I always hire people who are smarter than me," he bragged. He was awed by the knowledge of his staff members with law and business degrees, and he seemed to absorb all that they told him, no matter how intricate. Thus in negotiations he often surprised the opposing parties with his grasp of the situation.

Roy involved himself in matters other than company affairs during his work day. He remained active in charities, particularly the Motion Picture Relief Fund (later the Motion Picture and Television Fund), and in the Society of Independent Motion Picture Producers (SIMPP).

Founded in 1942, SIMPP gathered all the important independent producers into an organization to combat the stranglehold the major studios maintained on distribution. Most of them operated theater chains which favored their own pictures. They also indulged in the practice of block booking, by which theaters contracted annually for a major company's entire product. Such practices made it difficult for the independent producers to acquire bookings.

Roy Disney was one of the ringleaders in organizing SIMPP, along with Samuel Goldwyn, David O. Selznick, Charlie Chaplin, Howard Hughes, Mary Pickford, Hal Roach, and Walter Wanger.

Roy became a member of the executive committee, and Disney head counsel, Gunther Lessing, served as committee chairman. Later Ellis Arnall, former governor of Georgia and a power in the Democratic Party, was enlisted as president of SIMPP to provide the independents with political clout.

During the afternoon, with his office work and appointments finished, Roy enjoyed roaming around to chat and discuss company affairs (despite his open-door policy, the office of the president could be a lonely place). In the early 1950s he liked to drop in at Don Escen's office to see the new computer. At the urging of another associate, Paul Pease, Roy had purchased a RAM 500 computer to handle the corporate finances.

"Don, let's take a look at your latest trial balance," he would tell Escen, who entered instructions into the cumbersome machine. "Wow, look at that!" Roy gasped as the up-to-date assets and liabilities poured out of the machine. It was a revelation for a man who had once kept the company's finances with a sharpened pencil in a tiny notebook.

After a full work day, Roy enjoyed the relaxation of a cigar and a glass of scotch in his office. The door was open, and whoever wanted to drop in could do so. The cigars were the best that five cents could buy. He refused to buy anything more expensive. On one of his birthdays, his daughter-in-law Patty gave him a box of high-priced cigars. Roy opened the wrapping, looked at the label, and handed the package back to Patty. "I only smoke the nickel cigars," he said.

After an hour of schmoozing, he drove home for a quiet dinner with Edna. Roy seldom brought work home, though in times of crisis, such as the ABC lawsuit, he studied piles of documents in the evenings. Not an easy sleeper, he often read books in bed, usually biographies. His favorite subject was Thomas Jefferson, and he collected a small library of Jeffersonia. He frequently woke at night, complaining of a "nervous leg." At such times he retired to the exercise room and tried to tire himself enough so he could sleep again.

R oy Edward Disney remembers watching his father conduct a stockholders meeting in the theater on the Disney lot: "He was up at the podium making most of the presentations. I remember seeing how nervous he was. He was so good at meetings; If you didn't know he was nervous, you'd never guess it. It was a whole new world to me, because I had always thought of Dad as this great, self-confident person who said what he meant. I realized for the first time that he didn't like this sort of thing either."

Almost every year, one of the stockholders rose and complained, "How come we never get tickets to Disneyland? We're shareholders, and we deserve them."

Roy's reply: "We're not in the business of giving things away. If we gave away everything, you people wouldn't want our stock."

At another meeting, an angry stockholder rose to complain about the minuscule Disney dividend. "I own General Motors stock, and they pay a substantial dividend," the man scolded. "Thank you for the comparison," Roy responded, and he continued with the meeting's business.

In his late years, Roy developed a tremor in his right hand that caused him great embarrassment. Doctors told him it was not the result of Parkinson's disease or any other discernible ailment. Roy did everything he could to avoid exposing his shaking hand. He shunned situations where he had to sign his name in public. Only a few of his closest associates were aware of the disability.

Roy's regular churchgoing ended with his puritanical, Congregational upbringing as a boy in Chicago. "Dad's religion was absolutely inside his head," his son says. "He didn't go to church, but I think he believed in a very strict moral code. I'm certain he believed in God, although I don't think anybody ever asked him to define God. I'm not sure he would have said anything beyond, 'Well, he's there, and we all know that, don't we?' "

Throughout his adult life, Roy received a disability check from the U.S. government for having contracted tuberculosis in the navy. Again and again he tried to return the check, declaring that he wasn't disabled and had experienced no return of TB. He was unable to penetrate the government bureaucracy, and the checks continued.

"Roy had a quality that you don't find in many people today," remarks Mike Bagnall, a member of the financial staff. "It was part of a different generation in business. Their word was their bond, they were very sensitive of others, nonpretentious, no big egos, deliver service, the customer is always right, don't always take the last penny on the table, if a deal was good everybody would make enough money. Roy tried to be fair not only with his employees but with the deals that he made."

His attorneys say that when they were negotiating a difficult contract with outsiders, Roy would sometimes say, "Let's go easy on them."

Roy's health remained good in his later years, though he was subject to colds and bouts of pleurisy. Remembrance of his post-war illness stayed with him, especially when he had colds. He made sporadic efforts at exercise regimens, installing various machines and equipment in his basement.

In 1962, Roy and Edna sailed to England on the *Queen Eliz-*

abeth. Roy visited the ship's gym and became fascinated with a mechanical horse. He liked the realistic movement of the machine and decided he had to have one. Thus began months of inquiries and negotiations.

He questioned the Abercrombie and Fitch store in New York and was told they knew of no American manufacturer of mechanical horses. Next he asked Andy Thewlis of the London Disney office to search for the English manufacturer. Thewlis located the maker of the horse in Lancashire.

"Go ahead and order it," Roy told Thewlis. "And make sure it doesn't arrive at the studio rusty."

The Olympic Gymnasium Company, Ltd., agreed to ship the equipment, officially listed as "1 (one) Mechanical Horse Riding Machine, complete with Gent's Hunting Type Leather Riding Saddle and Stirrups; variable speed A.C. Motor with control switch for 110 volt single phase 60 cycle alternating current." The Disney company would pay for the purchase and the shipping, which amounted to $971.18, and then Roy would reimburse the company.

Before the shipment was made, Roy asked Thewlis to travel to Lancashire and give the horse a trial ride. Thewlis pleaded his ignorance of horses, alive or mechanical, but Roy insisted. Thewlis decided he needed an expert opinion. He engaged a Manchester chiropractor, and both went to the factory, where a red carpet led to a dais on which the horse stood. Both Thewlis and the chiropractor took a ride, approved, and Thewlis said, "Ship it."

After eight months, Roy received his horse and installed it in the basement. He rode it every night, much to Edna's disdain. A few years later, the story would have a sequel involving the Internal Revenue Service.

• • •

Roy and Edna reminded me of Bess and Harry Truman," Patty Disney observes. "They had the same set of Midwest values, the same simple lifestyle. And they were devoted to each other."

They were home folks who preferred an evening together rather than joining the industry dinners which Roy was sometimes obligated to attend. With the help of a housekeeper, Edna maintained an immaculate house. She did her own grocery shopping, always searching for bargains. She saved any string that came into the house, and at Christmas time she insisted that paper be carefully opened, to be kept for wrapping presents the following year.

Edna held strong opinions and often vented them. She was probably the only one who could shut up Walt Disney. Having known him since he was a newsboy of ten, she had no awe of him as Hollywood's maker of miracles. Their son remembers an evening when the Roy Disneys entertained guests including the Walt Disneys at dinner in the 1950s: "Walt was still preparing the script for *The Shaggy Dog*. It was one of the early 'Let's do a black-and-white comedy with some special effects and not much money' approach to the question, 'What else do you do besides animation?' There must have been ten-twelve people sitting around the table enjoying fried chicken and corn on the cob. Walt began his I'll-take-over-this-meeting thing, so he started: 'We're working on this wonderful story about a kid who turns into a dog.'

"He usually could keep people enthralled with his storytelling. He got a little bit into it, and Mother says, 'That sounds kinda dumb.' He went further on, and mother says, 'That really sounds like an awful stupid picture, Walt.' Every time she said something,

Walt's distraction got a little bit worse. He got to the halfway point in the story and just gave up on it."

Patty adds: "I would be shocked sometimes when Roy's mother would do that, then his father would look at her right there at the table and say, 'Edna, shut up.' I finally realized that if you didn't stop her when she got going, you couldn't stop her."

Edna had sympathy for the lonely, the disheartened, and others in need. Joe Reddy was a special friend. A short, roly-poly leprechaun of a man, he was one of Hollywood's most respected publicists, having guided the careers of Harold Lloyd and Shirley Temple. His skill as publicity chief for Disney helped the studio over many rough patches. Joe was a convivial man with an Irish fondness for spirits, and after work he often joined buddies in a Toluca Lake bar. When he realized he had passed the stage of negotiating the freeway, he would drive the few blocks to the Disneys' house and knock on the back door. Edna would lead him to the spare bedroom, where Joe would snooze until early morning.

One dark morning he awoke, left the house quietly, and began driving home. A motorcycle officer noticed his slow pace and flagged him down. "Where are you going at this hour?" the cop asked. "I'm going to five o'clock Mass, officer," Joe replied. "That's where I'm going; follow me," the cop said.

When Joe finally arrived home, his wife demanded, "Where have you been?" Joe replied, "Ruby, if I told you, you wouldn't believe me."

Roy Disney seemed ambivalent about whether he wanted his son to work at the studio. He was "less than enthusiastic," recalls Roy Edward, as he was usually called to differentiate him from his father. Roy probably was responsible for his son's first job, which was not for Disney, but at the studio. During the 1950s, Roy created some extra income by renting studio space to outside productions, notably Jack Webb's hit television series, *Dragnet*. The show's producer, Stanley Meyers, hired Roy Edward as an apprentice editor, somehow managing him admission to the film editors' union.

Roy Edward speculates that his father may have thought that if the son didn't like the work, there would be no bridges burned, as there might have been if he had worked for Disney.

The work was hard, but Roy Edward enjoyed a look into a new world, with people who were bright and fun-loving. He operated the splicing machine, putting together reels with the cuts marked by paper clips. *Dragnet* was a quick-cut show, and every reel had as many as two hundred splices. He worked long days, always ending with stained hands from the ink sprayed on each cut to eliminate a popping sound.

Roy Edward was laid off at the end of the *Dragnet* season. He walked next door to the Disney cutting rooms and asked the department head, Dick Pfahler, "Have you got a job for me? I just got fired." Roy Edward worked a few months in the shipping room, rewinding and repairing film then sending it off again. He served as assistant to Lloyd Richardson, who was finishing the edit of *The Living Desert* and starting *The Vanishing Prairie*.

Roy was "not displeased" to learn of his son's employment in the company. "I think he was apprehensive that if I did get involved in doing things for Walt, that Walt might not treat me as well as he did other people," Roy Edward speculates. "Of course he treated everybody pretty tough.

"I have always said he was very, very fair to me. If I did crappy stuff, he told me so. If he liked what I did, he told me that too.

He never patted anybody on the back. I always figured if I could get a laugh out of him in the sweat box [where rough cuts were screened], that was cool."

Roy Edward worked on the True-Life Adventures for the producer, Winston Hibler, then in 1962 he told Walt: "I kinda think I could do one of these things myself." Walt's reply was brisk: "Why don't you go ahead and try it?" Roy Edward submitted two scripts to Walt and drew no response, a sure sign of disfavor. Finally he clicked with an idea called *An Otter in the Family*. He made four more television movies before Walt died.

Roy Edward's work required long periods in the wilds, patiently waiting for animals to produce the desired footage. Despite his absences, he was able to court Patricia Dailey, the New Orleans–born daughter of Pete Dailey, a newspaperman who became a studio publicist and later an editor for *Look* magazine. She was slim and lovely, as outgoing as Roy Edward was shy.

In the summer of 1955, Roy Edward was working in Utah as one of the cameramen on *Perri*, first (and only) of Disney's True-Life Fantasies. He flew to Los Angeles to pick up a car and was greeted at the airport by his mother and Patty. "Well, Roy, are you going to kiss her?" Edna demanded. Roy Edward and Patty spent an innocent ten days together, and, Roy recalled, "decided we liked each other on a different level than we had before."

Roy Edward recalls that when he started on the trip back to Salt Lake City, he looked at Patty in the rearview mirror and decided, "I've got to go back and propose to this girl." With customary shyness, he didn't. When he reached Salt Lake City, he wrote a five-page letter, ending with, "By the way, I think we ought to think about getting married." He received a telegram in response: "Hell, yes."

The engagement was announced on the night before the opening of Disneyland. When they arrived at the gate the next day, Walt greeted them. Usually undemonstrative, he embraced Patty and exclaimed, "Great news! My nephew's marrying a girl with some spunk!"

The Disneys and the Daileys joined for a joyful engagement party, unattended by the groom-to-be, back filming in Utah. Patty commented to Edna: "You're so gracious to give up your only son." Edna's reply: "Thank God there's somebody else to pick up his socks." Roy merely grinned and grinned, his mind occupied by thoughts of grandchildren.

Three days before the wedding, Pete Dailey arrived home shamefaced and announced, "That's it, call off the wedding; I ruined it!" He explained that he had left the *Look* office and was driving home on the Hollywood Freeway when he encountered a vintage Cadillac traveling thirty-five miles per hour in the fast lane. Dailey sounded his horn again and again to no avail. Finally he pulled around the Cadillac and shouted some ungentlemanly comments to the woman driver. To his horror, he recognized Edna Disney.

It turned out to be no problem. Edna always drove at her own pace in the fast lane, eyes straight forward, oblivious to other cars. She never saw him.

The wedding took place as scheduled on September 17, 1955, at St. Charles Catholic Church in North Hollywood; then the newlyweds embarked on a lengthy European honeymoon. Roy kept them informed of the happenings at home. In December, he dictated a four-page letter to Madeleine Wheeler full of news about the Disney film releases, gossip at the studio, and family happenings.

The Living Desert was drawing crowds around the world, Walt was pleased with the footage on *Perri, The Great Locomotive Chase* was being filmed, bad weather had hampered Disneyland attendance but 67,000 came during Thanksgiving week, the

Mickey Mouse Circus was well presented but people preferred the rides on the short winter days. Edna had bought an exercise table and was following Roy's custom of using it when she couldn't sleep. The dog Prince kept running away and had to be confined to the backyard.

Roy ended by telling of a letter from a Disney representative in France who said "that you and Pat were nice folks and we should be very proud of you. That listened awful good to us— and we are!"

On April 16, 1957, Roy Patrick Disney was born at St. Joseph's Hospital, across the street from the Disney studio. The name followed the precedent of avoiding juniors and honoring mothers; Roy Edward derived from Edna, Roy Patrick from Patricia. Walt came to the hospital to congratulate the parents and admire his new grandnephew. Gazing over the nursery crowded with baby-boom infants, he gloated, "Look at all those babies in there. Another audience in seven years!"

Susan Margaret Disney arrived on May 12, 1958, and later Patty became pregnant with her third child. Roy and Edna served as faithful babysitters, although he had his limits. One weekend the grandparents volunteered to take care of Roy and Susan, then three and two, to give their parents two days of rest. On Friday, the two children went off with their grandfather in their best clothes.

Roy and Patty were still sleeping on Saturday morning when the doorbell rang. Grandfather Roy stood in the doorway, his car in the driveway, engine running. He held the hands of the two children, each bearing a suitcase, tears running down their faces. "Here," said Roy, handing them over, and he retreated to his car. That morning he had said, "You do that one more time and I'll take you home." He had to keep his word.

Abigail Edna Disney arrived on January 24, 1960, and Timothy

John Disney on June 13, 1961, four children within four years. They became the delight of their grandfather's later years. Once he said to Patty, "When I was in Kansas City, we used to run around town throwing rocks at the Catholics. Now I have four Catholic grandchildren!" He attended every Baptism and First Communion for all four grandchildren.

A Mason for decades, he later confided to Patty that he had resigned his membership in the order, which had a long history of anti-Catholicism. He felt he owed it to his daughter-in-law.

Roy Disney was a man who detested sentimentality, though he sometimes indulged in it. Once he said to Patty: "The street doesn't say 'dead end' anymore in my life. It says 'through road.' I look at those grandchildren, and I know that I'm never going to really die." Tears glistened in his eyes.

Walt Disney once remarked to a reporter that he envied his brother Herb. "All he wants to do is deliver the mail," Walt said. "He's a very happy man."

Herbert Arthur Disney possessed none of the ambitious determination of his two younger brothers, Walt and Roy. His job with the post office suited him and provided for his modest needs. He and his wife Louise, also a Midwesterner from Sedalia, Missouri, shared a bungalow in Hollywood, close to where Walt and Roy had lived on Lyric Avenue in the twenties. The house was within walking distance of the post office. Herb owned an Airstream trailer, and the big event of his year came when he and Louise would load up the trailer and tour the parks and beaches of the west during his two-week vacation.

After the studio became successful, Roy and Walt made regular gifts of stock to Herb, Ray, and Ruth. At one time, Roy offered Herb a job at the studio, where he could earn much more than he did from the post office. "No thanks," Herb answered. "I've got a nice pension coming from the postal service when I turn sixty-five, and I'm not going to jeopardize that."

Herb retired in 1953, and Louise died that year. Herb remarried, and he spent a comfortable retirement, enjoying his three grandchildren by Dorothy and Glenn Puder and taking longer trips in the Airstream. In 1961 he died in the same house he had occupied since coming to Los Angeles.

Ruth Disney Beecher was the only member of that generation of Disneys who didn't settle in Los Angeles. She had moved with her parents to Portland, Oregon, and remained there after her marriage to Theodore Charles Beecher. They had a son, Theodore Warren Beecher.

Ruth's husband never seemed to hold a job, and she often wrote to Roy for financial help. Unless her proposals seemed unsound, he complied. In 1956, she typed an eight-page, single-spaced letter detailing some of her needs. She told of her desire for their son Teddy to attend a summer camp: "He is so extremely high-strung and nervous lately, and I think a summer spent in the outdoors as much as possible would be the best thing for him."

She discussed buying a new house and the need for financial assistance—"we have had very little working capital to go on, as our funds have been mostly used up for necessities and medicine." In a postscript she added that a dentist had discovered thirty-two cavities in Teddy's teeth. When the dentist advised cutting back on sugar and brushing his teeth ten minutes after eating, Teddy replied, "Why, I couldn't do that; I'm eating something sweet every ten minutes."

Ruth was the last survivor of the children of Flora and Elias Disney. In 1995, she died in Portland at the age of ninety-two.

· · ·

Walt once remarked to John Hench: "Is that guy a character!" He was referring to his brother Ray, who was indeed the family eccentric. Ray had followed Roy and Walt to Los Angeles, and he had established himself as an insurance agent. His major client: the Disney studio and its employees.

Ray had complete access to the studio, and in the thirties and forties he roamed the halls, looking for workers who might need to insure their homes or cars or lives. He left them with matchbooks, pens, and rain ponchos as reminders of his available services.

Says Roy Edward: "People would begin to believe, as Ray wanted them to believe, that if they didn't buy insurance from him, their jobs would be in jeopardy."

After the strike, when Walt explained to the workers that there would be different conditions at the studio, one of the former strikers piped up: "Does that mean we don't have to buy insurance from your brother anymore?"

Ray walked into story meetings, sometimes interrupting Walt's train of thought. Frank Thomas and Ollie Johnston recall a meeting for *Pinocchio* that concerned what the fox, Honest John, should look like. Ray appeared at the door, looking for a client. Walt glanced at Ray's lean, eager face and commented: "There's your fox."

Walt and Roy became so exasperated by Ray's intrusions that they finally forbade him to roam the studio. Ray was incensed at what he considered his brothers' betrayal.

Ray Disney never learned to drive a car, never married, never appeared to have any girlfriends. He lived a few blocks from the studio and rode his bicycle back and forth. The apartment was small, and insurance clients who visited there—Ray became invisible when claims were filed—say that it took him fifteen minutes to open the door, so encumbered was it with locks and safety devices. In the 1930s, Ray began taking in cats. His collection grew, and the odor of cats and cat excrement was overwhelming. Edna complained that Ray always smelled bad because of the dead cigars he always had in his mouth.

His bicycle was the kind young boys rode: balloon tires, fenders, high handlebars. He pedaled along Riverside Drive in a suit and hat, his right pants leg in a clip to avoid catching in the chain. Shortly after Roy Edward and Patty were married, they were driving through Burbank in a heavy rain. They saw a figure pedaling a bicycle along the rain-soaked street, erect in a plastic cover. "Who is that?" Patty asked. "That's my uncle," said Roy. She commented, "He looks like Margaret Hamilton in *The Wizard of Oz*."

Ray was the last survivor of the four Disney brothers. He died in 1989 at ninety-nine after years of senility.

TWENTY-THREE

⁓

A s Walt Disney Productions expanded rapidly in the wake of the Disneyland opening, the intimate relationship between Roy and Walt Disney began to erode. Both faced overwhelming responsibilities.

Roy maintained close ties with the banks and investment houses, oversaw releases of the films through Buena Vista, supervised the foreign sales offices and made regular visits abroad, kept a watchful eye on the merchandising and pursued infringements, dealt with the board of directors and stockholders, and controlled all legal aspects of the corporation.

Walt made regular tours of Disneyland to improve all aspects of the park, oversaw animation though not as much as before (*Sleeping Beauty* required four-and-a-half years of production partly because of his preoccupation with Disneyland), contributed to live-action scripts and visited European locations, filmed his introductions to the television show, decided on scripts and casting for all the features and television shows, and spent time with WED in plotting new attractions for Disneyland and other plans for the future.

Gatherings of the two families became more infrequent, and Walt and Roy rarely visited each other's offices. They appeared at lunch in the Coral Room, which was reserved for executives, writers, directors, and visiting press and dignitaries. (In the egalitarian studio years, everyone took meals in the commissary. Roy had opposed adding the exclusive Coral Room, but once it had been built, he lunched there daily.) Walt's table was the first on the right, and he often entertained celebrities or reporters. Roy's was a table away, and he was usually joined by members of the law and financial departments.

One day Roy invited Dick Irvine, one of Walt's important executives at WED, to lunch with him to discuss a legal matter. Walt glanced over at the table with a glowering look and the upraised eyebrow that indicated his discontent. When Roy returned to the office, the phone was ringing. It was Walt. "You leave my men alone," he snapped. "Dick Irvine works for me, and I don't want him responding to you. I've got plenty for him to do." The complaint was typically Walt. Yet when one of Roy's Boys lunched with Walt, his brother made no complaint.

Increasingly, Walt and Roy went through periods of chilly relations; usually Walt, the short-tempered brother, was the instigator. One day Roy attended a screening of *Ten Who Dared* in an animation building projection room. The story of one-armed John Wesley Powell's exploration trip down the Colorado River in 1869, the film had been one of Walt's favorite projects, and he invited Roy to the screening with much anticipation. Alas, *Ten Who Dared* proved to be dismal ("It's hard to think of another

Disney film so totally bad," wrote Leonard Maltin in *The Disney Films*).

The lights came up in the projection room amid embarrassed silence. "Well," Roy remarked, "I guess everybody's got their stinkers." Walt steamed, and he refused to speak to his brother for weeks.

The annual stockholders meetings became a matter of contention between the brothers. Roy urged Walt to attend, but Walt adamantly refused. One year Roy said it would be a nice gesture if Walt just dropped in and said hello to the stockholders. After all, the meeting was being held in the studio theater, a few steps from the animation building.

"If I'm down there," Walt replied, "I'll be wasting time I should be spending up here making movies."

He maintained the same attitude toward board of directors meetings. No longer an officer of the company, he was not obliged to attend.

Everyone at the studio who dealt with Walt and Roy became aware of the undercurrent of discord between them. None of their associates heard either man lash out at his brother. But there was frequent grumbling about Roy's pennypinching or Walt's profligacy.

Bill Cottrell cited an example: "Walt wanted to get an airplane, something like a King Air or a Queen Air. He just thought for the things we were doing and talking about doing, it would be handy to fly over the project or fly back and forth. He could also fly to film locations.

"Roy said, 'We don't need that, we're not big enough.' Walt mentioned other companies that had airplanes and said, 'I don't know why I can't have one.' When Roy wouldn't budge, he said, 'Well, I'll buy it myself.' I guess Roy figured to keep peace in the family; the company would buy it."

Walt reveled in his new toy. He acted as bartender for his fellow fliers and enjoyed sitting next to the pilot of the Queen Air, sometimes taking the controls himself. This gave the studio's insurance officer concern. To tease him, Walt spoke of doing some stunt flying.

Walt once explained his attitude toward money: "People look at me in many ways. They've said, 'The guy has no regard for money.' That is not true. I have had regard for money. It depends on who's saying that. Some people worship money as something you've got to have piled up in a big pile somewhere. I've only thought about money in one way, and that is to do something with it. I don't think there's a thing I own that I will ever get the benefit of except through doing things with it. I don't even want the dividends from the stock in the studio, because the government's going to take it anyway. I'd rather have that in [the company] working . . .

"Everybody who's ever befriended and helped me I've tried always to see that they came out all right. When Roy helped me back there [in Kansas City], I was all alone and Roy had no connection with this business at all. When I came out here, I wanted Roy and me to be partners . . . Roy not knowing the business didn't know what we were in, but Roy had faith in me, the same as he did when I was in Kansas City and he sent me those checks.

"Roy has done a lot of things against his better judgment, because he felt that I wanted to do it. Most of our arguments and disagreements, I think, have been because Roy felt he had to protect me."

•　•　•

W e need more product," the Buena Vista salesmen complained to Roy.

Traditionally, the studio's releases had been geared to hol-
idays, when children were out of school. With the downfall of
the restrictive Production Code, the major companies could
now explore profanity, sex, nudity, and other content deemed
unsuitable for tender minds. A Disney movie was the safe
choice for parents.

But holiday releases were not enough to sustain a fully
staffed, worldwide releasing company. Roy decided Buena Vista
would need to release films from other producers, who would
be partly financed by Disney, if necessary.

In 1958, the Buena Vista salesmen mounted a campaign for
The Missouri Traveler, a period film with Brandon de Wilde as an
orphan moving into a Southern town. The rich socialite, C.V.
Whitney, financed the movie, which featured Lee Marvin, Gary
Merrill, Paul Ford, and Mary Hosford, an unknown actress who
happened to be Mrs. Whitney. *The Missouri Traveler* created little
enthusiasm from the critics and less from film buyers.

Roy decided to aim for bigger attractions. He was approached
by Rowland V. Lee, a producer-director who had been in films
since 1915. He had acquired the film rights to *The Big Fisherman*,
a novel about St. Peter by Lloyd C. Douglas, pop writer of reli-
gious themes. The adaptation of his *The Robe* had been the first
film in CinemaScope and had helped rescue 20th Century-Fox
from bankruptcy in 1953.

Lee, who hadn't directed a film in a dozen years, hired Frank
Borzage, another Hollywood veteran who had won the first Oscar
for a dramatic film, *Seventh Heaven*. Roy had known Borzage
from their polo playing days in the thirties. *The Big Fisherman*
would be Borzage's last picture.

Walt disapproved of the subject matter; throughout his career he had eschewed any film material dealing with religion, reasoning that a portion of the audience would be displeased by the depiction of a particular sect. He would have nothing to do with *The Big Fisherman*, leaving all the corporate responsibility to his brother. Roy was uncharacteristically free with the budget: $6 million, a huge amount for a Disney film. But he flinched at one outlay. He offered the role of the Arab princess to Elizabeth Taylor. She responded that she might be willing—for a million dollars. "A million dollars!" Roy exclaimed. "*Walt Disney* doesn't get a million dollars." The role was played by Susan Kohner.

Casting the role of Simon Peter presented a problem. Most of Hollywood's important leading men were either not interested, tied to studio contracts, or wanted more money than Roy would pay. The role finally went to Howard Keel, who had been a star of MGM musicals.

Roy decided to road show *The Big Fisherman*, opening in 1959 with a reserved-seat, two-a-day appearance at the Rivoli Theater in Manhattan. The critics responded negatively, as did the public. *The Hollywood Reporter* sounded the death knell: "The picture is three hours long, and except for those who can be dazzled by big gatherings of props, horses, and camels, it is hard to find three minutes of entertainment in it."

Buena Vista released a few other films, including imports from Germany, England, and Japan, but none produced much revenue. Roy abandoned the policy, adhering to Disney-made films exclusively and vowing never again to venture into the creative arena. Walt, of course, was secretly delighted.

Many years later, Roy told Charles Champlin of the Los Angeles *Times*: "[The Disney company is] blessed with a president who doesn't think he knows how to make pictures and doesn't put his two cents in. One thing we have to learn in this town is what we do and what we don't do."

• • •

The huge success of Disneyland prompted other companies to build theme parks. CBS converted an old amusement pier at Ocean Park, south of Santa Monica, into a collection of thrill rides and other attractions. It failed. The most ambitious new park was Freedomland in New York, built on a patriotic theme by real estate mogul William Zeckendorf. After the initial crowds, attendance dropped dramatically, and word spread that Freedomland was in deep trouble. Zeckendorf pleaded with the Disneys for help.

In a 1960 memo to Walt, Roy outlined Zeckendorf's statements: that changes were being made at Freedomland; that losses and depreciation provided $28 million in tax protection; that he had a cheap long lease on land in the middle of population centers; that Freedomland had a cash flow of $2.6 million ("How can he have a cash flow when he's in the red?" Roy mused).

"We are real estate people, not showmen," Zeckendorf confessed. "We respect you people and want to go into partnership with you on Freedomland. We will be the junior partners."

Roy told Zeckendorf that he doubted if Walt would want to assume "anybody else's headaches." As for Roy, "I had no inclination for it at all." The Disneys gave Zeckendorf their final decision: no. Freedomland soon closed its gates forever.

In 1960, an executive of Kidder, Peabody & Co., which had helped in the financing of Disneyland, wrote to Roy inquiring about the possibility of selling the park and leasing it back. When the executive received no reply, he again wrote Roy to complain: "When a feller takes a friend out to lunch and introduces his best girl, is it cricket for the friend to look up the girl without telling?"

Roy replied that he had been away from the studio when the first letter arrived; at any rate, "it didn't seem to need an answer because we never had in mind the sale and leaseback of Disney-land and by that time we had completed arrangements for some Disneyland financing, current and long-range." He added that he had never overlooked Kidder, Peabody, but didn't feel that the situation called for an outsider.

He concluded: "I don't think your analogy to a fellow and his girl is good, because in love they say anything is fair, but in business we try to be a little ethical."

I n 1960, Roy wrote to a Los Angeles patent attorney, beginning, "You probably hear from a lot of screwballs, so here's another one!"

Roy complained about wet feet. Traveling throughout the world, he often encountered rain. Rubbers were too bulky. He had a plan for a better design. "When I retire," he wrote, "I can put ads in *Good Housekeeping* and *Sports Illustrated* and other magazines that carry small ads that the suckers answer, and I can stay home and take care of the answers and not only keep busy, but I might accidentally make a buck!"

He described in intricate detail the molding of a soft, yet firm rubber which could be folded and carried in a pocket. His enthusiasm rose: "I think I could sell tens of millions of them if we ever get a good working model and get them on the market."

Roy concluded: "So these are the worries of an old traveler who is supposed to be president of a very important and busy company—but I haven't anything better to do today, so I thought I would lay a little plan for my retirement days."

The patent attorney replied that Roy's idea had been patented long before. Roy admitted defeat and paid the lawyer's bill of $117.10, which he carefully noted for the files "not tax deductible."

Roy's inventor dream had quickly ended. And retirement was something he would never achieve.

P rotecting the Disney characters remained a passion for Roy throughout his career. Whenever an infringement was uncovered, he directed the lawyers to pursue the offenders. "You can't let people be infringing," he once said. "We found manufacturers picking up and using [our characters] without our permission. So we moved in and decided the best way was to license them."

The volume of offenders created a constant headache for the studio's legal department. "It just went on and on," recalls Dick Morrow, who succeeded Gunther Lessing as chief counsel. "There were so many of them that we almost didn't want to respond, because we didn't have the staff. If [the infringers] were just a minor operation somewhere, it would cost too much to go get 'em. We'd rather do something where we'd get newspaper coverage, headlines about how tough we were, and try to frighten people off."

A Disney lawyer in New York acted as the character "cop." He sent out letters that got progressively tougher. Usually the offender became a licensee or desisted from pirating the Disney characters. Court cases were rare, reserved for the most visible infringements. Roy instructed the lawyers not to seek damages; he merely wanted the practice stopped.

Tracking down merchandise pirates in foreign countries was difficult, especially in Latin America. For years the law department fretted over a Mexican manufacturer of mineral water with a picture of Donald Duck on the bottle. Attempts at litigation always failed, and the company seemed impossible to locate.

Gunther Lessing, who claimed expertise in Mexican matters

because of his association with Pancho Villa, made the Mexican mineral water matter a personal crusade. He thought he saw an opening when the wife of the president of Mexico asked for a print of *Snow White and the Seven Dwarfs* to show at a charity event at Chapultepec Castle. Lessing believed he could ingratiate himself with the first lady and seek her help in the case.

His hopes were dashed. He learned that the president's wife received a penny for every bottle of water that was sold. And the water had no minerals, except those that came out of the Mexico City faucets.

Walt often talked about his Irish heritage in interviews and general conversation. Roy never did. His son believes Roy's reluctance stems from his childhood in a time when the Irish, who had come to America en masse in the latter part of the nineteenth century, were somewhat in disrepute. IRISH NEED NOT APPLY was not uncommon on help wanted signs. But if Roy did not proclaim his ancestry, he like Walt sometimes displayed an Irish temper.

With Walt's restless desire to achieve as much creativity as possible in his lifetime, patience was not his long suit. Not so with Roy. He was patient with mistakes, particularly those by younger members of his staff.

"Roy had a great respect for his lawyers' judgment and opinions," observes Robert Foster, who had been a member of the law department. "He could be very curt, very abrupt if he sensed that you were equivocating. If you spelled out your reasons for your opinion and they were logical, he was respectful. He could be a little rough if he sensed that you were equivocating and weren't positive.

"He used to jump on Spencer Olin's back; Spence had a tendency to equivocate rather than give a positive answer. Roy showed intolerance for that. I've been at meetings when he would jump on Spence for explaining both sides of an issue rather than taking a position. Roy could be unmerciful. He would say, 'Dammit, Spence, which is it?' "

During the desperate search for Disneyland financing, Roy had tried to interest other lenders besides Bank of America and Bankers Trust. An official of Interstate Bank came to the studio to meet with a financial officer about a possible loan. During the meeting, the banker was called to the phone in the outer office. The secretary heard him say, "I'm out here at Disney wasting my time about this Disneyland thing." The remark was relayed to Roy. He summarily halted any negotiations with Interstate, and Disney never again had dealings with the bank.

TWENTY-FOUR

⚛

After Disneyland, then what?

Walt Disney's raging imagination demanded new challenges, new vistas. "I've always been bored with just making money," he once said. "I've wanted to do things, I've wanted to build things. Get something going. What money meant to me was to get the money to do that."

He maintained a watchful eye on the live-action features and was pleased with the success of *The Shaggy Dog*, which had attracted the scorn of both Lilly and Edna. *Pollyanna* was a moderate success, but it produced a new Disney star, Hayley Mills. Walt grumbled about being coerced to cast her father, John Mills, as Papa Robinson in *Swiss Family Robinson* in order to assure Hayley for future films. But the forced booking was worth it. *The Parent Trap*, with Hayley as twins, attracted a large audience, especially teenagers. *The Absent-Minded Professor* continued the run of hit comedies with special effects.

Walt relied more and more on producers, Bill Anderson and Bill Walsh, and for the nature movies, Winston Hibler. Yet he denied them credit that producers at other studios received.

In 1964, Card Walker decided the annual report should feature the producers in order to show that the company had filmmakers who could carry on in case something happened to Walt. Walker and Marty Sklar, who was preparing the report, took the concept to Walt, who immediately vetoed it.

"I don't mind sharing the pictures," Walt commented. "But I don't want to talk about 'a Bill Walsh production for Walt Disney,' or 'a Bill Anderson production for Walt Disney.' I've worked my whole life to create the image of what 'Walt Disney' is. It's not me. I smoke, and I drink, and all the things we don't want the public to think about. My whole life has been devoted to building up this organization that is represented by the name 'Walt Disney.' I don't want you breaking that down by doing this in the annual report."

The pace of the animated features had slowed considerably. Walt had told the animators, "You're on your own," and he provided none of the scrutiny that had inspired them in earlier features. He devoted as much attention to the partially animated *Mary Poppins* as he had to his animated features of the thirties. Walt had been fascinated by the Mary Poppins book ever since he discovered it on Diane's bedside table. In 1944, Roy tried to buy the property from the author, P.L. Travers, in New York. She declined, and Walt persisted over the years. Finally in 1960, Travers agreed to sell him the rights.

Walt was enchanted by his choice to play the levitating nanny. "I'm in love with Julie Andrews, and I'm going to marry her," he told me devilishly. "Of course I'll have to divorce my wife first."

His passion for Disneyland continued unabated. He looked forward to the winter weekends, when he could wander the park with few people to interrupt his musings. Often he would stay overnight in his firehouse apartment, prowling through the park after the public had gone, inspecting where a coat of paint was needed, studying empty spaces that could be filled with new and tantalizing attractions.

He once said: "That's what I like about Disneyland: I can always keep 'plussing' it. I'll never be finished with it. Now when I finish a picture, I ship it off and I'm done with it. I can never bring it back and fix it, no matter how much I want to."

Walt often remarked in interviews that there would never be another Disneyland. He may have believed that in the early years of the park, but his mind soon changed. As early as 1959, he was scouting the possibility of a second park in the East. This time Roy offered no opposition. He had seen Disneyland help propel Walt Disney Productions to a new plateau of prosperity (after twenty-two years of indebtedness to the Bank of America, the company paid off the last loan in 1961). Roy had become a believer.

Buzz Price had been commissioned by Walt to study the feasibility of building a park in the eastern part of the country. The results were overwhelmingly favorable. Disneyland drew its guests from only one-quarter of the nation's population, the preponderance being from California. "To achieve the kind of penetration you get from the western side of the Mississippi, you had to be in the East," Price reported.

Walt next ordered a survey on location. Washington, D.C., and Florida seemed the likeliest places. An opportunity arose in Florida. John D. MacArthur, the insurance billionaire, owned 12,000 acres in North Palm Beach. He was joined by RCA and Disney in a venture to convert the property into a second Disneyland. The enterprise was progressing when RCA encountered a decline in business and withdrew. Walt also backed out. "Then he threw his energy into the New York World's Fair," says Price, "and used it as a proving ground for the future—the biggest R&D lab forever."

Some financial people considered Walt Disney a dreamer who devised grandiose plans, then told his brother, "Here—find the money."

In fact, Walt never entered any project without meticulous planning. The process started with Buzz Price's Economics Research Associates, which conducted more than a hundred surveys for Walt over the years. If the auguries were favorable, Walt proceeded with planning, which could take months or years. Sketches and models were prepared and carefully analyzed. Everything was mapped out before Walt would signal the go-ahead.

"Walt was cautious," observes Mike Bagnall, a Disney financial officer. "One reason he went to the New York World's Fair was to try some ideas for shows on East Coast audiences. We were 'way out here where the Indians were; most of our attendance was local or from the western part of the country. He was concerned whether his attractions would be accepted by the perhaps more sophisticated East Coast."

Another reason for participating in the World's Fair: Walt could acquire attractions for Disneyland at little or no cost. Sponsoring corporations would pay for the exhibits, then be offered the opportunity to move them intact to Disneyland following the 1964-1965 run of the fair. The corporate subsidy would help finance WED's development of new technologies, such as the Audio-Animatronics presentation of a lifelike Abraham Lincoln.

In 1960, the Disney staff contacted top corporations, offering to create attractions for the fair. If interest was expressed, Walt made his own persuasive pitch. General Motors was intrigued but decided to build its attraction in-house. Ford accepted the Disney offer, along with General Electric, the State of Illinois (for the Lincoln exhibit), and Pepsi-Cola (for the "It's a Small World" attraction, a benefit for UNICEF).

The New York World's Fair was commanded by Robert Moses, the legendary, autocratic builder of many of New York's public places. His chief aide was William E. (Joe) Potter, a retired U.S. general and onetime governor of the Panama Canal Zone.

Potter was quick to recognize the resemblance of Moses to Disney: "They despised people with reluctant or negative attitudes; they were tougher than hell; they had goals that defied problems such as the lack of money; they were both geniuses."

Moses had first suggested that Walt build an attraction similar to the Tivoli Gardens in Copenhagen, Potter recalled. Although Walt had found inspiration for Disneyland at Tivoli, he rejected the proposal.

"Walt was a pragmatist," observed Potter. "He figured it would be impossible to earn a profit with an attraction that would appear for only two years. He began to see a different goal: letting corporations pay the bill."

The Disney attractions at the World's Fair proved to be immensely popular, demonstrating to Walt that his brand of three-dimensional entertainments was equally embraced, East and West. As an afterthought to his deals with Ford and General Electric, he had asked for and received $1 million for the use of his name. He offered to apply that amount to shipping costs if the two corporations would move their exhibits to Disneyland. Ford declined, General Electric accepted, and its "Progressland" was installed in Tomorrowland, which sorely needed new attractions. "It's a Small World" and "Great Moments with Mr. Lincoln" also came to Disneyland.

• • •

Amid all the successes, something was tugging at Roy Disney's sleeve, and it wouldn't go away. In the end it would threaten the entire structure of Walt Disney Productions.

The beginnings came in late 1952, when Walt had committed himself to the planning and building of Disneyland. In the face of Roy's lukewarm approval of the venture and the banks' wariness of investing in an amusement park, Walt needed another source of financing. The solution came from Roy himself, who had advised Bill Cottrell that Walt should take some steps to provide for his family. The message was conveyed to Walt, who asked Cottrell to start the process of forming a personal services company.

Cottrell hired outside lawyers to negotiate the contract with the lawyers of Walt Disney Productions. Walt reasoned that since he had created the cartoon characters and the merchandising of them bore his name, he was entitled to a percentage of the profits from the merchandising. He also proposed to build and own the steam railroad that would circle Disneyland; after all, the train stemmed from his hobby, the Carolwood Pacific Railroad that he had built around his residence.

After lengthy and sometimes heated negotiations, an agreement was reached. Walt's company, WED, would own the railroad and would receive 10 percent of all merchandising. WED would conceive and engineer attractions for the park and would sell them to the company at cost, plus overhead. Walt would receive $153,000 in salary from Walt Disney Productions, plus a percentage of profits from the films. Roy had serious misgivings about the deal, fearing that stockholders would accuse Walt of profiteering from things he had created for the company. Still, there was no arguing with Walt once he had set a course for himself, and rather than risk a fierce and perhaps disastrous battle, Roy acquiesced.

To avoid too much public controversy, Roy decided on a potentially dangerous course: He would seek approval of the contract from the board of directors only, not the shareholders. Three of the directors, fearing they would be held liable in case of a shareholder suit, resigned. The rest of the board warily gave their approval of the contract.

Walt got what he wanted. He was able to retain control of his beloved railroad. He would have a steady inflow of revenue to finance his plans for Disneyland. After the park opened, he became intrigued with the possibility of a transportation system that would be an eye-catching exhibit for Disneyland and might have application to relieving the ever-increasing traffic on America's streets and highways. He learned of a monorail system being built by the Alweg company of Germany, went to the plant to inspect it, and decided it would be ideal for Disneyland. It opened in the park in 1959 and was extended to the Disneyland Hotel in 1961. Walt and Alweg tried to interest cities in adopting the monorail, but never succeeded. The monorail joined the railroad as part of WED's assets.

As Roy had feared, a shareholder sued the corporation over Walt's contract, charging that it should have been presented for a vote by the shareholders. The Disney lawyers saved the day. At that time, California law decreed that plaintiffs in civil suits were required to post a bond to cover the defense's legal fees in case the suit was lost. The first question posed in the courtroom was whether the shareholder was able to post the bond. He was not. Case dismissed.

Roy was greatly relieved that no other challenge was made over Walt's contract. The two brothers resumed their relationship, but there was an unspoken rift between them. Never in their thirty years as business partners had they been placed in a legal, adversarial relationship. Through WED, Walt had become almost an independent contractor with the corporation, making major decisions without necessarily consulting Roy. If Roy resented this erosion of their once-close partnership, he told no one.

Walt created Disneyland without having to seek approvals for his every move. He did not seem motivated by greed. His salary and percentages didn't appear excessive, considering that he supervised everything that was produced by the studio; production chiefs of other studios earned far more. His style of living never changed. He enjoyed the peace of mind in knowing that he was building a legacy for Lilly and for Diane and Sharon.

Most of the studio employees were unaware of the coolness between the two brothers, but it was obvious to those who worked closely with Walt and Roy. It followed that the breach between Walt's Boys and Roy's Boys increased correspondingly.

B y 1963, Roy realized he could no longer postpone the matter that had been nagging at him for years. Something had to be done about WED. As Walt Disney Productions expanded, so did the number of shareholders. Gadflies had become the bane of corporations, and Roy feared that one would rise at the next annual meeting to challenge Walt's 1953 agreement. The resulting controversy, perhaps involving lawsuits, would be harmful to the company's reputation. Now that the Disneys had committed themselves to their biggest challenge yet—a new Disneyland in Florida—they could ill afford a financial scandal.

Roy was forced to do something he dreaded: to confront Walt. It was not the best of times. Walt had been driving himself extremely hard. Besides the films and Disneyland and the television show, he was making plans for a winter resort in the California

Sierras, a model city as part of the Florida project, and a college of the arts. His old polo injury pained him constantly, and he was easily irritated.

Roy contemplated a strategy. He concluded it would be best to confront Walt not amid the pressures of the studio, but in a remote and peaceful place, such as Walt and Lilly's desert retreat at the Smoke Tree Ranch area in Palm Springs. The two couples went there for a long weekend, but the atmosphere was anything but peaceful. Roy never talked to his family about his troubles with Walt, but Edna did. She told her daughter-in-law Patty that the two brothers shouted and railed at each other for three days. Edna and Lilly cowered in another part of the house.

Ron and Diane Miller were also visiting her parents at the time. They were outdoors, and Ron remembers hearing "a lot of yelling and screaming and everything else, though I'm probably dramatizing that a little bit. Walt just made it very clear that 'Dammit, I want to be on a par with what other people are making in this industry, Roy. If you don't do that, I'm going to leave.' "

The "peace" meeting ended in dreadful accusations. Never in their lifetimes had the two brothers exchanged such harsh words.

For months they would not talk to each other. For pressing corporate matters, they sent curt, impersonal memos. Other matters were conveyed by messengers who were acceptable to both men.

"Sometimes I would talk to Roy about things that Walt didn't want to get into a confrontation about," says Royal (Mickey) Clark, an attorney for WED. "One time they were having a stockholders meeting in the studio theater, and Walt told me, 'I want you to go down and sit in.' He didn't want to go, because it was the time when he and Roy were not seeing eye-to-eye. I came back and told Walt, 'It was just a standard stockholders meeting;

everything went along fine.' He would ask me to do things like that.

"It wasn't in any sense prying or spying. Walt just wanted to have a feeling of how things were going on. He and Roy couldn't converse. In a lot of ways, it was a silly kind of situation, where two very strong men couldn't see eye-to-eye, and neither one wanted to give in to the other. They both had fantastic egos. Maybe 'ego' is the wrong word to use in characterizing Roy. He was very strong-willed."

Serving as emissary between the Disney brothers required the diplomatic skill of a Henry Kissinger.

Neal McClure, then an attorney for WED, recalls: "I tried to explain to Walt one time that even though everything [concerning WED] was proper and above board, he had to be like Caesar's wife—above suspicion. Walt blew. 'What do you mean? I haven't done a damn thing that's wrong.' I said, 'That's exactly what we want to do: We want to clean it up so you'll never be accused of it.'

"It came to my attention that Walt and Roy were rather cool to one another. I tried to intercede there, and I learned a valuable lesson: never get mixed up with family arguments. As you can see, I was more brash than wise . . .

"Even though they were cool to one another, there was no doubt in my mind that they were devoted to each other. I tried to tell Walt, 'You know, Roy is favorable toward you.' Walt replied: 'That's between Roy and me!'

"In many respects, everybody else was invited to butt out. A writer in a business journal reported, 'Things are quite informal [at Disney]; they all use first names. But Mr. [Walt] Disney made it abundantly clear that informality is not to be confused with familiarity.' "

A major matter the brothers needed to agree on was the Disney Foundation. They had established the foundation as a means of handling the hundreds of requests for charitable donations. Though Walt was at first reluctant, Roy convinced him that the best way to fund the foundation was with their own company stock. Roy adhered to the adage that charity should begin at home. Most of the foundation's bequests went to causes and institutions in the Burbank and Los Angeles area, and many benefited children—the Boy Scouts, Girl Scouts, etc. St. Joseph's Hospital, directly opposite the studio on Buena Vista Street, was a major recipient.

When CalArts became one of Walt's passions, he urged Roy to agree to a contribution from the foundation. Although Roy was sympathetic to CalArts, his natural conservatism prompted him to delay any decision. As the school neared the construction stage, Walt repeated his request.

Mike Bagnall of the treasurer's office, who oversaw foundation matters, advised Roy that the foundation had enough money that a donation to CalArts was possible. Roy directed Luther Marr to compose a memo to Walt stating that the foundation could give a million dollars to CalArts. The memo ended: "Do you agree?"

Marr, one of the designated shuttle diplomats, delivered the memo to Walt. "Did Roy say this?" Walt asked amazedly. Marr answered yes. "Roy said this?" Yes. Taking his familiar grease pencil, Walt wrote on the memo: "OK OK OK OK OK." When Marr returned the memo, Roy said, "Did Walt write this? Did Walt write this?"

The schism between the brothers sometimes reached ridiculous proportions. Walt had managed to get two of his "Boys" elected to the board of directors: Card Walker and Bill Anderson. One day Walt made a rare appearance at a board meeting, and he told the members, "I told Bill and Card to learn everything they can here, but don't spend too much time on this crap."

On one occasion, the board was considering a measure that Walt opposed. The outside directors were attending, but Walker and Anderson were needed for a quorum. They didn't appear. After an hour of waiting, Roy appointed the company attorney, Luther Marr, to hunt for them. Marr went upstairs to the offices of Walker and Anderson and was told that both were in a sweat box watching footage.

Marr opened the door of the darkened projection room and said, "Roy needs you for a quorum at the board meeting." No reply. Marr tried again in fifteen minutes. Again no reply. On the third time, Marr heard Walt's annoyed voice: "Tell 'em to go ahead without them." Finally, two hours late, Anderson and Walker appeared at the meeting and the measure was voted.

Dick Morrow, general counsel for the corporation, observes that despite the lack of direct communication between Roy and Walt, "the love between the two brothers never diminished in the slightest, and I heard that from each of them individually. People who tried to take advantage of [the situation] and tried to play off one against the other faced trouble.

"It was a general conflict between who was running the company and who was going to prevail: Walt and the creative side or Roy and the administrative side. [The brothers] just weren't on track together, although each of them recognized the genius of the other one and had great respect for it.

"It probably went back to the time when they were youngsters, when Walt had to obey Roy. I think there was a sibling thing there—I can't call it a rivalry because Roy absolutely worshipped Walt. He would do anything for him."

But now, with Walt's contract coming up for renewal, Roy decided things needed to change. Walt Disney Productions had achieved respect in the financial world; the stock was now traded on the New York Stock Exchange, having started on the Over the Counter Exchange. Security laws had changed since Walt's personal services contract had been instituted. The Disney lawyers were warned to avoid any public reference to the contract.

Lawyers for the two parties conferred at length, but they could find no common ground. Walt refused to accept Roy's terms, and Roy refused to amend them. Stalemate.

One day Walt said to Bill Cottrell: "I want you to have lunch with Roy. He wants to buy the trains and the monorail, and I don't want to sell. You'd better see what it's all about. I can't talk to him."

Cottrell, who had come to the studio because of Roy and had remained a good friend, met with Roy over lunch and learned Roy's terms. "The studio is getting big," Roy reasoned, "and there's always a chance of some disgruntled stockholder suing over WED. These things do happen, and I want to save Walt the embarrassment and the aggravation and the pressure they'll put on him if they get him in court."

It was a terrible position for a friend of both brothers, but Cottrell agreed to convey Roy's message. He told Walt: "Roy is a tough guy to negotiate with, but he has to be. He's representing the company and the stockholders. I understand his position and I understand your position."

Walt instructed Cottrell to ask Walt's own attorney, Loyd Wright Jr., and the Disney company's New York attorney, Shorty Irvine, to analyze the personal services contract. Walt said it was a personal matter, and he, not WED or the Disney company, would pay their fees.

The attorneys' decision: sell everything back to the studio— the trains, the monorail, the architectural and engineering company, and the name use. "Now they want to take back my name!"

Walt exclaimed in despair. He directed Cottrell to hire the best law-yer in Los Angeles to conduct the negotiations. Herbert Sturdy of the prestigious firm of Gibson, Dunn and Crutcher, was chosen.

The talks between the two sides began unpromisingly, none of the lawyers ceding any ground. Joining Walt's team was Loyd Wright Sr., attorney for many of the important figures in Holly-wood and the Los Angeles business world. A blustery veteran of courtroom battles, he was accustomed to making bold statements.

Roy was present during a conference concerning Walt's com-pensation. Wright became impatient that the company would not accede to the amount he proposed. Finally Wright blurted, "Well, it looks as though I'll have to take my client to an agent and have him negotiate the terms." The implication was that Walt would sign up with a high-powered agency that might take Walt to an-other studio.

"That was the first time I witnessed Roy explode in anger," Cottrell remembered. "He was angry with Loyd, Mickey Clark, and myself for bringing him some bad news. Roy said it was a conspiracy; I never had any idea that Roy would say anything like that. Anybody around Walt knew that he wasn't going to go through some agent.

"Roy was so mad that Loyd would have the audacity to sug-gest that he was going to take his brother and get an agent. This was pouring gasoline on the fire. The conversation ended very quickly."

When Cottrell reported about the meeting, Walt told him, "I don't want to quarrel about this thing anymore. Let Loyd Jr. han-dle the negotiation; he's calmer than the old man. There's a clause in there that I can make one picture off the lot with any other stu-dio. If they don't want that, let them take it out. Let's get it settled."

On a late afternoon, Roy returned to his office from a meeting. The negotiations over Walt's contract were being conducted in the conference room next door to Roy's office. He could hear the raised voices and sense the undercurrent of anger. It became obvious that the studio had taken an intransigent attitude, conceding nothing. Roy strode into the conference room and the lawyers fell into a respectful silence. Bill Cottrell recalled what Roy said to his own negotiators: "Let me say a few words. You seem to forget how important Walt Disney has been to you and your lives. None of us would be here in these offices if it hadn't been for Walt. All your jobs, all the benefits you have, all came from Walt and his contributions. He deserves better treatment than what's being shown here."

The tenor of the negotiations immediately changed, and an agreement was reached. Walt would get a ten-year extension on ownership of the trains and monorail, and his royalty contract would remain intact. The studio would buy WED, with its architectural and engineering departments (WED would later become Walt Disney Imagineering). Walt's company became Retlaw (backward spelling of his name).

The end of the brotherly feud became part of the Disney lore. Walt appeared in Roy's office bearing a birthday present, an Indian pipe of peace. Both laughed and reminisced. Later that day, Walt sent a letter to his brother:

> It was wonderful to smoke the pipe of peace with you
> again—the clouds that rise are very beautiful.
>   I think, between us over the years, we have
> accomplished something—there was a time when we
> couldn't borrow a thousand dollars and now I understand
> we owe twenty-four million!
>   But in all sincerity, Happy Birthday and many more—
> and—
> I love you.

TWENTY-FIVE

✧

"I remember spending the weekends at my grandparents' house," Susan Disney Loughman reminisced. "It was always great fun, it was an adventure. They had a great backyard with all kinds of toys. There was a sloping hill, and we would ride down it in big barrels. The backyard was like a wonderland; there were steps, a wishing well, a potting shed that was mysterious and scary and full of spiders but somehow attractive to kids. Grandpa loved to sit on the back porch and watch us play."

These were the times that Roy Disney liked best, when he could leave the myriad concerns at the studio, loosen his tie, and enjoy watching his grandchildren. All four retain warm memories of their visits to Edna and Roy's house.

"We were always excited to see our grandparents," says Tim Disney, "because they obviously valued seeing us. We always looked forward to it. My earliest memories were when we lived in Glendale, and they would come by for Saturday afternoon. It was always a festive atmosphere.

"I used to stay with them when my parents were out of town. It was a very close relationship. My grandfather was very generous with his time with us, it seems to me in retrospect. He used to walk us down to the five-and-dime down the road and buy us something. I recall that he always had a roll of cash; he paid for everything in cash. As the product of an older generation, he didn't believe in credit cards.

"Now I realize that he and my grandmother were a link to a previous time. My father was born when she was forty, so the space between the generations was quite large."

"I always thought my grandparents were so funny because they were so proper," says Susan. "There was always a tablecloth on the kitchen table, and my grandmother would always set out her beautiful china. There were always berries or melon, and a toaster would be on the table."

Roy had mellowed from the time he brought the very young and unmanageable Roy Patrick and Susan home to their parents on a Saturday morning. Susan observes: "I think Grandpa would have let us do anything. We were all a little afraid of Grandma; we knew she meant business. If she gave us a stern word, we obeyed."

Tim adds: "I do not remember my grandfather disciplining me in any manner. He was always a nice old man, kind to us, boxes at Christmas, and that sort of thing. We saw Grandma more, because he was at work. She was a pretty stern person.

"She was the kind of woman who was so neat and organized and in control of everything that was going on in her household that she actually put white carpet in her kitchen. I spilled grape juice on the white carpet soon after she'd had it installed. She was very angry about that. But I was an accident-prone child, so I incurred her wrath more than my brothers and sister."

A Disney Christmas was marked by the huge box from Walt, full of toys and other merchandise individually wrapped by his secretaries.

"I remember on Christmas morning, after we had Santa Claus, Roy and Edna would show up," says Susan. "We ran outside, and they would open the trunk of their car. It was joyous to see the presents in there. We all would carry them inside, and it was just like a second Christmas."

One of the delights of Roy's life was to take his grandchildren to Disneyland.

"He loved to watch us have fun; that was *his* fun," remarks Roy Patrick. "He was partial to Adventureland, the western end of the town; those were his roots, of course. I think he was more comfortable in that portion of the park than any other section. He also loved toys; he was fascinated by the Jet Pack [the flier propelled by jets attached to his back].

"He took us to WED to see some of the developing rides. I remember walking through Pirates of the Caribbean, which was fascinating. It was originally planned as a walk-through, but it played better as a ride-through. He also took us on the set of *Mary Poppins* when they were preparing the key sequence of flying around the room. He loved that stuff."

Susan recalls a special treat: "He went along with my sister and me on the Matterhorn and encouraged us to scream our lungs out. He loved to hear us screaming."

Abby has her own special memory of a visit with her grandparents to Disneyland: "They always parked the big gold Cadillac in the employees' parking lot. There was a little cafeteria outside for the employees. I looked over and saw Mickey having a cup of coffee with Snow White! His head was on the table and he was smoking a big cigar! It was a bizarre way for a child to perceive Mickey. They had this one Mickey who was very short and had a deep voice, though of course he never talked when he was in character.

"He came over to my grandmother and gave her a big hug. 'Edna! Edna! Glad to see ya!' he said in this deep voice. That's how I remember Mickey Mouse; he's emblazoned on my brain that way."

The children of Roy Edward and Patty have only hazy memories of their famous greatuncle. They were growing up at a time when Walt was totally immersed in a number of groundbreaking projects, and he rarely socialized with his relatives or anyone.

In retrospect, Abby offers an analogy out of the Disney lore: "I watch *Pinocchio* over and over again with my kids, and being an English major, maybe I read too much in it. But I see *Pinocchio* as the perfect parable of Walt and Roy. Jiminy Cricket speaks exactly as I remember Grandpa speaking; he always had this Midwestern, middle-America way of speaking—'Gee whillikers' and all that. Jiminy is always letting Pinocchio go off into his creative impulses and then pulling him back at the last minute and getting him on the right course again, then letting him run wild again and pulling him back. I'd love to know if the animators had Roy in mind when they drew Jiminy." (Ward Kimball, who designed Jiminy and served as supervising animator, says no.)

At the end of 1963, Roy Disney reached the age of seventy. Most of the other pioneering founders of movie studios had died or been deposed. Roy had sometimes spoken of retiring to enjoy his grandchildren and take pleasure trips with Edna. But he found himself busier than at any time in the forty years of the

Disney company. He faced the major challenge of financing the Florida project and helping Walt fulfill his twin obsessions, the city of tomorrow and the college of the arts.

Roy worried about his brother. Walt seemed to be driving himself harder than ever before. He was easily irritated and short-tempered; he could be brusque with associates. His trademark hacking cough seemed more prevalent. Yet despite his periodic resolves, he continued smoking cigarettes.

While he never questioned Walt about his finances, Roy worried about that, too. He knew that Walt never concerned himself with his bank account, and he knew nothing about Walt's investments. One day Roy asked Walt's secretary, Dolores Scott: "How are his finances? Don't let him get involved in some crazy scheme. Let me know if there's something that doesn't seem right."

Both Disneys maintained their support of Republican politics. The strike had helped make them resolutely anti-Communist, and Walt even made an out-of-character appearance as a friendly witness before the House Un-American Activities Committee in 1947.

Walt and Roy supported Richard Nixon and other Red-hunters of the 1950s with campaign donations. Roy continued to contribute to Republican candidates, often sending shares of Disney stock that the campaign could sell. In 1968 he wrote to his old friend, Senator George Murphy, telling of his "very substantial contribution" through Nixon's fundraiser, Henry Salvatori. Roy promised that he would also donate $5,000 worth of Disney stock to the fund for Republican candidates.

In 1971, Roy agreed to donate $5,000 worth of stock to buy a table for the "Salute to the President" (Nixon) dinner at the Beverly Wilshire Hotel. In a memo to his secretary, Madeleine Wheeler, Roy added: "I forget how many the table seats, but if it's a ten table, I will have to find four other Republican suckers and their wives . . . I will pay for the table so it will be gratis and let them off the hook, but they can make some donation on their own."

Many of Roy's onetime associates remark on his paternalistic nature. He was concerned about his employees and offered them job security, health care, pleasant working conditions, adequate pensions. Many of them remained at the studio for forty years or more.

Even though Lilly and Edna had worked for the studio in the 1920s, Walt and Roy instituted the rule as the studio expanded that husbands and wives could not be employed. That was re-pealed after so many artists married women from the ink-and-paint department. The brothers also hired a number of old friends from Kansas City, notably Walt Pfeiffer, Walt's boyhood vaude-ville partner, who became manager of the story department.

Following Hollywood tradition, relatives became part of the studio personnel. Roy Edward produced nature films for the tele-vision show. Walt was grooming his son-in-law, Ron Miller, to produce movies. Bill Cottrell, Walt's brother-in-law, helped guide WED and Retlaw.

Roy encouraged hiring the sons and daughters of longtime Disney employees and associates, such as Ub Iwerks' two sons and Mike Bagnall, son of board member George Bagnall. Roy once told me his philosophy: "I figure if the parent turned out well for us, the children would too."

Roy's paternalism did not extend to overpaying the employ-ees. While many of the animators and other artists received sal-aries above the average for cartoon studios, those in other categories generally received less than the film industry norm.

Roy saw no reason to change an attitude that dated back to the days of the Disney Brothers Studio. He and Walt had sacrificed their own paychecks during times of financial straits. Even in periods of prosperity, the brothers took salaries that fulfilled their needs, preferring to invest the rest in the company. He expected his employees to go along with that sense of frugality.

In the 1960s, Roy's staff experienced a number of resignations. He was distressed by losing men he had relied on. The reason for the departures was evident: better pay at other studios. Roy pondered what to do, and he decided to lower the number of years when employees could be vested for pensions. The move helped convince many of his associates to stay with the company.

Despite their conservatism, the Disney brothers were not noticeably antilabor. Virtually all of the studio's job classifications were unionized, and the Disneys made no apparent effort to deter the guilds and unions.

"Roy was a compassionate person," comments Bob Foster, a company attorney. "He had a genuine interest in the people, the employees, the staff. Those that he was closest to, of course, were his accountants, his attorneys, the administrative staff. Roy would inquire of your family, and you were free to discuss family affairs with him.

"In labor negotiations, Roy would say, 'Those poor guys, struggling down there, trying to put their kids through school. Can we do something to help them along?' You could see his compassion for these guys who were out there sweating."

Roy often had well-known guests at his lunch table. Casey Stengel, the baseball legend who was operating a bank in nearby Glendale, was a frequent visitor, and Foster noted that Roy often made a point of introducing Stengel and other notables to employees, knowing they would be pleased.

Even though Disney was rarely in direct competition with other studios, Roy felt obliged to keep abreast of their product. Screenings of current films were held every Tuesday afternoon at five in the Disney studio theater, and Roy attended regularly with Edna. They sat in the back row, holding hands like teenagers.

By the 1960s, Roy and Edna had become veteran travelers, having made annual flights to the major capitals of free Europe as well as trips to Asia. Edna became an expert packer, though on one occasion she slipped. Roy telephoned his secretary from Florida: "Edna forgot to pack her girdle, and she can't get along without it. Would you please see if someone from the studio is coming down here and can bring it? You'll find it in the top right-hand drawer of her dresser." Madeleine Wheeler located the girdle, and a Disney executive carried it in his attaché case and delivered it to the owner.

Edna went everywhere with Roy. Harry Archinal remembers a trip to Japan that included trips to Tokyo, Yokohama, Osaka, and Sapporo: "We had one stormy flight to Hokaido. We couldn't see a thing, never saw the ground. Roy and Edna remained calm throughout."

In March of 1961, the Disneys embarked on a three-month trip around the world, accompanied by Edna's sister Jenny and her husband, Henry Vogel. The itinerary: Tokyo, Osaka, Hong Kong, Bangkok, New Delhi, Cairo, Athens, Istanbul, Rome, Paris, Milan, Verona, Copenhagen, Stockholm, Oslo, London, Edinburgh. Edna was seventy-one, Roy was sixty-seven, but they behaved like youthful tourists.

Roy wrote notes at every stop, carefully making entries in a 3-by-5-inch notebook with the same tiny script he used in his ledger entries for the Disney Brothers Studio. He recorded his business meetings at each stop. He later reported to TWA: "I had previously bought and paid for a round trip from Paris to Milan. Then I would be in step with the world-trip tickets. But because of an airport strike, we had to go by train to Milan. So we are entitled to a refund from TWA for Paris to Milan for two people."

Roy had always deducted Edna's traveling expenses from his income tax, meticulously separating what pertained to his business affairs and what was essentially pleasure. He instructed his associates to file expense accounts for their wives' travel on the same basis. Inevitably, his practice came to the attention of the feds.

In 1966, the Internal Revenue Service ordered Roy and Edna to pay $4,245 because of deductions he had made for Edna's traveling expenses in his tax returns of 1962 and 1963. Despite the advice that you can't fight city hall, much less the IRS, Roy challenged the claim in a lawsuit. In a pretrial statement, his lawyers pointed out that Walt Disney Productions made $115 million in gross sales from a business of providing family entertainment. Thirty-five percent of that amount came from foreign sales. The statement reported merchandising representatives in twenty-six countries dealt in 5,000 items, forty-two magazines in twenty-three countries in twenty languages, plus 16mm film distribution, musical records, and sheet music.

Both Roy and Edna testified in federal court. Roy declared it was a company policy that wives travel with husbands in order to present a wholesome image, that the husband could entertain and be entertained without any embarrassment. Having a wife along would add to the company's image in interviews and other publicity.

Edna took the stand and indignantly countered the government's contention that she accompanied her husband for pleasure alone. She testified of handling the details for receptions, dinners, screenings, and other social events and of making visitors at ease and getting to know the wives and families of Roy's associates and clients. She also declared that she took care of her husband's personal matters. "Who else would do his socks?" she demanded.

U.S. District Judge Thurmond Clarke ruled that Edna's accompanying her husband on the world trip and two journeys to Europe "served to enhance the firm's image abroad." He said her travel expenses were a proper tax deduction. The IRS appealed to the 9th Circuit Court of Appeals, which upheld the decision unanimously.

Roy won one, lost one. He had sued to allow deduction for the mechanical horse he had bought in England and installed in his basement gym. The judge denied his claim, stating, "It was not specifically recommended by the taxpayer's physician."

Both Walt and Roy had lively senses of humor, a gift from their mother. When I was researching my first *Art of Animation* book, I was struck by the brilliance and dedication of the principal animators, the famed Nine Old Men. While lunching with Walt in the Coral Room one day, I expressed my amazement at how they could spend hour after hour at their desks, their pencils bringing movement to a variety of characters. "It's almost like having a mistress," I burbled. "Yeah," Walt muttered with a wry smile, "that's why we call it 'this fucking business.' "

Buzz Price recalls when he made the presentation of his analysis of the Palm Beach proposal for a Florida Disneyland. The big brass of RCA and NBC were present, along with Walt and Roy. After Price had rehearsed his charts and conclusions, Roy commented: "Buzz, your presentation will be much more impressive if you will zip up your fly."

TWENTY-SIX

C·an management produce Disney product after Disney?"
Walt mused to a magazine writer. "That's the $64 question.
As well as I can, I'm untying the apron strings."

Indeed he seemed to be freeing himself from other duties so
he could concentrate on EPCOT and CalArts.

Those two visionary projects absorbed Walt's thinking in his
early sixties. A wealth of other matters occupied his days—the
movies, the animated features, the television show, the unending
improvement of Disneyland, and the planning of the Florida Disneyland. But those were things he had done before. His passion
for innovation led him to areas not concerned with entertainment.
He looked to the future, envisioning a city that would be free
from modern urban woes and a college that would nurture new
generations of artists.

Walt would not live long enough to realize either dream. That
would be left to his brother.

• • •

The origins of EPCOT cannot be easily traced. Perhaps it was an outgrowth of his lifelong search for better ways of doing things: adding sound, color, full-length stories, and dimension (via the multiplane camera) to animation; revolutionizing outdoor entertainment. He had planned the Burbank studio down to the contour of the chairs. Disneyland itself had been hailed by noted architects as the ideal city—clean, wholesome, carefree. Except that nobody lived there.

Walt had originally been opposed to a second Disneyland. He hated to repeat himself, and he wanted the park in Anaheim to be unique. But as his ideas for EPCOT blossomed, he saw value in a Florida park.

"That will be the weenie for EPCOT," he reasoned. "Weenie" was a familiar term at the studio; it was the lure that would encourage movement to different attractions—e.g., Sleeping Beauty Castle was the weenie that drew Disneyland visitors down Main Street.

Roy did not completely share his brother's vision of an ideal city. "Let's build the park first so we can get some income flowing into the company," he argued. "You can build EPCOT later." He was able to convince Walt.

Although he plunged into planning what he called Disneyland East, Walt remained obsessed with EPCOT. Marvin Davis, one of his planners at WED, recalled: "It was his philosophy not to build a city that would solve all the urban problems all over the world, but to give a chance to American industry to experiment and show to the world just how the problems of traffic and housing could be solved . . .

"It would be a place not only for testing physical things, but educational developments and all forms of communication. He was greatly interested in solving the young adult problem that faces everybody. If we can successfully show to the world an area in which teenagers are properly controlled and given an opportunity to express themselves and are kept occupied—'this is something we really want to work on,' he said.

"So the amusement park was really a secondary thing. He was interested in solving the urban problem. It's a big scope, but that's exactly what he was thinking."

Davis said that Walt would bring him plans written on a paper napkin: "It seemed that over breakfast he got his most creative ideas and would scribble them down and bring them in. I would use them, and I tried to grab the napkin after he showed it to me, but he would wad it up and throw it in the wastebasket, and I would [later] dig it out. For some reason he had a fetish about anybody grabbing his scribbles."

CalArts had a longer history. It dated back to the 1930s, when Walt sought to improve his artists' skills by sending them to the Chouinard Art Institute near downtown Los Angeles. Nelbert M. Chouinard, who founded the school in 1921, didn't charge for the classes when Walt and Roy couldn't afford them. When the school fell into bad times in the late 1950s, Walt offered to help Mrs. Chouinard. Buzz Price and his Economic Research Associates surveyed the situation and discovered someone had embezzled $75,000. A Disney attorney, Luther Marr, straightened out the institute's tangled finances and helped establish a more sound organization.

The Los Angeles Conservatory of Music, which had been a local institution since 1883, also had been victimized by an embezzler and was struggling to survive. Walt heard of the school's plight and met with its major supporter, Lulu May Von Hagen, wife of a wealthy lawyer and businessman. She proposed combining the Conservatory and Chouinard and adding other disciplines to form an all-inclusive college of the arts in the manner of the California Institute of Technology, which encompassed the sciences. Walt embraced the idea.

Walt had entered an extraordinary phase in his career. He had committed himself to two unique ventures: a city of the future and a college of the arts. Besides his other duties, he was faced with planning and building a park far grander than Disneyland, one that might cost $100 million. Now he gathered his formidable powers of persuasion to sell others on his visions.

Edna Disney told Richard Hubler in 1968: "Walt had a way of telling you about what he wanted to do and explaining it to you in a way that you fell right in line with him. You would go right along with him; you couldn't help it. He just had a way of telling it to you that way.

"Walt had very expressive brown eyes, and he used his eyes a lot. He'd use his eyes and his hands and tell you all about everything and explain it all to you. That was his way of making you believe it all—and he was usually right."

Walt was now firmly decided on Florida as the location for Disneyland East and EPCOT. He called on Buzz Price to help find the best area in Florida. Miami was too far south, Price decided. He determined that 40 percent of the tourists went to southern Florida, 40 percent to the central part of the state, and 20 percent further north. Those who went south, of course, had to pass through the central portion.

"It was clear that we needed to be in the center of the state," Price says. "Then we used the logic that we developed on Disneyland that we didn't want to be on the ocean and compete with the beach. We figured that the freeways that were coming from east and west were crisscrossing in Orlando."

The first white settlers founded the town in 1824, naming it Jernigan. The name was later changed to honor Orlando Reeves, a settler who was killed in an Indian fight. By 1875 it had grown enough to be incorporated with the name Orlando. By a curious coincidence, the town was located in Orange County, as was Anaheim on the other side of the continent. Orange orchards provided the initial industry, later came manufacturing.

"As for tourists," wrote Edward L. Prizer of the *Orlando Magazine*, "we caught a few who couldn't afford Miami. You saw them sitting in rocking chairs outside the little motels along 17-92 in Winter Park or the South Orange Blossom Trail, but they were, at best a curiosity."

Orlando enjoyed a boom in the mid-fifties as the space program at nearby Cape Canaveral heated up. In 1956, the Martin Company opened a plant that employed thousands of local citizens. A few years later, Orlando was struck by triple blows: cutbacks in the space program caused wholesale layoffs at Martin; the Cuban missile crisis dealt a devastating blow to tourism; a freeze ruined the citrus crop. Despite boosterism by the chamber of commerce, the Orlando economy languished. An ideal situation for a company to amass huge acreage of land at reasonable rates.

When Price suggested that a 5,000-acre site would be sufficient, Walt exploded. He wanted more, to protect this park from the neon jungle that had grown up around Disneyland. Price suggested four sites that ranged from 10,000 acres to 100,000 acres. He recommended one in Orlando, but a large part of it was in escrow. When it fell out of escrow, Walt said, "Let's go for it."

Thus began a two-year cloak-and-dagger saga of deception, false identities, and dummy corporations.

•　　•　　•

Bob Foster was the self-confessed "Disney's official clod-kicker" of the law department. His quiet, homespun manner made him the ideal candidate as the decoy to negotiate for millions of dollars of real estate owned by Florida citizens.

He was no backwoods hick. Foster had graduated from Loyola Law School in Los Angeles with Dick Morrow and Luther Marr, Disney attorneys who had recommended his hiring in 1956. One evening Roy was surprised to find Foster working in the Disney law library. The lawyer explained that he was preparing for a law class he was teaching at Los Angeles City College. Roy, the high school graduate, was impressed, and he sometimes bragged, "I've got a lawyer on my staff who teaches in college."

Foster quickly understood the workings of the Disney studio. "I learned early that Walt didn't particularly like attorneys," he said. "The reason was that attorneys essentially are negative people, cautioning their clients about what not to do. Walt didn't like being told what not to do. I learned not to avoid him, but not to bother him. The important thing with Walt was to state things positively."

His relationship with Roy was easier. Foster began at the studio by negotiating the terminations of contracts with outside lessees at Disneyland. By 1963 he had become counsel at Disneyland. That was the year he was summoned to Roy Disney's office. Roy, surrounded by top executives, made his proposal.

At the beginning of his manuscript, *The Founding of a Kingdom*, Foster writes: "What does a fellow do, how does he react, and what does he say when called to his boss's office and asked if he will go into the hinterlands and in a quiet manner, surreptitiously buy a piece of real estate, somewhere between 5,000 and 10,000 acres?"

What he did was say yes. The job turned out to be even bigger than anyone expected.

With his customary caution, Roy laid down one restriction: whatever was acquired had to be justified as "a sound real estate investment for a public company." Roy knew that many bridges had to be crossed—financial, legal, and legislative—before Walt's dream could be realized. If one element fell out, the entire project could collapse. Roy wanted to be able to tell the stockholders that the real estate could be sold at no great loss to the company.

Foster began by studying geodesic maps, locating large parcels of land, whether for sale or not, reviewing Orlando, Ocala, and Lakeland newspapers for real estate ads. In January 1964, a group of top Disney executives visited Florida to inspect available properties; Walt was asked to stay home for fear he would be recognized. The search was narrowed down.

In April 1964, Foster decided it was time to start operating in Florida. He needed a contact, preferably a lawyer, who could aid in searches and negotiations. Disney's New York attorney, "Shorty" Irvine, recommended a Miami attorney, Paul Helliwell. He had been a colonel in the wartime O.S.S. under William (Wild Bill) Donovan, co-founder of Irvine's law firm.

Foster visited the New York World's Fair the day before its opening on April 14, 1964, and made a point to be seen by as many Disney people as possible. On the way back to Manhattan in a limo, Walt winked to Foster. Both understood but didn't want others in the car to know that Foster was leaving the next day on a surreptitious journey to Florida.

The plane reservation bore his first two names, Robert Price, which would be his nom de guerre in the coming year in Florida. Meeting with Helliwell in his Miami office, Foster revealed his true name but not his employer. After determining that Helliwell had no conflict of interest and had a staff capable of handling a complex matter, Foster explained that his client was a large corporate client, listed on the New York Stock

Exchange, seeking as much as 10,000 acres in the middle of the state. The parcel would be large enough for recreational use and for land use as well.

Helliwell recommended a Miami real estate dealer with state-wide experience, Roy Hawkins, to help in the search. At first Foster used Bob Price with Hawkins but later he revealed his true name. Hawkins and Price-Foster spent a month hunting down and inspecting possible locations in central Florida.

In late May, Bob Foster reported back to Walt, Roy, and the seven-man committee for the Florida project. Pointing to a large map, Foster outlined three possibilities: in the north between De Land and Daytona Beach; near Osceola City; in Orange County near Orlando. His presentation obviously favored De Land-Daytona Beach.

"I felt a certain uneasiness," Foster recalls. "Then came the unequivocal signal of Walt's disapproval. He always telegraphed his punches of disapproval, no words, no gestures, just an arched eyebrow . . . if that left eyebrow went up, you were in trouble. I was in trouble. Walt's only comment was, 'What the hell are you doing away up there?' "

Foster didn't know that the committee had decided that locations north of Orlando would be too chilly in the winter to entice visitors and to sustain the subtropical landscaping of the park. The most promising properties were two near Orlando, but one had title problems and the other might or might not have been for sale. Foster needed answers, and he felt more comfortable discussing matters with Roy—"he was a good listener, was quick to get the relevant issues, and asked probing questions."

Roy decided to take a closer view of the Florida proceedings, and he joined Foster and Donn Tatum in Miami. He attempted to remain incognito. He wrote to his good friend, Ellis Arnall, former governor of Georgia and associated with Roy in the Society of Independent Motion Picture Producers:

> ... Behind dark glasses and a false beard, and posing as Mr. Roy O. Davis of New York, I embarrassingly ran into Elliott [Levitas, a congressman and Arnall's law partner] in Miami the other night, but it turned out all right and we had a nice dinner together ... The matter that took me to Miami is progressing favorably. Other than that, I am not talking ...

Roy was acquainted with Paul Helliwell, but not Roy Hawkins. Introduced as Davis, Roy soon reverted to Disney and formed an immediate rapport with Hawkins, both being veterans of the First World War. Roy also discovered he had worked for Hawkins' uncle in the Kansas City bank. During the Miami meetings, Roy gave the go-ahead to acquire 12,400 acres owned by three Orlando home builders—two of them cousins named Demetree—who bought the property in 1961 for less than $100 an acre. It had been optioned by the Chiang Kai-shek family of Taiwan, but the option had been dropped.

The owners asked for $165 per acre. After lengthy negotiations, both sides agreed to an option to the purchase of the Demetree property at $145 per acre. Some of the "bean counters" in Burbank criticized the deal, but Roy sent hearty congratulations, raising the morale of Foster, Hawkins, and Helliwell.

The Demetree property had one potential snag: The mineral rights were owned by Tufts University. The owners had struggled to obtain the rights without success. After a thorough investigation and lengthy negotiations with Tufts officials in Boston, the mineral rights were obtained.

The acquisition team continued the hunt for land, tying down two important properties: 1,250 acres on the north side of Bay Lake, owned by an Orlando investment group; a cattle ranch of approximately 8,500 acres in Osceola County owned by a member of a pioneering Orlando family, Irlo Bronson.

The three major properties had been assured by August 1964, then came the massive problem of acquiring the smaller ones, or outages. Many of them had been bought by individuals during a 1913 subdivision, the ownership passing down to relatives who lived all over the country. As each piece of property was acquired, it was entered on a huge map in a conference room at the Burbank studio.

Roy Disney remained in close communication with the acquisition team, conveying the information to Walt by phone or memo. In June 1966, as the campaign was drawing to a close, Roy sent a lengthy memo to Walt:

> . . . The negotiations on the Eassey property have not broken off, but they have reached the point where it looks to me as though this could be a serious holdup and we might really have to pay through the nose to get it. . . .
>
> I wasn't trying to go around you. I was trying to fortify Bob Foster and Roy Hawkins with a stronger approach or argument and was talking from the angle of what could be our logical alternative and how difficult and costly the alternatives might be . . .
>
> The Eassey property is forty acres, located within the first mile off Hiway 530. If working this "out" (in case we don't buy it) proved to be very troublesome and therefore expensive, we might be better to buy it now, even at what seems to be a ridiculous price, but what might be cheap in the long run . . .

Roy considered the asking price of $6,500 an acre excessive, but concluded that the company might pay it to "remove this nuisance." He suggested an alternative of moving "the front of the park back to the Orange County line, which is one mile from Highway 530, and to keep that one mile as an area of beauty and completely screen the forty acres so it wouldn't bother us." He recommended sending Donn Tatum to Orlando to help in the negotiation.

Though the purchase of large land holdings caused widespread speculation in Orlando, the identity of the buyer remained unknown. Ford, Hughes Aircraft, Martin-Marietta, and Disney were among those suspected. Even though some of the smaller properties had not been assured, Walt insisted on viewing the property. He was told that if he was recognized by anyone, he had to deny he was Walt Disney; otherwise his presence would hit the papers and balloon the prices of acquisitions still in negotiation.

On his first night in Orlando, Walt was dining with some associates in a hotel dining room. The waitress kept eyeing him. Finally she approached and commented, "You know, you look like Walt Disney." He replied indignantly, "What do you mean, I 'look like Walt Disney'? I am Walt Disney!" He pulled out his driver's license for proof. Fortunately, his identity didn't reach the newspaper.

In the end it was Walt who blew the cover. By mid-September 1965, all but a handful of the land purchases had been assured, and they had mounted to 27,000 acres. Bob Foster was still masquerading as Bob Price and trying to keep a low profile in Orlando. Reporters for the *Orlando Sentinel* hunted for possible clues. Because Bob Price sometimes flew from Orlando to St.

Louis (en route to see his mother in Kansas), one writer concluded the buyer was McDonnell-Douglas, which was headquartered in St. Louis. Another failed to find a Bob Price listed as a Disneyland employee and tried other big corporations. When he found a Bob Price at General Dynamics in San Diego, he was convinced he had located the mystery corporation.

In October, a group of reporters from southeastern newspapers visited the Disney studio, one of several visits by journalists on the occasion of Disneyland's tenth anniversary. Emily Bavar, Sunday magazine editor of the *Orlando Sentinel*, joined a round-table lunch with Walt Disney. She asked him if Disney was the company buying big land holdings in Orange and Osceola Counties.

"Why would we want to locate away out in that area?" he replied.

Bavar considered his avoidance of an outright denial to indicate confirmation. She telegraphed a dispatch to the *Sentinel*, which downplayed the story with a small headline: "Disney Hedges Big Question—Mystery Site Left up in Air." After consulting with Bavar, the editors changed their tack four days later. The *Sentinel* ran a 72-point banner on October 24: "WE SAY OUR 'MYSTERY' INDUSTRY IS DISNEY."

For Roy and Walt, the *Sentinel* revelation was more of a relief than a shock. The major properties and many of the lesser ones had been assured, and the holdouts could be dealt with. Now Disney could address the next big step: convincing the politicians to vote for the company's bold plan.

The office holders reacted favorably—some of them ecstatically—to the Disney offer to infuse millions into Florida's economy. The governor, Haydon Burns, was running for reelection, and he embraced the plan as a campaign bonanza. He telephoned Walt with his idea of a parade through Orlando that would rival New York's ticker-tape spectacles. Walt tried to explain that such an event was not the Disney way. He became so annoyed with calls that he told Bob Foster to try to call the governor off.

The Disneys did agree to a press conference at the Cherry Plaza Hotel in Orlando on November 15. That morning they saw for the first time the entire 27,000 acres that the company's $5 million had bought. They flew around the periphery of the property, an assemblage of swamps, tundra, and murky lakes. To Walt, it was a heartening view. At last he had unlimited land to pursue his goals, which had become dominated by his vision of EPCOT.

The press conference was jam-packed with media and politicians eager to be associated with the advent of the Disneys. Governor Burns basked in glory, praising Walt as "the man of the decade" and Roy as "the financial wizard of Walt Disney Productions." Walt explained the company's plans for central Florida and put special emphasis on his interest in EPCOT.

He told the gathering that he and Roy had been in business for forty-two years and remarked, "He's my big brother, and he's the one that when I was a little fellow I used to go to with some of my wild ideas, and he'd either straighten me out and put me on the right path—or if he didn't agree with me, I'd work with it for years until I got him to agree with me . . . In this project, though, I'd just like to say that I didn't have to work very hard on him. He was with me from the start. Now whether that's good or bad, I don't know."

On the flight back to California, chief counsel Dick Morrow engaged Walt in a conversation about legislation for the Florida project. The Donovan, Leisure law firm in New York proposed that the best solution for the local regulations needed to operate the park and its surroundings would be a municipality. Morrow had been persuaded, and he told his reasons.

Walt was strongly opposed. His good friend, Jules Stein, head of MCA, had advised him against a municipality, citing his experience with Universal City. Carl Laemmle had founded the Universal Studio as a 230-acre municipality within the city of Los Angeles, just northwest of Hollywood. When MCA bought Universal in 1952, Stein said he inherited the headache of dealing with city and county politicians, particularly over the company's popular Universal Tour.

"Jules Stein said it was a bad idea, and that's good enough for me," Walt insisted. Morrow pressed his argument, and the tone of the exchange rose to alarming heights. The conversation ended with no result, and the question of a municipality was shelved for a later time.

The Florida Project, as well as Disneyland, *Mary Poppins*, and other successes aroused interest recorded in financial journals about the innovation and prosperity of the Disney company. In its May 1966 issue, *Fortune* featured an extensive article by John McDonald about the Disney phenomenon. Walt was spotlighted, but because the story dealt with intricate financial matters, Roy also played an important role.

"Walt Disney is one of the few executives around who are actually treated as assets, i.e., in the corporation's report to stockholders," the article stated. "Any elaboration of his role has to distinguish between the two functions: He is a man who has long worked for the company in several executive capacities; he is also its most important piece of property."

The intricate relationship between Walt Disney Productions

and Retlaw was reported, including Retlaw's 10 percent investment in twenty-eight movies. The 1953 agreement allowed him to invest in 25 percent, but he declined. Roy explained: "It's money. Ten percent costs Walt about $1,250,000 a year." A hit like *Mary Poppins* could bring him more than a million dollars in profit. This in addition to Walt's personal salary of $182,000 a year, plus $2,500 a week in deferred salary.

The article traced the up-and-down history of the Disney company and analyzed the relationship of the brothers. It quoted a member of a group of Florida businessmen and politicians who had come to the studio to hear about the Disneys' plans for the development in their state:

"I think these two men offer as effective a combination as I've ever worked with. It is more effective than any I've seen in Wall Street, Miami, anywhere. Roy is the hard shell, the tightfisted, conservative businessman, the financier. He'll keep asking you when you are going to be specific.

"And Walt is the best politician I ever saw. The night we said good-bye, he came in and said, 'Let me show you what we can do with a mallard duck.' He had some plastic ones . . . He said, 'How do you think 500 of these would look on the lake near Kissimmee?' He described how he would put lights on the lake so it would look pretty at night. Then, later, when Walt was not there, Roy was back in business, asking, 'What about those tax liabilities?' Walt keeps giving you confidence that you are going to be there, and Roy keeps sharpening the pencil."

In his interviews with McDonald, Roy maintained his usual modesty about his contributions to the company, saying about Walt: "I just try to keep up with him—and make it pay. I'm afraid if I'd been running this place we would have stopped several times en route because of the problems. Walt has the stick-to-itiveness."

TWENTY-SEVEN

ᴄᴘ

On July 1, 1966, Roy Disney dictated a newsy letter to a banker friend who was touring Europe with his wife and daughter:

> Walt left yesterday for a two-week cruise on a
> chartered yacht. It is big enough to handle the entire
> family of daughters and grandchildren. They went aboard
> at Vancouver, B.C., and will cruise through the island
> waterways along the Canadian coast. It sounds like a very
> enjoyable trip. It must be a pretty good-sized yacht. It has
> a crew of eight, and I understand Bobby Kennedy has
> chartered it for his family the week following Walt's return.
> I do hope Walt has a relaxing time, though I understand
> he took along a big pile of scripts and other things to read.
> But then one has to have something to turn to and get
> away from the grandchildren for a little bit.

We have all been well and things are rocking along about as usual—pretty busy. The park is doing about $1.5 or $1.6 million a week now for the past three weeks. The "Small World" ride seems to be pleasing everybody. It's certainly beautiful. I think you know the Bank of America sponsors it. I understand they are happy about it—or reasonably so, anyway.

Our picture business has been perking along well. Little old *Bambi* is headed for $5 million or close to it in the U.S. and Canada. In the last couple of days we started out with our new picture, *Lt. Robinson Crusoe, U.S.N.* While it is too early to get a good feel of it, it is going very well and looks like it is headed for $7.5 to $8 million domestic gross.

Right now we are shooting what I think is going to be a really wonderful picture—*The Happiest Millionaire.* It looks especially good. It's a musical and has a fine cast. I wouldn't say at this stage it will outgross *Mary Poppins,* but there's no harm in hoping . . .

I notice that you are going through the Château country of France and that you have one stop in Mont St. Michel. Right in that country is where the Disney family originated—at d'Isigny-sur-mer. They are supposed to have crossed the channel with William the Conqueror in 1066 . . .

With land for the Florida Project secured, Roy allowed himself to feel sanguine about the company's future. Disneyland, the movies, merchandising, and other divisions continued making increased profits every year. As always, Walt found new ways to spend the company's money, but Roy saw no reason to dampen his brother's enthusiasms. With the help of Buzz Price's Economic

Research Associates, Walt located an ideal site for a winter resort, Mineral King Valley near Sequoia National Park.

In 1965, the United States Forest Service put Mineral King up for sale, and Walt made a successful bid of $35 million. He worked closely with WED planners to design a ski resort that would resemble the place he had admired while making *Third Man on the Mountain* in Switzerland.

The Florida project and Mineral King would require immense amounts of financing, yet Roy seemed little concerned. Perhaps Roy had mellowed, recognizing that Walt's other big ideas, no matter how tortuously funded, had contributed to the company's immense growth. Roy realized that Disney Productions' record of performance had created great goodwill and ready lenders in Wall Street. Roy revived his long-held dream of retirement. He evidenced no diminution of his faculties and acumen. But he felt he owed it to Edna and to himself to seek a more peaceful existence in their seventies.

By mid-1966, Roy and Walt were working more closely than they had in years. Intermediaries were no longer required in their communication with each other. Roy often mentioned his desire to withdraw from daily contact with corporate affairs. Walt wouldn't hear of it. The thought of not having Roy always at hand to soothe the company's problems and fulfill its needs was abhorrent to him. Walt even attempted subversive work with Edna, hinting that she might not enjoy having Roy underfoot all day.

"I'd like to just get in the car with Edna and start driving and never come back," Roy sometimes remarked to his son. Driving wasn't simply a recreation for Roy; it was a contest of wills. He was as bold as Edna was cautious behind the wheel. Roy Edward and Patty shudderingly recall a thrill ride on a New Year's Day.

The two couples were returning from the Rose Bowl football game amid the usual crush of traffic. Roy decided he could make better time by driving Chevy Chase Drive, which snaked through a Glendale canyon. Trouble was, other football enthusiasts had the same idea, and Roy discovered the stream of cars was inching southward. He glanced to the left and saw that no cars were advancing northward. He swung to the left and advanced down the canyon at a rapid speed while his three passengers cringed. Fortunately, Roy encountered no oncoming traffic, and he arrived home in record time.

John Tobin joined the Donovan, Leisure law firm in 1959 and became a partner a few years later. He was assigned to the Disney account, and one of his first duties was to explain a tax matter to Roy Disney. He viewed the task with misgivings, thinking, "I've got to explain to this high-powered businessman that he can't have what he wants." Such things, Tobin's experience told him, did not result in a pleasant response.

They met in Roy's office, and Tobin analyzed the tax matter as tactfully as he could. He had barely finished two-thirds of his presentation when Roy interrupted, "John, what you're telling me is that it's exactly the way it oughta be." Tobin was greatly relieved.

Tobin also became involved in an intensively secretive matter involving General Electric.

With the land secured for the Florida Project and the plans progressing, Roy faced the formidable task of financing. Disneyland opened at a cost of $17 million. Early estimates for Disneyland East started at $100 million. Bankers and financiers told Roy such an investment was too great for a company the size of Walt Disney Productions. He was advised to seek a large corporation as partner. General Electric was approached, and its executives proposed a merger.

On a visit to Burbank, Tobin was told by the chief counsel, Dick Morrow, that Roy wanted to see him privately. Tobin reported to Roy's office expecting a solemn pronouncement. "I'm going to have Dick take you out to Disneyland," Roy announced. "If you're going to do work for the company, you have to know what we're all about. I want you to spend the day at Disneyland, and I'd like you to take some photographs, not for us but for yourself."

Tobin listened unbelievingly. He was sent to the camera department, where he was presented with a camera and instructed in its use. "Roy was right," Tobin recalls. "I was so impressed with the way the park was run it gave me enthusiasm for doing my own work for Disney."

The merger talks with G.E. progressed, and Tobin was sent to the studio to explain the terms to Roy and Walt. Tobin had been instructed to reduce the terms to a one-page memo. He had known little contact with Walt, and he presented the page with a degree of nervousness. Walt read for a few moments, then stopped. "What's this word 'employee'?" he asked.

"Well, Mr. Disney—"

"My name's Walt."

"Walt, sir, if they buy the company, they own you. You will continue at their convenience. They will be able to fire you at any time."

Walt's left eyebrow shot up. The negotiations with G.E. ended soon afterward. For a time, the possibility of a merger with Westinghouse was discussed, then abandoned. Roy decided to go it alone.

With outside help no longer a possibility, Roy realized that Walt Disney Productions alone would be forced to find the money to build the Florida project. His brother needed him. For Roy, it meant that retirement was indefinitely postponed.

• • •

Roy was alarmed by Walt's appearance when he returned from the cruise with his family. He looked thinner, the cough rumbled deeper, his leg had stiffened. Still, Walt maintained the same strenuous schedule, spending long hours at WED, conferring on the new animated feature, *The Jungle Book*, flying across the country in the company plane. He visited the Florida property with Roy and other executives, viewing the land from a helicopter and admiring the vastness of the place.

He grew more irritable and was quick to criticize his associates, usually feeling contrite afterward. One night at dinner in Florida, he launched a two-hour castigation of Donn Tatum, alleging that he had tried to drive a wedge between the two Disney brothers. Other Disney officials at the table slipped away in embarrassment.

"As time went on, Walt grew more serious," commented Bill Cottrell, who worked closely with Walt at WED. "He might have been taking on more responsibility or feeling more responsibility. I don't think Walt was having as much fun as he should have had. I don't know, maybe he had too much on his mind. He grew older, and Roy seemed to be more easygoing as time went by."

Walt blamed his physical condition on the old polo injury, and he entered UCLA Medical Center on July 24 for tests. Doctors found that calcification had increased and recommended an operation to relieve the condition. Walt decided to wait until the end of the year before undertaking it.

In September, Walt appeared at Mineral King for ceremonies with California Governor Edmund G. Brown to announce state and federal support for a highway into the valley. To reporters, Walt seemed pale and breathless, but his public relations man attributed that to the cold and altitude. He returned to the planning of the Florida Project at WED, and he grew impatient over

293

talk about how to operate the theme park. "I don't want to discuss what we learned in the past," he said irritably. "I want to talk about the *future*." His eyes were on EPCOT.

After flying to Williamsburg for an award, Walt returned to California. The pain was so severe that he had to face the surgery UCLA doctors had recommended. He made a date to enter St. Joseph's Hospital.

Perhaps in an effort to cheer his brother, Roy wrote him a memo on October 24 telling of an early screening of *The Happiest Millionaire*. Sounding more like a press agent than a company president, Roy called the movie "a wonderful package of enter-tainment—just wonderful . . . I was especially impressed with John Davidson—maybe because I have not been too impressed with him on his NBC shows . . . Tommy Steele is terrific and Lesley Ann Warren is lovable and beautiful and does a very fine job. Fred [MacMurray] is great as the father . . . The ending bothered me a little. I suppose romantic, softhearted me wanted to see those nice young kids again . . . [The movie] should be before a community for as long a time as possible—like *Sound of Music* has been—so that the kind of people who are not regular thea-tergoers can have an opportunity to see it."

Roy added that the company had closed the fiscal year with almost $12 million in profit and $5 million in depreciation, "plus everything written off—such as R&D, story write-offs, and picture amortizations to the bone. Also over half our taxes for this year are already paid—all of which is very comforting."

He wrote that he and Edna were taking a two-week vacation and would return "on your 'D' date. I will be thinking of you and praying that you get everything out of that operation that you hope for. I am sure, if I were in your spot, I would do the same thing, so good luck!"

Doctors at St. Joseph's found something more serious than calcification in Walt's neck: a walnut-size spot in his left lung.

Walt refused to acknowledge his own mortality. He had always avoided any discussion of death, and he hated funerals. Herb Ryman told about the funeral of Charlie Phillipi, a veteran art director at the studio. Walt called Ryman and asked if he could ride with him. Ryman recalled: "So we sat together at the funeral. Walt drummed his fingers and rubbed his hands; he was emotionally upset. Afterward we saw [animators] Marc Davis and Milt Kahl, and Walt shouted to them: 'Okay, let's get the hell back to work.' He was covering up his emotions. That was one of the last funerals Walt ever went to."

On the day after the X rays, Walt returned to the studio for a full day's work, which included a CalArts board meeting at which the building plans were first displayed. He viewed rushes of various films in progress, and he met in his office for a drink with his producer, Bill Anderson.

"They found a spot on my lung," Walt said casually.

"Oh, my God!" Anderson gasped.

"Don't worry, now," Walt replied. "I'm gonna whip it, I'm gonna whip it. They're going to go in and take a biopsy."

Three days later, he drove himself to St. Joseph's, and the operation took place on the following morning. He didn't want Lilly and his daughters to make any fuss, but they came to the hospital anyway. They received the shocking news: The left lung was cancerous and had been removed. The prognosis was grim: he had six months to two years to live.

Roy sought information about the extent of Walt's illness, but the doctors were evasive. Finally he went to Walt's principal doctor and said, "We run a large corporation. As chairman of that corporation, I need to know what is wrong with Walt and what the prognosis is." The doctor wrote on a slip of paper and handed it to Roy.

That evening, Roy stopped by Roy Edward's and Patty's house for a drink. "This is what he said is wrong with Walt," he said, handing over the paper. Patty perused it and said, "Grandpa, in Latin that says 'small-cell cancer of the lung.' "

"Goddamn!" Roy exclaimed. He grabbed the paper and stormed out of the house. Patty was stunned; her father-in-law had never talked to her like that before. "I realized later he didn't want to hear it," she said. "It was like hitting him in the gut."

The public remained unaware of the severity of Walt's illness. His family and Roy's informed no one, partly out of unwillingness to accept reality. But doctors and nurses at the hospital had no such restraints, and the results of the operation became known to a few individuals.

Walt grew restless with the inactivity, and he was allowed to leave the hospital after two weeks. He returned to the studio, and those he encountered tried to hide their shock at his appearance. His face was gaunt, and his usual tan had faded. His clothes seemed to hang on him. He inquired about production plans on several movies, but he spent most of the time with his WED planners. That was obviously where his interest lay: the future. He inquired about plans for EPCOT and Disneyland East and conferred with Roger Broggie about the Pirates of the Caribbean ride, which had been a favorite of Walt's. It had been shipped to Disneyland but needed more tests before it could be unveiled to the public.

For two more days, Walt came back to the studio, and he conducted a few meetings, chatted with Peter Ustinov and the director Robert Stevenson on the set of *Blackbeard's Ghost*, and paid a visit to the machine shop, where he had spent fond days building his home railroad.

John Hench recalls a last lunch in the Coral Room: "Walt came over to the WED table and said he was awfully tired of hospital food. His voice wasn't very good at first, but it got stronger and stronger. He talked about the Pirates of the Caribbean, which he was interested in. He said [about the operation], 'I think they got it all; I'm convinced they got it all.'"

Walt and Lilly spent Thanksgiving at Diane and Ron's house. He thought he might feel better at the Smoke Tree Ranch house, but after one night he felt weaker and returned to reenter St. Joseph's on November 30.

Roy visited him every day, always bringing good reports about progress of the company. Walt's decline was more rapid than the doctors had anticipated. Cobalt treatments robbed his strength and appetite, and painkillers sometimes confused his mind. When Roy paid a call on the night of December 14, his brother seemed totally lucid. He imagined the Florida property on the ceiling, and he pointed and said, "Roy, you have this north-south road, and we can build on both sides of that. We can put Disneyland at the far end, then we need an east-west road." Roy returned home elated, and he told Edna, "I think he's got a good chance of making it."

At nine-thirty the next morning, Walt died.

TWENTY-EIGHT

✑

Walt's family and Roy's gathered at the hospital to embrace and console each other and gaze on Walt, now gaunt and gray, his great vitality gone. When Roy's son and daughter-in-law arrived, they found Roy outside Walt's room, his back turned, shoulders shaking. Patty walked to him and held her arms around him and buried his chin on her shoulder. He sobbed uncontrollably.

Across the street at the studio, there was disarray. Shocked by the loss of the company's guiding force, the executives below Walt and Roy were uncertain as to how to proceed. Marty Sklar, who had been responsible for writing annual reports and other important documents, was summoned from WED to Card Walker's office.

"Walt's dead," Sklar was told. To his astonishment, neither Walker nor Donn Tatum nor anyone else had made any preparations, even though they had known Walt was dying. Roy refused to talk to them that morning. Sklar was told to go in the next office and summarize Walt Disney's life and career for release to the press. That was done, and the news was released. The cause was announced as "acute circulatory collapse." No mention of cancer.

The news shocked the nation, not only because a beloved American icon had died. People had not been prepared for it. The studio had maintained all along that Walt's hospital stay had merely been to correct his old back condition. Only his family and a few company people were aware that cancer had been raging through Walt's body.

The funeral contributed to the mystery. The studio gave out no information except that the funeral was private, family only. The lack of public knowledge gave raise to a variety of fantasies, the most prevalent being that Walt had been preserved by cryonics, for thawing at a later date. The fact that the body had been cremated did little to end the speculation.

Walt had often said that he didn't want a public funeral; he had seen enough of the spectacles when Hollywood celebrities died. Walt's funeral was austere in the extreme. Lilly, her two daughters and their husbands, Roy and Edna and their son and daughter-in-law sat in a tiny chapel at Forest Lawn Memorial Park in Glendale. The only flowers were a wreath sent by Roy Edward and Patty.

The funeral compounded Roy's distress over his brother's death. "When I go, don't do that to me," Roy told his son later that day. When he mixed a drink for himself, he put it down, saying, "I'm not going to have any more Scotches. I am so sad, I should not be drinking at a time like this." And he didn't drink for a long period afterward.

His family and those who dealt closely with Roy believe that he was never the same after Walt's death. It appeared as though he never thought Walt would die, certainly not before Roy himself died.

"I think the whole family was like that," observes Roy Edward. "Walt had become a kind of mythical being even then to a lot of people, and especially to his own family. It was a sense of 'he'll be around forever.' "

Solemnly, Roy Disney returned to his responsibilities as the surviving co-founder of Walt Disney Productions. He issued an open statement to the public, the stockholders, and the more than 4,000 Disney employees assuring them that "we will continue to operate Walt Disney's company in the way that he has established and guided it." He stated that Walt had gathered a team of people "who understood his way of communicating with the public through entertainment. Walt's ways were always unique, and he built a unique organization."

Roy now needed to enlist the support of Walt's Boys, those who owed their allegiance to Walt and for whom Roy was a casual figure. He was unfamiliar with WED, for example, principally because Walt didn't want anyone, including his big brother, poking around in his future projects.

A week after Walt's death, Roy gathered the major executives, including Card Walker and Donn Tatum, the principals from WED, department heads, and creative people in a projection room at the studio. He had regained much of his composure, but his listeners noted that his voice was hoarse and he occasionally choked when he spoke of Walt. The company would continue on the same course that Walt had charted, Roy said confidently. Speaking of the Florida project, he declared: "We're going to finish this park, and we're going to do it just the way Walt wanted it. Don't you ever forget it. I want every one of you to do just exactly what you were going to do when Walt was alive."

Roy also went to Disneyland and spoke to a gathering of

supervisors and department heads. Nothing would change in the operation of the park, he told them, adding that Walt's plans for new attractions and expansion would be carried out.

I n January 1967, I interviewed Roy for the Associated Press, his first interview since Walt's death. He was genial as usual, but markedly subdued. He spoke of Walt's planning of Disney World, as it was now called, on the hospital ceiling as he lay on his deathbed.

"He drove himself to the end," Roy remarked. "Sometimes I think he drove himself too hard. You never know about these things, but maybe all the work helped bring on his death. But maybe he was driving against that day when he wouldn't be here to spark the ideas. He may have felt if he got the projects started, we would be able to carry on." The company had enough film, television, and Disneyland projects for three years, he added. Building Disney World might take a decade.

This was my first extensive interview with Roy, and the contrast with Walt was evident. With Walt, a reporter needed only to toss out a subject and he would run with it in dazzling display of creativity. Sometimes he began the soliloquy with no inducement.

Roy answered every question in a succinct, homespun manner. Their offices also offered a contrast. Walt operated in a third-floor suite, with a formal office and a spacious conference room complete with bar and kitchen. Roy's second-floor office was no bigger than others in the animation building. The office was dominated by a large, pensive portrait of Walt. Above it was the peace pipe Walt had presented after their long, acrimonious battle over WED.

Roy explained that the company was now operating by committee, which he admitted was not the best system—"but we will have to do it that way until the new leadership develops."

The committee consisted of Bill Anderson, production chief; producers Bill Walsh, Winston Hibler, Harry Tytle, and Jim Algar; Card Walker, marketing chief; Roy Edward Disney, television producer; Walt's son-in-law, Ron Miller, now producer.

I asked Roy why the Disney stock had risen after Walt's death.

"I think that was part of a growing realism that motion picture stocks were underpriced," he replied. "Our stock was selling at six times our earnings, which was ridiculously low. I thought it should go up to twelve or fifteen times our earnings, and it has been rising accordingly."

Some Wall Street observers believed that speculators had been buying the stock with the hope that with Walt gone, the company would be subject to a takeover, resulting in its divisions being sold off.

"God help us if we had to be absorbed into some big conglomerate mess," Roy commented. "We'd have to be running pretty scared to agree to that sort of thing. And we're not scared."

Roy discussed a number of other matters, but always he returned to Walt.

"He was a very practical guy," Roy said. "He would dream, dream, dream, but then he would come back to reality. The main thing was to get the job done. He would try for the utmost, and then he would retreat to a position he could handle . . .

"Success changes everyone, especially in Hollywood, where success is exaggerated. With Walt, I think success made him drive harder. He was always saying, in effect, 'You ain't seen nothin' yet.' If he had a big success, he was eager to go on to the next one. For that reason, he would never make sequels.

"I remember we had a big success with the reissue of *Snow White*. I thought Walt would be pleased, but all he said was: 'So you're in the secondhand business now.' "

TWENTY-NINE

✑

"W hen Walt died, Roy had been in the WED building only once, to my knowledge," recalls Marty Sklar, "and Card and Donn not at all. This was Walt's place—'I'll take care of it; you guys stay out of it. I'll tell you what I want you to know about what we're doing.'

"In the year after Walt died, many people were extremely frustrated because we had already started on Disney World and were well into it. We didn't make any progress for a year. What the [decision makers] didn't realize was that there were talented people at WED who could carry on the projects for Disney World particularly. Since they had no direct insight into what went on here or even who the people were, there was this big gap that Dick Irvine [chief executive of WED] and others had to fill. They had to be convinced that this was still a viable organization that could do this kind of project."

Jack Lindquist agrees: "The process slowed down following

303

the initial shock of Walt's passing. Nothing happened because nobody would pick up the gauntlet and move forward. From December 15 for almost a year, there was doubt whether there would be a project. They went forward and secured the legislation, and some of the legal work was done. But nothing as far as the design and what the project would be."

Partly the situation was due to the numbing void in Roy's life following the loss of his intimate partner of forty-three years. From the very beginning, Walt had provided the creative impetus for the company, often leading it into unexplored territory. Roy had been the tempering force, challenging Walt to prove his visions practical, then supplying the means to accomplish them. Probably if Walt had lived, his relentless drive would have made the Florida Project proceed apace. Roy now was forced to make creative and financial decisions unilaterally, taking counsel from others, then acting as forthrightly as Harry Truman.

Florida clearly would be the biggest thing the company had ever attempted. Where would the money come from? Did Roy dare plunge the company into debt that would take years to pay off?

Again the suitors came calling. Litton Industries, Gulf and Western, and other conglomerates expressed interest in merging with Disney and providing financial help for Disney World. Although he and Walt had rejected General Electric's proposal, Roy gave consideration to an offer from Westinghouse Electric.

Jonathan Bell Lovelace, a Los Angeles lawyer long associated with the Disneys, in August 1967 mailed a letter so confidential that it was sent to Roy's home rather than the office. He wrote: "I would think you might be far happier and live much longer if you were to make a partnership move now when you could be assured of continuing and expanding opportunities for the loyal and able men in the Disney organization and the orderly development of Disney World as you visualize it."

Lovelace observed that Roy had been "besieged by suitors, many of them pure opportunists" after Walt's death. Westinghouse was not one of those conglomerates, he said, but a company involved in the entertainment field. The future status of key Disney executives would be assured—"you would in effect be replacing your present stockholders with a new single stockholder."

Roy was not swayed by the blandishments of Westinghouse. He had learned from the double-crossing of Pat Powers and Charles Mintz to share ownership with no one. He would go it alone.

But how?

Nolan Browning, an attorney and financial expert, provided the solution: convertible debentures. The idea was to sell bonds which could be converted into stock when the stock rose to a certain price.

In January 1968, Roy wrote to his Georgia friend, Ellis Arnall: "Things are going well with the company. Our Florida project is gaining momentum rapidly, although at this writing we have our first labor troubles on the job. Perhaps you noticed that we sold on the market last week $40 million of Walt Disney Productions Convertible Debentures. The deal went over in a big way and that gives us our first basic Florida financing."

Don Escen, one of Roy's financial aides, remembers: "We went out with the first $40 million in convertible bonds; they hadn't been out but eight-nine months and we converted them. We turned around and went out with another $50 million in convertibles and converted those a short time afterward. Then we went with a stock issuance of $72 million. We came back with another convertible issue of $50-75 million after that."

An admiring article in *Forbes* magazine in 1971 reported: "Because Disney stock sold for between thirty and fifty times earnings, the equity dilution involved was remarkably small. The new stockholders, in effect, contributed half of the company's current equity and yet ended up with only about 25 percent of the company. Since Walt Disney pays only nominal dividends, the carrying cost of the new money is very slight—about $600,000 a year in cash dividends, for an effective cost of 0.4 percent after taxes."

Roy confidently predicted that Disney World would open entirely debt-free.

With the land secured and the financing in place, the next step was to win approval from the Florida legislature for the extraordinary powers that Disney needed for the structure of Disney World. In the months before his death, Walt still insisted, based on Jules Stein's advice, that he didn't want to create a municipality. Bob Foster, who had been responsible for the land purchases and was now preparing a proposal for the legislature, disagreed.

Foster was summoned to make his case before Walt and Dick Morrow, the company's general counsel. Foster had prepared cards that outlined the plan and had rehearsed his presentation before associates. Meeting in a conference room at the studio, he methodically explained to Walt and Morrow how certain functions could be distributed: building streets, establishing a library, electric power, distributing water, erecting bridges, etc. He came down to a stack of cards listing elements that didn't fit into any existing authorities.

"My God, Bob, you talk slowly!" Walt commented. "We can put those in a municipality!"

Walt's acquiescence averted a multitude of problems.

"Without a municipality, Walt Disney World could never have been built," says Foster. "We would have had multilayers of governmental influence, building permits, inspections, zoning matters, both local and state."

In 1967, Foster presented to Roy the plan for the Ready Creek Improvement District, which would circumvent governmental interference with the building and operation of the Florida project. Roy had been keenly involved in every step of the plan's development. "Are we asking too much?" he inquired. "What do private companies get from state governments when they go into a state?" He commissioned Buzz Price to make a survey in the southeastern states on governmental incentives for industrial development. The survey showed that the Disney proposal was on firm ground.

The massive legislation, amounting to 481 pages, was presented to the lawmakers. It gave Disney rights to operate virtually its own government, with its own police and fire departments, utilities, building codes, zoning, environmental control, and taxing. Nothing so thorough had ever been proposed in Florida, and some of the legislators were skittish about dispensing such power. The legislation was stalled in committees.

There was another political complication. Governor Haydon Burns, who had embraced the Disney plan, had been denied the Democratic nomination for reelection. Claude L. Kirk had been elected governor, the first Republican to hold the office since 1872. Like most politicians, Kirk was unenthusiastic about his predecessor's initiatives.

Roy's instruction to Foster was firm: "Tell them if we don't get that legislation, we're not coming."

A clincher was needed. The legislators were not inclined to hand over such extraordinary rights to an area twice the size of

Manhattan merely to build another Disneyland. They needed to be told that something vital and visionary would be built. Enter EPCOT.

Shortly before he died, Walt had appeared in a short film explaining his concept of the city of tomorrow. In an unprecedented move, the EPCOT film was screened to both the House of Representatives and the Senate. Opposition melted, and the bills passed both houses with a wide majority.

Roy came to Tallahassee to attend signing of the bills. As Kirk led the Disney party through the governor's mansion to the garden for the signing, he looked quizzically at Roy. He said, "Roy, I have studied your legislation, I have read it carefully, studied and restudied it. There's one serious omission, and I can't understand it."

Roy was perplexed. "What's that, governor?"

"There's no provision in the kingdom for the crown."

Roy Disney stood in the gondola of a cherry picker and surveyed the Magic Kingdom. Gas balloons of different colors rose toward the sky, each signifying the location and height of landmarks—Cinderella Castle, the railroad station, Tomorrowland, the carousel. In the distance, balloons marked the hotels. On the ground, earthmovers carried tons of earth down Main Street to elevate the land. In the drained bottom of Bay Lake, bulldozers scooped up centuries of ooze and roots down to the white sand so the water would be clear and blue.

Roy could gaze over the flat land to the distant horizon knowing that the company owned everything. But what an unprepossessing sight. Barren dunes of white sand. Black-water swamps tangled with roots and decaying trees. An occasional grove of palmettos and pines. But it was mostly a primordial wasteland right out of *The Rite of Spring*.

"We're all mad, this is totally crazy," Roy commented to a meeting of his top officials afterward. "We've got $90 million in this project, and we don't have a single thing above ground."

Building Disney World was different from building Disneyland. Both adhered to crash schedules to meet announced opening dates: Disneyland on July 17, 1955, Disney World on October 1, 1971. The site for Disneyland was compact, flat, sandy, and dry; it was cleared by bulldozing the orchards. Disney World was hugely sprawling, honeycombed with streams, canals, lakes, and swamps, with deeply rooted plant life that needed to be dug up and cleared. The water table lay four feet under ground level, so the base for the Magic Kingdom had to be raised sixteen feet to accommodate underground offices and service facilities.

The difference in command was significant. Walt knew exactly what he wanted in Disneyland. All looked to him for decision making, and his word was law. His associates feared the raised eyebrow and scornful look.

Roy occupied the top command of Disney World. But he also commanded a huge corporation, and although he made frequent trips to Florida, he could not afford the project his complete attention. In matters of design and engineering he deferred to the experts at WED, led by Dick Irvine. He relied heavily on the two military men, Joe Potter, the general who brought his vast experience with the Army Corps of Engineers, and Joe Fowler, the admiral who built navy ships during the war and headed construction for Disneyland.

Without Walt's dictatorial control, power struggles developed on the Florida project. Not with Potter and Fowler, whose service backgrounds disciplined them to get the job done, but with others in the hierarchy who tried to extend their areas of influence. This was a source of constant bedevilment for Roy. "He had to play referee in all of the internal fights among the Disney people," says Marty Sklar.

Roy also became increasingly distressed by the escalating costs. Of course, all major Disney projects, from *Snow White* to Disneyland, soared far above the original estimates. Jack Lindquist suspects that Walt studied the estimates of his associates, and viewed them more realistically before submitting them to Roy. Thus the blow that came with the final tally was somewhat softened.

Now the estimates came directly to Roy, and he was furious when they doubled and tripled.

"Without Roy, [Walt Disney World] wouldn't have happened," says Jack Lindquist. "It was not just Roy saying, 'Go ahead, build it.' Everyone else was so in awe of Walt that they could not step forward and take his place. It took a Disney to do it, and that was Roy.

"I've always felt how fortunate the two guys were, Walt and Roy, how much they needed each other. I don't know if they knew it or ever thought about it. But I've often wondered what might have happened if they hadn't been together. Walt might have ended up working for Walter Lantz, because he wasn't a businessman. And Roy could have ended up manager of a Bank of America in Glendale."

Despite his enormous duties, Roy found time to dictate letters to friends and family. In 1967 he answered a letter from an old friend at King Features Syndicate, which had handled the Disney comics.

"I have often thought of retiring," Roy commented. "In fact, for the past five years I have been trying to do so, but now it is out of the question. While, in some ways, I wish I could retire, when I see how difficult it is for some fellows I think maybe I am better off working. So that's the way the ball bounces.

"In any event, we are busy as a cat on a tin roof and we have a lot of work ahead of us and frankly I am having a lot of fun doing it."

In 1969 Roy wrote to his niece, Dorothy Puder, in Bakersfield: ". . . We miss Walt very much around here. I only wish he had been given another ten years to reap some of the rewards of all the labor of forty years before. Certainly all that this company is today is rightfully attributable to Walt's ideas and drive . . . But we have made the transition without him very well indeed, and I think the company is now in its soundest condition in its history and I feel sure the next ten years will know spectacular and continuing growth . . .

"Just the other day, when she reached her seventy-ninth birthday, Edna said she had nothing whatever to complain about and everything to be happy and grateful for, but she was darn sick and tired of getting so old."

Both Edna and Roy viewed the passage of time with concern. Although Roy's health remained good, the prospect of retiring looked ever inviting. Before that could happen, he realized, he would need to assure an orderly transition. In the first two years, the committee system of management, with all its limitations, worked reasonably well. Roy kept close track of all that was going on and strove to prevent intramural rivalries from developing into disputes.

Still the future leadership needed to be set in place. The obvious candidates were Card Walker and Donn Tatum.

E. Cardon Walker came out of UCLA in 1938 to work in the traffic department at the Hyperion studio at $15.95 a week. Like most recruits who were not artists, he shifted from one department to another—camera, story, shorts, budget control, then made his mark as head of advertising and publicity. An imposing man with the size of a basketball player, he had a firm voice and a persuasive manner. Having risen through production, he was one of Walt's Boys.

Donn Tatum, a solidly built man with a ready smile, was a rarity among Disney executives; he had not risen from the ranks. He had studied at Stanford and Oxford and had earned a law degree, and his early business training had been in radio and television for RCA and ABC. Both Walt and Roy had been impressed by his sharp intelligence and pleasant attitude during their relationship with ABC, and in 1956 they brought him to the studio as business manager for Walt Disney Productions. His shrewd analysis of administrative issues helped raise him to higher posts, and by the time of Walt's death he had been chosen vice president and administrative assistant to the president and the executive committee. That made him one of Roy's Boys, but his loyalty extended to both sides.

As he agonized over the succession of power, Roy concluded that neither Walker nor Tatum possessed the qualities necessary to lead the company. He devised an alternate plan. Roy had long admired the sagacity of Clark Beise, president of the Bank of America and a Disney board member. Hearing that Beise was planning to retire from the bank, Roy made his move.

He and Edna drove to San Francisco, where he made an eloquent plea for Beise to assume the presidency of Walt Disney Productions. The banker replied that he felt ill-equipped to guide an entertainment giant; furthermore, he welcomed the retirement from his everyday duties. No amount of argument could dissuade him.

Roy was crestfallen. When they arrived home, Edna told her daughter-in-law: "I've never been so scared in my life. He kept driving over the double center line. He was so upset that Beise had turned him down. He doesn't know what he'll do next."

S ix months after Walt's death, Roy made his decision. In a memorandum to the board of directors, he told of his "careful consideration to the long-range plans of the company."

He continued: "For some time I had planned to retire or at least materially cut down on my active participation in the management of the company. The death of Walt has forced me to reappraise this plan. I am increasingly mindful of the fact that the Disney name is a vital asset of the company. The people on whose advice I have relied were unanimous in their view that it is important that the Disney name be retained in top management, and that I remain as its chief executive officer and president and chairman of the board."

He was willing to continue in those capacities, he stated, but wanted to be relieved of the day-to-day problems so he could devote his time "primarily to the overall future planning of the business, particularly overall financing and matters affecting the stockholders and public relations."

He proposed electing Donn Tatum executive vice president (administration) and vice chairman of the board, with responsibility for administrative and functional planning. Operational responsibilities would fall to Card Walker, his title being executive vice president (operations).

"In making these recommendations," Roy concluded, "it is my hope and firm belief that Mr. Tatum will demonstrate to all his fitness to succeed me as chairman of the board and chief executive officer, and that Mr. Walker will demonstrate his fitness to succeed me as president and chief operating officer of the Company."

As always, the board voted in favor of Roy's recommendations.

In November 1968, Roy relinquished the presidency of Walt Disney Productions in favor of Donn Tatum, who would continue as vice chairman of the board of directors. Card Walker, whom Roy had proposed as the future president a year before, was elected to the new post of executive vice president and chief operating officer. Roy was not ready to hand over his posts as chairman of the board and chief executive officer.

On the surface it seemed that Roy had put into effect a smooth transition, providing a dual leadership for the time when neither founder would be present to guide the company.

THIRTY

❧

O ver a period of four years, Roy made dozens of trips to Florida, almost always accompanied by Edna. At first they stayed at the new Hilton Inn in Orlando, then in one of the cottages for executives on Bay Hill. Roy's place was next to the house of Joe Fowler, with whom he developed a warm relationship. The two men were close in age, and both had accomplished much in their lives, Roy with the company, Fowler in the navy. Roy admired the admiral's "can-do" attitude. No matter how difficult the chore, Fowler always responded in a positive manner.

Joe Potter was another favorite of Roy's. He was also of the same vintage, and his experience in commanding huge projects for the Army Corps of Engineers proved invaluable in converting the wet expanses into manageable terrain. Like Fowler, Potter believed no task was too difficult to accomplish on time.

Roy was in command. He did not deal in creative matters; he left that to Dick Irvine and his crew from WED. In all other aspects, Roy made the final decisions. As he had in all his company dealings, he listened to the proposals and then decided what would be done. Those who tried to ignore or override his will did so at their own peril.

Overseeing such a huge construction project would have been an immense responsibility for anyone, especially a man in his mid-seventies. Roy didn't complain. He saw the Florida project as a great opportunity to expand the company. Perhaps more important, it was something Walt had wanted. That was always uppermost in his mind. He had decided on the name Walt Disney World, so that everyone would be reminded of the creative genius behind all that the Disney company had accomplished. Everyone knew Ford cars, he reasoned, but not all people remembered that Henry Ford had built the company.

Most of those around Roy did not agree with his choice. They believed it should be called Disney World. When someone referred to Disney World in a meeting, Roy stopped him. His eyes narrowed behind the glasses, and he said firmly: "I'm only going to say this one more time. I want it called *Walt* Disney World. Not Disney World, not Disneyland, not anything else. *Walt Disney World.*"

One of Roy's major decisions concerned the positioning of the Magic Kingdom. The Disney financial people wanted to place it at the corner of the two highways, I-4 and 192. That would make it readily available to the public and preclude the huge expense of building the infrastructure of roads and canals and preparing the land for later use. The construction people fought against that.

Dick Nunis comments: "We said, 'Walt left us the road map, we ought to stay with it. We have forty-three square miles, and if we put Disneyland in a corner of the property and everything else behind it, it doesn't make any sense. We ought to spend the money on the main road corridor and draining the property, because some day it would be more difficult to do.

"That's what Walt had said: 'We've got to prepare the land—now.' He brought in experts from all over the country to study the land.

"Roy was very supportive of carrying out his brother's wishes. Without Roy it would never have happened. He told the financial people, 'I want to continue with Walt's plan. So let's quit wasting time on these meetings.' "

Two years had passed since the Florida legislature had granted Disney its kingdom, and little had been heard from the property except the rumble of heavy machinery. In April 1969, members of the press were invited to the new Ramada Inn tower in Ocoee, west of Orlando, for the unveiling of the master plan for Walt Disney World. The politicians had their say, especially the Florida-boosting Governor Kirk. Then came Roy Disney.

"This is a big day for our company," he said in his plainspoken way. "I know Walt would like what his creative team is doing, because these are the ideas and plans he began. Everything you see here today is something Walt worked on and began in some way."

The room darkened, and a screen lit up with a depiction by Disney artists of what Walt Disney World would look like. It was a dazzling production, evoking awe from the audience. Afterward, the guests loaded onto buses for a trip around the site. It was still raw land, littered with tree stumps and root masses, with gas balloons indicating the future landmarks. It was difficult for anyone to believe that in less than two-and-a-half years this wilderness would be converted into a wonderland for millions of visitors.

With above-ground construction beginning, Roy's presence in Florida became essential. Decisions had to be made, squabbles settled. One of the early disputes concerned the Contemporary Resort Hotel. It had been designed as a showpiece, an A-frame with room floors rising to the peak and the monorail running through the fourth-floor concourse. Construction people said it would be impossible to accommodate the monorail in a hotel. Walt's planners argued that without the monorail the hotel's interior would resemble, as one wag put it, "a place where the Goodyear blimp comes to mate."

Roy realized that the monorail would remove the Contemporary Resort from the Hyatt style of atrium hotels. "Build it," he said.

The Contemporary presented an impressive sight as the steel exterior rose fifteen stories above the Florida flatlands. During a visit Roy announced he wanted to see the view from the top. Elevators had not been installed, and the only route was on open steel stairways. Accompanied by men half his age, Roy made the climb without stopping. When he reached the top, he was afforded the best view he had seen, except by helicopter, of the vastness of the property. "Wow! This is unbelievable!" Roy exulted.

Labor problems proliferated. Orlando couldn't supply the labor needed for such a huge undertaking, so workmen were enlisted from all over the South and East. Many arrived unsolicited in pickup trucks pulling trailers. Others moved over from the Kennedy Space Center, where their jobs had been eliminated in a downsizing. This created a mixed collection of workers, some of them antagonistic toward each other and to the management.

Strikes became endemic. One discontented worker with a placard at the construction entrance could cause hundreds to refuse to enter. Jurisdictional disputes became common. The uniqueness of Disney attractions required plastics, resins, and other materials the workers had no experience with. Two unions would claim jurisdiction, and work stopped until the matter was settled. In desperation, Disney management sought help from union headquarters in Washington, D.C., and gradually the disputes were resolved.

In the building of Disneyland, the studio art directors who had designed the buildings and rides were accustomed to California workers who provided a full, constructive day on the job. Now the designers found the work day in the South was far different. Accustomed to the heat and humidity, the workers toiled at a slower pace, sometimes not at all.

Roy had no patience for such habits. Marvin Davis recalls accompanying Roy and others on an unannounced walk-through at the Contemporary Hotel: "It wasn't a planned thing, because we didn't want people to know we were coming. It wasn't lunch time, but there were guys lying around on their backs, leaning over for a sip of coffee or something, their feet in the air. As we came through, so help me God, they didn't move. They just stayed there. We had to ask them to get out of the way so we could get through. This just infuriated Roy. When we got back to the office, Roy said, 'Whoever those guys are, see that they are fired.' "

A major factor in the financing of Walt Disney World had been a partnership with U.S. Steel in building two hotels, the 1,000-room Contemporary Resort and the 500-room Polynesian Resort. The contract called for U.S. Steel to build the hotels at its expense, then Disney would operate them and share the returns. Though he was instinctively opposed to partnerships, Roy had agreed to this one. He knew he could go to Wall Street so many times before the convertible debentures lost their charm.

The wedding of U.S. Steel and Disney seemed doomed from

the start, if only because their corporate cultures were radically different. The steel company had sought to use the hotels as a showcase for its modular method of hotel building. Each room would be built and fitted on the site and set in place like a piece of a Lego set. But the technique encountered production and union problems, and building fell dangerously behind schedule. It appeared that neither hotel would be completed before the October 1, 1971, opening date.

One day Roy called Donn Tatum and Mike Bagnall into his office and announced, "I want to buy out U.S. Steel." Tatum, who had negotiated the contract with U.S. Steel, was forced to return to the steel executives and tell them of Roy's decision. They were disappointed, believing that the association with Disney would be a shrewd corporate move. Roy explained to U.S. Steel top management that the company had made a profit from building the hotels, and now Disney wanted to control its own destiny by owning and operating the hotels, especially since they both connected with the monorail.

Some of Roy's associates argued against the buyout. Dick Nunis, who had risen from a summer job at Disneyland to top management and was troubleshooting on the Florida job, commented that the $90 million was needed for more boats and capacity.

"I'm doing you a favor," Roy replied. "We're not going to be good partners with them."

It was a bold move. Disney had no experience in hotel operation (the Disneyland Hotel was owned by Jack Wrather; it was bought by Disney in 1987). The cost of Walt Disney World, originally estimated at $100 million, had doubled and would ultimately reach $400 million. The Disney treasury was dwindling at an alarming rate. Roy was gambling that Walt Disney World would create the same sensation as Disneyland. The future of the company depended on it.

In many ways, CalArts proved a weightier and more frustrating endeavor for Roy than Walt Disney World. The Florida project was vast and incredibly complex, but it could be grasped and reasonably controlled. Roy's decisions became law, and his underlings recognized that. All united under a common goal: to create a superior entertainment and get it done on time.

The California Institute of the Arts was dwarfed by comparison: a campus that would accommodate less than 1,000 students and faculty. Roy entered the world of academia, something with which he was totally unfamiliar. He could not make unilateral decisions, as he had during four decades as head of a business. Now he needed to seek the approval of the board of directors and to deal with a sometimes fractious faculty and student body.

The toll on Roy seemed measurable. In her more acerbic moments, Edna Disney in later years sometimes referred to CalArts as "the place that killed my husband."

Harrison (Buzz) Price and his Economic Research Associates made several surveys concerning the feasibility and location of CalArts, and he served on the board of directors for more than thirty-five years. He recalls: "After Walt died, Roy had the job of implementing a bequest and a commitment. It was a tough time to build a school. There was a lot of flak; a lot of the people in the city wondered why the hell we were doing it. [Dorothy] Chandler [wife of Los Angeles *Times* publisher Norman Chandler and patroness of the arts] wanted it downtown. No one understood Walt had a mission, and it was a smart one. Many guys in the corporation thought it was a stupid idea to take the assets of time and money represented by the corporation and to throw them into this strange thing that Walt wanted to do.

"Roy never for a minute bought that message. Roy was the lonely man supporting that school after Walt died. I think CalArts took more of his time and energy than the Magic Kingdom in Florida. The corporation was in place to do that job."

In the beginning, the sole supporters of CalArts were Roy, Price, and Lulu May Von Hagen, the patroness of the Los Angeles Conservatory of Music who had given Walt the notion of a college of the arts. Mickey Clark, an attorney at WED, and studio attorney Luther Marr also gave support. Soon outside directors were added to the board.

At the time of Walt's death, a model of the CalArts building had been created and the site chosen: the Disney studio's location ranch, Golden Oak, in the north San Fernando valley. A geological survey disclosed potential dangers, and the site was eliminated. Roy and Price negotiated with Newhall Land and Farming, a big agricultural and development company, for fifty acres in the Santa Clarita Valley at $5,000 an acre. The land seemed more seismically sound (the 1994 Northridge earthquake caused $36 million in damage).

Under Roy's supervision and with Walt's endowment of half his estate (more than $40 million), CalArts progressed toward reality. The school headquarters—which followed Walt's concept of everything under one roof—began construction. The board, now a mixture of finance and the arts, chose a president, Robert Corrigan, who had supervised interactive programs at Carnegie-Mellon and New York University. Because construction was delayed by strikes and other matters, the first year of classes would be held at a location a few miles away. It was a former Catholic girls school, Villa Cabrini, which was converted to CalArts' needs.

Mel Powell, the jazz pianist turned academic, had been lured from Yale in 1968 as the founding dean of the music school.

"My impression of Roy O. was that he appeared to be an extremely faithful citizen of CalArts," Powell recalls. "He wanted very much to have it mounted and be successful. He was sort of custodian of his brother's dream; he felt very responsible about it.

"Considering his task as chairman of the Disney corporation, that was quite remarkable. His attendance record for CalArts was spotless. He was always there when needed."

Both Powell and Nick England, who also joined the music department and later served as dean, remember Roy in hard hat conferring with builders on the construction site. Powell and Roy had many telephone conversations, and Roy expressed a desire for a school of architecture to be included in the curriculum. Because of the expense involved, it never happened.

"Roy was always the enabler," England comments. "He made things happen that Walt wanted. During that first year when we ran into money problems, Roy began to be around a lot."

Powell, who served as provost in that early period, recalls a meeting at which H.R. Haldeman was chairman. Haldeman mentioned that the school was short $5 million. Roy merely nodded his head, and the problem was solved.

Afterward, Roy mentioned to Powell that Haldeman would be the next president's right-hand man. Powell assumed he meant the next president of CalArts. "I was thinking small," Powell laughs.

The brave new college of the arts opened the doors of its temporary campus in September 1970. Both faculty and students were caught up in the excitement of their adventure, pioneering an innovation in American education. Though some of the classrooms seemed makeshift, the buildings were functional and appropriate for the sylvan setting. The surrounding area was peaceful, removed from traffic and commerce. Ideal for the nurturing and expression of artistic talent.

Peace was not to be achieved, not in the era of the Chicago riots, freedom marches, campus sit-ins, Vietnam protests, the sexual revolution, Haight-Ashbury, flower children, and "turn on, tune in, drop out."

The first sign of things to come occurred when nubile women students began appearing at the swimming pool without swimsuits. They swam in the cool water and sunned on the warm decks to the delight of the male students, who were similarly unattired. Members of the faculty were unconcerned, commenting, "They're artists, after all."

When staid members of the board of directors learned of the nudity at the pool, they were horrified. Roy himself was appalled; this was not what Walt had in mind for the college. The matter was raised at a board meeting, where outside members demanded that something must be done.

"What is wrong with viewing the human body?" questioned a teacher of photography who was a board member, and he launched into a lecture on the beauty of the human figure. As he did so, he removed his coat, shirt, shoes, pants, and undershorts and stood naked in front of the full board, including Roy, Lulu May Von Hagen, and other women. The chairman, a school dean, gazed at the naked body and commented, "What have you got to be so proud about?" The meeting ended in chaos.

Nude swimming was banned, and the flap ended up in the newspapers, causing great embarrassment to Roy and his family and to Lilly and hers. He decided to rescind his commitment for another gift to CalArts of many millions of dollars. When one of the school's deans was told of the event and the subsequent loss of revenue, he quipped, "My God, that's thirty million an inch!"

Thievery on the campus became rampant. Cameras, tape machines, electronic equipment, musical instruments, even pianos disappeared from the classrooms. "The students felt that everything was common property," observes Nick England.

"It was a moment of luminous madness," Mel Powell agrees. As provost, he devised the principle of "omniety," meaning that no meetings would be held without student representation. He reasoned that if students understood the big expense of replacing the equipment they would realize they were only hurting themselves by stealing. One of the conservative board members complained: "That's like turning the asylum over to the lunatics." But Roy accepted Powell's reasoning. The thievery did diminish.

The student dormitories were redolent with the sweet smell of marijuana, as were the faculty offices. Unidentified dogs roamed the campus in packs, creating a wasteland atmosphere. Protest meetings for various causes gathered at regular intervals. The student unrest was abetted by members of the faculty and administration.

Although Roy had paid the salaries of hundreds of artists at the studio, he simply did not understand the artistic mind and temperament. He could negotiate business deals with total confidence. Artists baffled him.

As Roy's frustration grew, he considered firing the entire administration. But he learned that such a course was not easy in an academic situation. This wasn't the studio, where he could summarily dismiss those who were at odds with company policy (though he rarely exercised that power). The academic world was bound by procedures, and the board of directors had been loaded with those who sympathized with the administration.

"Roy was seething," Buzz Price recalls. "Those two Missouri boys [Roy and Walt] could laugh and joke and tell stories, but they had been brought up right. They didn't go for that kind of nonsense. Roy decided he was going to dump the school. He asked me to make a deal with USC to take it over."

Price gave top officials of the University of Southern California a sub-rosa tour of the CalArts building then under construction. They were extremely impressed, and it appeared a deal was in the making. Roy assigned Price to negotiate with Justin Dart, chairman of the USC board of trustees. Dart, president of the Rexall Drug and Chemical Company, had long been a power in Republican politics and backer of Richard Nixon.

"Roy says he will give you $15 million cash and the school, lock, stock, and barrel, if you make it a school of arts for S.C.," Price told the drug magnate.

"Tell him we want $21 million," Dart replied.

Price carried the message back to Roy. "Tell Justin Dart to go fuck himself," Roy responded. It was the only time Price had heard him use that kind of language.

An attempt was made to involve Pepperdine University, but nothing developed. Roy decided to persevere with CalArts, and the headaches continued. In time the top administrators were fired, the flower children disappeared into communes, and the school became a prestigious institution. Roy didn't live long enough to see his efforts vindicated.

Two days before Roy died, Donn Tatum, seeing the upset CalArts was causing Roy, asked, "Why don't you give it up?"

"Godammit, Donn," Roy replied vehemently, "Walt wanted this school, and I'm going to get it for him."

THIRTY-ONE

⌘

Opening Day, Walt Disney World, October 1, 1971.
The news had been proclaimed three years earlier that Disney's second Magic Kingdom would open on that date. The choice had been strategic. Jack Lindquist explains: "We selected October, which had the smallest number of tourists in Florida, and Friday, the slowest day of the week. That would give us several weeks before the first major holiday crowd, the Friday after Thanksgiving, and two months before the Christmas rush." The planners did not want to duplicate the Disneyland opening, which came in July, the heaviest period of the summer season. The park had not been shaken down to accommodate the onrush of visitors, and Walt Disney World, given its breakneck completion schedule, would not be ready, either.

The Disney publicity forces had been whipping up the hoopla for months prior to the unveiling. National magazines, major newspapers, and television shows were invited to Orlando to see the work in progress. *Forbes* magazine featured a lengthy article in the May 1, 1971, edition that detailed Roy's financing of the project through convertible debentures. The article concluded:

"The chance of Disney World breaking the company are slight indeed. Disneyland movies, TV shows, and a vast array of merchandising contracts provided close to $44 million pretax profits last year, enough to cushion any conceivable operating losses and write-offs.

"And then, there is that lovely, clean balance sheet. This will be Roy Disney's legacy, just as the cartoon characters and the fantasy were Walt's."

Rosy predictions such as that one helped buoy the Disney stock high enough to retire two of the convertible debentures and issue another $100 million offering that financed the buyout of U.S. Steel. The massive expansion of the stock base benefited Walt Disney Productions, but it was less advantageous for the Disney families. In the early years of the company's stock, Walt and Roy and their wives owned 51 percent of the total. After the debentures to build Walt Disney World, the Disney holdings had shrunk to 7 percent. Thus the company could be the target of a hostile takeover by corporate raiders—as happened in the 1980s.

E ven three years was not enough time to clear the dense growth, drain and refill lakes, build forty miles of canals, erect the Magic Kingdom and three large hotels, and perform thousands of other necessary tasks to complete Walt Disney World. At one point a major contractor declared that the October date couldn't possibly be met. Roy ordered him replaced. As the date of opening approached, Roy learned the bad news: the Contemporary Resort would not be finished in time. As with Disneyland, Tomorrowland was a trouble spot. The lake for the 20,000 Leagues under the Sea submarine ride remained unfilled. Several other attractions had not been completed.

The Disney media blitz had overwhelmed some reporters who grossly overestimated the opening day crowd. One newspaper suggested the ridiculous figure of 200,000. The chief of the highway police ordered all units on alert, calculating as many as 360,000 people would be on the road.

Everything possible had been done to avoid the disasters of Disneyland's Black Sunday. No festivities were planned; the press would not be invited until the dedication festivities on October 23-25, by which time the park would have gone through a shake-down. The Florida opening had its casualties. The trams, which had been carefully tested, broke down. Fortunately, the guests had access to the park via the monorail, which maintained its steady, silent circumference of the property.

Opening day attendance: 10,000. That was no surprise to the Disney planners, who had projected 12,000. But it startled the media, some of whom suggested that Walt's final dream had proved a bust. Wall Street, perhaps in response to this upstart from the West, followed suit. Disney stock dropped seven points in one day.

Roy was enraged. He summoned his top executives to a meet-ing on October 2, and he blistered them for the opening day figures. They tried to explain that the slowest day of the slowest month had been chosen and approved, that the tourist traffic would remain a trickle until the snowbirds started to flee the northern storms. Orlandoans had not been expected at the open-ing because they had been treated to three nights of previews as a gesture of goodwill to the locals. The arguments made no head-way with Roy.

He had other, more serious matters to discuss. He had been

reviewing some of the construction bills and found them hugely excessive. He accused the top men of hiding expenditures from him. Explanations were unacceptable. His complaints could be heard down the hall by other employees. They had never known Roy to be so angry.

The gloom brought on by attendance on opening day soon vanished as tourists began flooding in. The turnstiles counted 400,000 guests in the first month, which was ahead of projections. Weekends attracted as many as 25,000 people per day. Roy was able to approach Dedication Day in a more sanguine mood.

It was the end of a long journey, and Roy had been there from the beginning, from Walt's first musings about a city of tomorrow. Roy had directed the clandestine search for property, and he had slowed the project only under the devastating blow of Walt's death. Then he had moved forward, calmly and resolutely, always mindful of what his brother had wanted. As the decisions piled up, Roy became aware of the burden of his years. He did not show it to outsiders, but Edna recognized the toll exacted by being the sole authority for the direction of the company.

The final months of completing Walt Disney World had been the hardest. He had gambled the future of the company on one great project; having been in the entertainment business for nearly half a century, he knew its unpredictability. Financing had become scarce, and as new problems arose, they could only be solved by throwing more money at them. In the rush to meet the opening schedule, opportunities for corruption presented themselves. When he discovered an underling who was trying to submit false invoices for his own benefit, Roy excoriated him face-to-face with words he had learned in the navy and reserved for such occasions. For Roy, the greatest crime was betrayal of his trust.

He also was disturbed by hints that his successors were impatient to assume control of the company. Actions had been taken, and he became aware of them only later. He believed huge expenditures had been made without his approval. He used strong language with those he suspected. Denials were made, nothing was resolved.

The October 23 dedication displayed the Disney showmanly flair. Meredith Willson led a 1,076-piece marching band down Main Street to Cinderella Castle to the music of his "Seventy-six Trombones." Musicians from sixty countries formed the World Symphony Orchestra which was conducted by Arthur Fiedler. A choir of 1,500 voices sang "When You Wish upon a Star" and other Disney standards. Mickey, Minnie, Donald, Goofy, and all the other Disney stars waved to the crowd. The two Disney families were recognized: Roy Edward and Patty and their four children; Lilly, Diane and Ron Miller and their seven children; Sharon and Bill Lund with three children.

After giving his thanks to the people who had built Walt Disney World, Roy reminisced: "My brother Walt and I went into business together almost a half-century ago. And he was really, in my opinion, truly a genius—creative, with great determination, singleness of purpose, and drive; and through his entire life he was never pushed off his course or diverted by other things. Walt probably had fewer secrets than any man, because he was always talking to whoever would listen. Talking of story ideas or entertainment projects. My banker one day said, 'How is such-and-such a picture progressing?' And I said, 'Joe, I don't think we have a picture of that name in work.' He repeated the name and said he saw little sketches of the story. I said, 'Joe, Walt was just using you as a good guinea pig to see how you would react to the story.

We don't have any picture like that in work.' And that was the way Walt went through his life."

A television special had been produced to celebrate the opening of Walt Disney World, and Roy and Edna watched it at their Bay Hill house, along with their family. The show featured Hollywood celebrities with song-and-dance routines in major areas of the park. It had been taped in empty streets and attractions, and Roy inquired, "Where are the people?" When Disneyland was building, Walt had observed that people would be a major factor in the enjoyment of the park.

Roy began weeping. Partly it was because of his disappointment with the empty show-biz razzle-dazzle on the television screen. Partly it came from exhaustion. Suddenly it was over. The park had been constructed, the surrounding area prepared for whatever would come in the future. The friction, the worry about money, the overwhelming responsibilities, the unending sorrow over the loss of Walt—all these had exacted their toll.

Now he could return to California and pursue the goal he had sought seven years before: to retire. He would never return to Florida.

Roy received his vindication on the day after Thanksgiving. Traffic was piled up on I-4 from the entrance to Walt Disney World five and a half miles toward Orlando. Radio stations broadcast warnings about the gridlock dangers. The parking lots became jammed and had to be closed. Fifty thousand people crowded into the Magic Kingdom.

In his studio office, Roy listened with growing satisfaction to reports from Florida. Now the management was faced with the problems of how to make parking more accessible and how to handle larger crowds so that all of the guests would leave the park happy. Those were problems Roy enjoyed having.

At last he had fulfilled his two vows to Walt's memory: the Florida park had opened and was prospering, the future of CalArts had been assured. Roy made arrangements for passage on the SS *Monterey* to Australia, sailing on February 20. On December 8, the Pacific Far East Line confirmed his reservations for adjoining staterooms on the promenade deck. The fare: $10,250.

For decades, Roy had been forced to fly to all parts of the world because of the press of business. Now he and Edna could enjoy a leisurely cruise across the Pacific with company concerns far behind.

Just as he was contemplating the idyllic cruise, Roy suffered a devastating blow. Mitch Francis died of pancreatic cancer. Mitch had been Roy's closest friend, perhaps his only confidante. They had worked side by side in the Kansas City bank, canoed together down the Mississippi. Roy had gone on a blind date with Edna at her brother Mitch's behest. The two young men had enlisted in the navy together. After the Disney brothers had established their company, Roy convinced Mitch to bring his family to California and work as purchasing manager at the studio. Roy and Mitch could sit in a lawn swing and talk for hours, not about studio affairs but their families and the memories of a lifetime. Roy's daughter-in-law Patty remembers, "When Mitch died, it took all the starch out of Roy O."

Roy's pleasure at seeing Walt Disney World successfully launched was tempered by his concern for the expenditures that had been made without his oversight. He placed the blame on several of the top executives, especially Card Walker. Several weeks after the opening of the park, Roy told one of his attorneys,

Luther Marr: "I want to clip Card Walker's wings. I want it put in the executive committee minutes that every expenditure will have to be approved by [WED chief] Mel Melton."

The following day, Donn Tatum came to Marr's office. Tatum had heard about Roy's request. He warned that if it was entered into the minutes, he would have to tell the outside directors that Roy was not thinking right, that he was forgetful about things that he had been told.

Donn and Card still rankled over the dressing down Roy had dealt them before their underlings on the day after the Walt Disney World opening. They claimed Roy had been informed about the expenditures. He said he had not been. Had Roy become senile? Neither Marr nor any of Roy's associates nor his family thought so. Were Card and Donn eager to establish their own primacy, since Roy had planned to retire? The question remains unanswered. The writing of the minutes was postponed, and events made it unnecessary.

Despite his discontent with Card and Donn, Roy still had to deal with the vital matter of succession. Originally he had envisioned a dual presidency, but, as in all corporations or any other organization, that rarely works. "Donn was not a real aggressive guy," observes Roy Edward Disney. "I think he would have been pretty happy to find a way to accommodate a dual presidency." Card had a different personality. He dominated meetings with his size and his persuasiveness. Donn was a conciliator, Card was a leader.

Roy agonized over how to resolve the matter. Then one evening, Roy and Edna had invited Roy Edward and Patty for one of Edna's Midwest-style dinners. While Edna and Patty washed the dishes, Roy invited his son out to the front porch for a chat. Roy lit a cigar, and the two men enjoyed the warm valley evening, silent except for the calling of crickets and the constant whir of the nearby freeway.

"I've been thinking a lot about who should run the company after I retire," Roy said, "and I've come to a decision. It'll be Card."

He asked Roy Edward for his opinion. "Well," the son replied, "I really like Donn Tatum an awful lot more than I like Card Walker."

"So do I," Roy said. "But this is how it's going to be."

One more matter needed to be settled. Roy had assembled a loyal group of financial and legal managers who had served him and the company with dedication and excellence. He wanted to make sure that their positions would be insured after his retirement. He knew that the company would be controlled by one of Walt's Boys who might want to install those loyal to him.

Roy summoned Donn Tatum and handed him a list of names. "I want you to be sure that the jobs of these men are to be protected," Roy said.

Now he could look forward to a carefree cruise across the Pacific with Edna. It was something he owed her after all the trying years that followed Walt's death. Luther Marr detected a different attitude in Roy. For a few years, Roy had watched his diet carefully, at the behest of Edna and his doctor.

"All of a sudden, I noticed that Roy was just eating whatever he wanted, he was doing everything to enjoy himself," says Marr. "I believe he was thinking, 'If it comes on, so what? I'm not going to sit around and mope about this stuff.' "

Roy's associates remember that whenever someone died of a heart attack or stroke, Roy commented, "That's the way I want to go. Fast. Not like Walt and Mitch."

I was in my room, and I had done something I wasn't supposed to do," remembers Susan Disney Loughman. "I had taken a TV from another room, and I was watching a Christmas show.

335

When my brother fell, he fell right outside my window. I heard some thumping on the wall, and then I heard this moaning. I'll never forget; it was horrible. I knew something was really wrong.

"I ran to the top of the stairs, and my little brother was there. 'It's Roy, he fell,' Timmy said. We ran downstairs and out the back door. He was laying there with a big pool of blood in front of his face. Obviously he was badly hurt. We dragged him inside; as a child I didn't know better, but I thought we should keep him warm."

Roy Patrick Disney, who was fourteen, had also done something that was forbidden in the family's new house in Toluca Lake. While his parents were vacationing in Florida, he and his brother Tim had climbed out of his bedroom window onto the slate roof. Rain had fallen, and the slate was slippery. Roy Patrick had stepped onto a canvas awning and fell through it.

"Susan, who was thirteen, was very levelheaded, thank God," says Roy Patrick. "We had a maid who was a live-in nanny, and she panicked. I was all crumpled up in a puddle of blood; I had bitten my tongue in half. The maid said, 'He's faking, he'll be okay.' Susan said, 'No, he's not, he's not!' "

Susan called her grandmother Dailey, who lived half a block away. She rushed to the house and called an ambulance. At St. Joseph's hospital, Roy Patrick was pronounced DOA—dead on arrival. "But we'll work on him," an attendant said. Two hours later, the report came: "He's alive, but we don't know what will happen to him."

Patty and Roy Edward heard the news at one o'clock in the morning and anxiously tried to schedule a flight home. In 1971 there were no direct flights from Florida to Los Angeles, and the frantic parents spent six hours in Atlanta waiting for a connecting flight. When they finally arrived at St. Joseph's Hospital, the situation was grim. Roy Patrick lay motionless in the white bed, his labored breathing the only sound in the room.

The two sets of grandparents consoled each other in the hallway. Roy looked ashen. It was the same hospital where Walt had died six Christmases before. Now Roy's oldest grandson, the bearer of his name, was barely holding onto life.

Roy Patrick remained in a coma, and his grandfather visited the hospital every day. Unfortunately, he always seemed to arrive at the worst time, when the boy was raving and seemed in unbearable pain. Roy's grief was compounded.

He masked his feelings when he crossed Buena Vista Street to the studio. On Friday afternoon, December 17, Roy seemed reluctant to leave his office. He signed papers that Madeleine Wheeler had prepared for him, and he dictated a warm letter to his friend Ellis Arnall in Georgia.

> . . . Edna and I are going to be around here until after the first of the year and then I will have to be here for our annual meeting on February 1. Then, if all goes well, we are going to be on a cruise ship sailing for Australia for a few relaxing weeks. Other than that, we have nothing planned for 1972.
>
> But 1971 has certainly been a hummer for us. We were all very pleased about the opening of the Florida park, and Edna and I are going to love going down there with you and Mildred and showing you around . . .

Roy poured himself his usual Scotch and water and went out to Madeleine Wheeler's desk for a chat. Roy reminisced about the good times at the studio during their long association, and he said that he expected to fully retire in a year. "But I might stay on another six months," he remarked. "That would be my fiftieth year in the picture business. Will you stick with me?" Madeleine assured him that she would. As he left the office, he said, "I may see you at the Disneyland Christmas parade."

Roy had decided that the family needed a break from the overwhelming sorrow over Roy Patrick's condition. Roy and Edna would take the three other grandchildren to the Christmas parade.

On Sunday morning, Roy got his hat and coat, then he put them down. He told Edna, "I don't feel like going down there. I don't think I'll go." He had been complaining about seeing something like a cloud over his vision. His eye doctor had examined him and delayed prescribing new glasses until blood tests could be made. Roy didn't take it seriously, and he postponed undergoing the tests.

Roy undressed and went to bed. Edna didn't know what to do with the grandchildren; she didn't want to disappoint them after promising a trip to Disneyland. She called Roy Edward and said, "Do you want to take the children to the park with me? Your father says he doesn't want to go." Patty said she would stay at home in case of any development with Roy Patrick, and Roy Edward agreed to accompany his mother and the children.

Patty called her father-in-law twice that day, and although he sounded grouchy, he said he was feeling all right. At Disneyland, Susan, Tim, and Abby rushed from one ride to another; their father and grandmother followed behind. Despite the gaiety of the crowd, Edna and Roy Edward felt an uneasiness throughout the day and into the evening, and even the children had trouble enjoying themselves. As soon as the parade was over, they hurried back to Toluca Lake.

Susan remembers: "Before we left the house, Grandma had put a pot on the stove with two cans of soup in it, in case Grandpa got hungry. When we walked in the kitchen, I saw it was still there, it hadn't been touched. I knew something was wrong, and I made a bee line to the bedroom. He was lying on the floor.

"I called my dad and my grandmother, and they came in. Grandpa said to her, 'I called you and I called you, and you didn't come.'"

Roy was lifted to the bed, and his son stood over him anxiously. "Dad, if you can hear me, say something," Roy Edward pleaded. His father opened his eyes and muttered, "What?" Then he fell into a coma.

Once again, the two families, Roy's and Walt's, gathered for their mournful vigil on the fourth floor of St. Joseph's Hospital. This time the anxiety was doubled. Roy lay in room 421, only his breath disclosing a sign of life; his grandson and namesake remained in perilous condition directly below in room 321.

Despite the brave words exchanged by the family members, Roy's condition was hopeless. The nuns spoke in whispers to Edna and explained that her husband's brain was dead, and only the life-sustaining apparatus was keeping him alive. Edna consented that the efforts should be discontinued.

Roy Oliver Disney died on December 20, 1971, of a massive brain hemorrhage. He was seventy-eight years old. The obituaries were modest in comparison to Walt's, understandably so for a man who spent most of his career in the shadow of his renowned brother. Because Roy was modest by nature, little was known of his accomplishments: how time after time he had rescued the studio from insolvency, how he had somehow found the financing for Walt's grandiose schemes, how he had kept the company on a sound financial basis, how he had fulfilled his brother's final dream of a college of the arts. His greatest achievement was Walt Disney World. The building of such an immense and lucrative project—without a cent of debt—provided the cornerstone over which a worldwide empire would rise.

President Nixon sent a message to Edna from the White House: "Our thoughts and prayers are with you as Pat and I share your sorrow at the loss of your husband and our dear friend . . . May you be strengthened in the years ahead by your pride and satisfaction in the long and rewarding life he lived and by your remembrance of the happy moments you had together."

Patty Disney obtained permission from the cardinal for the funeral to be held outside the altar at her parish church, St. Charles. Edna insisted that the casket be open, in keeping with Midwest tradition. All of the families were there, including the surviving siblings, Ray Disney and Ruth Disney Beecher. Four hundred people attended, including George Murphy, Ray Bolger, Meredith Willson, Dean Jones, Karl Malden, and John Gavin.

Monsignor Harry C. Meade, with whom Roy had often talked about business matters over drinks, made some remarks, and Donn Tatum delivered the eulogy. "He built an institution deeply entrenched in the hearts of people all over the world," Tatum said. "His love of Walt and concern with him were legendary."

The studio commissary provided ample food for the wake at Roy and Edna's house, and drinks were raised to Roy's good humor and accomplishments. Edna spoke with each of the guests, accepting condolences and praise for her husband with equal graciousness. "Edna was wonderful," Patty says. "Like a queen." She never allowed herself to cry.

The last good-bye was said and the commissary people packed up and left. "We didn't want to leave Edna alone," Patty recalls. "I didn't feel close enough to Edna, and Roy was kinda helpless. So Susie, our oldest daughter who was so much like her grandmother, spent the night with her. She sat there on Grandma's bed, and Grandma cried a lot. But it was all by herself. She didn't want anyone else but Susan to see."

Two days later, after the three Disney grandchildren had their Christmas at home, Edna appeared at their house in her big gold Cadillac. She opened the trunk to reveal an abundance of handsomely wrapped presents. This was the ritual that she and Roy had enjoyed every Christmas Day. The presents were signed, "From Grandma and Grandpa."

A week later, Roy Patrick had begun to regain his senses. He gazed out the hospital window and noticed that the studio flag was at half-staff. "What's that for?" he asked his parents. "Your grandfather has died," he was told.

A year would pass before the boy returned to normal.

With the two founders gone, Card Walker assumed control of Walt Disney Productions. Two members of the second generation continued the family tradition, Walt's son-in-law, Ron Miller, as film producer and executive producer of *Walt Disney's Wonderful World of Color*, Roy Edward Disney as producer of television shows. Both had been put on the board of directors by Roy.

Key members of Roy's Boys became casualties in the new regime. The list of associates Roy had entrusted to Donn Tatum was whittled down, one by one, until none remained at the company. The Mineral King Valley project, which Walt had planned as an innovation in winter resorts, was dropped. Buzz Price, whose research had helped the decision making on Disneyland, the New York World's Fair, Walt Disney World, and other endeavors, was no longer hired by the company.

The changes at the studio distressed Edna, and she exercised her customary candor in expressing her opinions. She continued living in the same house on Forman Avenue and looked forward to the times when her grandchildren's voices would fill the empty rooms. Her relatives and friends remarked how unchanged she was though she was now alone. It was against her nature to share the overwhelming loss she felt.

The will left $3 million to the Roy and Edna Disney Foundation, with specific bequests for scholarships and for the Motion Picture and Television Fund. Trust funds were established for Roy Edward and Patty and their children, as well as Ruth and Ray and other relatives.

One of Edna's pleasures was driving one or two of the grandchildren to Bullock's Wilshire, where she had her hair styled. The children always dreaded the drive from Toluca Lake to the store and back again. Edna's driving style hadn't changed.

"She drove that giant car into her nineties," says Abby Disney Hauser. "She used to drive the Hollywood Freeway forty miles an hour in the fast lane. People honked their horns, and she'd say, 'I don't know why everyone is in such a gol-darned hurry.'"

Edna often revisited Disneyland, particularly when new attractions were being added. She was there in 1976 during the trial runs of Space Mountain, one of the first thrill rides at the park. When she announced that she was going to try it, the officialdom became agitated. Edna was 86, the widow of a company founder. Space Mountain still hadn't been thoroughly tested. Edna would not be dissuaded. She climbed into the car, and it started the ascent.

Donn Tatum waited worriedly for Edna to return. "Are you all right?" he asked Edna anxiously. "Of course I'm all right," she snapped. "My sister and I rode all the roller coasters." She didn't add that had been seventy years before in Kansas City.

Although she later hired a housekeeper to help with the chores, Edna maintained her own household, shopping for groceries at Gelson's market.

"She was well and she was lucid until she was ninety-four," says Abby. "Nothing bothered her, she never complained. But she had one health problem after another, a lot of pain and difficulty getting around. She just didn't believe that people should complain."

In December 1984, the burden of her years became too much, and she was hospitalized at St. Joseph's. Family and friends visited her, but she seemed too weak to talk. Marge Davis, Lilly's niece, who had known Edna since she came to Hollywood to marry Roy, tried to console her. "Edna, I know how much you miss Roy," Marge said. "You know?" Edna said sadly, and she turned her face to the wall.

One night, Patty recognized that her mother-in-law was failing, and she placed a telephone call to Lilly. "I think you should be here," she said. "Oh, Patty," she replied, "I'm clear on the other side of town, and it's raining and—" She interrupted: "Lilly, I think you should be here."

Lilly arrived a half-hour later at the hospital where Walt and Roy had died in other Decembers. She walked quietly into Edna's room, sat beside the bed, and took Edna's hand. What a history the two women shared. Inking and painting in a Disney garage. The desperate times when the payroll couldn't be met. The glory years of Mickey Mouse and *Snow White*. Another brush with insolvency in the war years. Betting it all on Disneyland. Dealing with the Disney temper and the feuds between the two brothers. The final triumph with Florida, too late for Walt.

The time came for Lilly to leave. "I'll come and visit you tomorrow, dear," Lilly said. Edna answered with customary bluntness: "I won't be here."

Edna Francis Disney died the next day, December 19, 1984, at the age of ninety-four. The families buried her, as they had Walt and Roy (and would Lilly in 1997), a few days before Christmas.

AUTHOR'S NOTE

Roy O. Disney's life was as private as his younger brother's was public. Happily for a biographer, two vital resources were available: his family, friends and coworkers; and the Disney Archives. Roy Edward Disney and his wife Patty were exceptionally helpful with their reminiscences and family memorabilia, and in suggesting people to interview. Their four children, Roy Patrick, Susan, Abby, and Tim, provided insightful memories of their grandparents.

Others who graciously shared their memories and observations:

Bill Anderson, Harry Archinal, Mike Bagnall, Antonio Bertini, Armand Bigle, Bob Broughton, Royal (Mickey) Clark, Bill Cottrell, Marc Davis, Marvin and Marge Davis, Roy de Leonardis, Tricia Edgar, Nick England, Don Escen, Dan France, Bob Foster, Hazel George, Stanley Gold, Leonard Goldenson, John Hench, Dave Iwerks, Don Iwerks, Ollie Johnston, Bill Justice, Ward Kimball,

Bob King, Horst Koblischek, Jack Lindquist, Irving Ludwig, Gunnar Mansson, Luther Marr, Neil McClure, Diane Disney Miller, Ron Miller, Dick Morrow, Peter Nolan, Dick Nunis, Ken Peterson, Glenn Puder, Dorothy Disney Puder, Ken O'Connor, Mel Powell, Margaret Peet, Jo Sears, Harrison (Buzz) Price, Leonard Shannon, Janet Spurgeon, Marty Sklar, June Smith, Andy Thewlis, Frank Thomas, John Tobin, Jack Valenti, Card Walker, Ray Watson, Bob Wilson, Claude Winkler.

In addition, I was able to draw from interviews I conducted with individuals for *Walt Disney: An American Original.* Among them:

Ken Anderson, Edna Disney, Lillian Disney, Joe Fowler, Ub Iwerks, Wilfred Jackson, Mel Melton, Walt Pfeiffer, Joe Potter, Herb Ryman, Dolores Scott, Ben Sharpsteen, Donn Tatum, Larry Tryon, Harry Tytle. I also made use of interviews I conducted with Walt and Roy Disney for Associated Press.

One of Roy Disney's farsighted moves was to accept the proposal in 1970 by a UCLA bibliographer, David Smith, to establish a Disney Archives. Smith was authorized by Roy and Card Walker to assemble and catalog the mass of material accumulated during the studio's history. Roy also commissioned Smith to use his free time in assembling a genealogy of the Disney family, and Smith visited the family's sites in Goderich, Steuben, Ellis, Marceline, and elsewhere.

The Disney Archives, still conducted by Dave Smith, contributed invaluable help in providing research material for this biography. I quoted extensively from a series of interviews Richard Hubler conducted in 1968-69 with Roy O. Disney in preparation for an unrealized biography of Walt Disney. Hubler also interviewed Edna Disney and others. Another important source: the interviews Diane Disney Miller and Pete Martin conducted with her father for *The Story of Walt Disney*, published in 1956 by the

Saturday Evening Post and in book form by Henry Holt. Robert Tieman, Becky Kline, Collette Espino, and Adina Lerner were helpful in hunting down the material.

The Archives supplied boxes of Roy's business and personal correspondence, dating back to the earliest years of the Disney Company. Roy Patrick Disney, who lives with his family in his grandparents' home, found a box of Roy Oliver's personal correspondence in the garage, a welcome serendipity. Dan Viets of Columbia, Missouri, provided valuable research on Marceline, including books celebrating the seventy-fifth and one hundredth anniversaries of the city. Katherine and Richard Greene kindly supplied interviews with Ruth Disney Beecher. Charles Ridgway was helpful in the search for material on Walt Disney World, and his media guide to the park's twenty-fifth anniversary proved an excellent resource, especially Edward L. Prizer's history.

The amazingly comprehensive Walt Disney Company photo library, headed by Ed Squair, supplied many of the photographs, as did the Disney Archives. Roy Edward and Patty Disney opened their family albums and provided the vintage home movies, edited and transferred to videotape by David A. Chaparro.

Special thanks to Howard Green and Barbara Wilcox for their help at the studio. Also to my editor, Wendy Lefkon, for her counsel and patience, and to my agent, Dan Strone of the William Morris Agency.

Readers of both biographies will find certain similarities between this book and *Walt Disney: An American Original.* That is inevitable, since the brothers' careers followed parallel paths. Wherever possible in this book, I have striven to relate the events from Roy Disney's point of view.

INDEX

INDEX